SECOND EDITION

Serious Cycling

Edmund R. Burke, PhD

University of Colorado at Colorado Springs

Human Kinetics

Library of Congress Cataloging-in-Publication Data

Burke, Ed, 1949-
    Serious cycling / Edmund R. Burke.--2nd ed.
      p. cm.
    Includes index.
    ISBN 0-7360-4129-X
    1. Cycling. 2. Cycling--Training. I. Title

    GV1041 .B77 2002
    796.6--dc21

                             2001039843

ISBN: 0-7360-4129-X

Acquisitions Editor: Ed McNeely; **Developmental Editor:** Cynthia McEntire; **Assistant Editor:** Scott Hawkins; **Copyeditor:** Jennifer Thompson; **Proofreader:** Joanna Hatzopoulos; **Indexer:** Sharon Duffy; **Permission Manager:** Toni Harte; **Graphic Designer:** Nancy Rasmus; **Graphic Artist:** Francine Hamerski; **Photo Manager:** Tom Roberts; **Cover Designer**: Jack W. Davis; **Photographer (cover):** © SportsChrome USA; **Photographer (interior):** Tom Roberts unless otherwise noted; **Art Manager:** Craig Newsom; **Illustrators:** Denise Lowry and Dody Bullerman; **Printer:** Bang Printing

Human Kinetics books are available at special discounts for bulk purchase. Special editions or book excerpts can also be created to specification. For details, contact the Special Sales Manager at Human Kinetics.

Printed in the United States of America   10 9 8 7 6 5 4 3 2 1

Human Kinetics
Web site: www.humankinetics.com

United States: Human Kinetics
P.O. Box 5076
Champaign, IL 61825-5076
800-747-4457
e-mail: humank@hkusa.com

Canada: Human Kinetics
475 Devonshire Road Unit 100
Windsor, ON N8Y 2L5
800-465-7301 (in Canada only)
e-mail: orders@hkcanada.com

Europe: Human Kinetics
Units C2/C3 Wira Business Park
West Park Ring Road
Leeds LS16 6EB, United Kingdom
+44 (0) 113 278 1708
e-mail: hk@hkeurope.com

Australia: Human Kinetics
57A Price Avenue
Lower Mitcham, South Australia 5062
08 8277 1555
e-mail: liahka@senet.com.au

New Zealand: Human Kinetics
P.O. Box 105-231, Auckland Central
09-523-3462
e-mail: hkp@ihug.co.nz

Serious Cycling

Edmund R. Burke, PhD

CONTENTS

Part III   Planning

Part IV   Racing

FOREWORD

I have had the privilege of working with Ed Burke for almost 20 years. Throughout my career, both as an athlete and now as a coach, I have never known anyone so selflessly dedicated to the successful application of science to the sport of cycling. As a coach who works with developing athletes—some of the most successful in many sports—I am grateful to Ed for being such a positive force. Now Ed's expertise and insights are available to everyone in *Serious Cycling*. Not only is this book a top-rated synthesis on road cycling in general, it is also an invaluable tool for helping cyclists at all levels achieve their dreams of athletic success.

This book is for cyclists at any stage in their careers who wish to know more about the scientific basis of training principles and their application to cycling. Most people have a greater understanding of how their cars work than how their bodies work, although this is less likely to be true for athletes, who, in the process of pushing their bodies to the limit, acquire a lot of information about themselves. Many cyclists have little in the way of scientific education and need to work hard if they are to assimilate all the nutritional, physiological, psychological, and biomechanical information, training principles, and tactics now available in this book. The reward for this effort, however, is considerable, with the real possibility of using the information to improve performance. But even if this were not so, knowledge of what is going on under the hood can add greatly to the pleasure of cycling even for those of us who will win no medals.

Serious Cycling is highly educational. At the same time, Ed successfully presents and discusses complicated scientific events in a fluent and practical style that can be enjoyed and understood by cyclists with no formal background in the sciences. The only prerequisite is a curiosity about the function of the human body and the application of science to training. And this curiosity should have a high priority.

Every cyclist I know is trying to improve performance. If you are one of them, or if you are a cyclist who can't seem to improve, I hope you'll read this book and learn the most efficient way to reach your goals. I think most coaches would agree with me that you cannot progress in this sport unless you know how to train. To improve your training, let *Serious Cycling* help you develop a better understanding of the science and its application to training and competition.

While there is no best way to train, the information in this book will give you insights into your own training, as well as expert suggestions that may help you realize your full talents.

Chris Carmichael
Carmichael Training Systems
www.trainright.com

PREFACE

As the author of *Serious Cycling*, I could not be more pleased with the popularity of the first edition of this book. I have heard not only from elite cyclists and coaches, but also from many serious cycling enthusiasts, about the information provided in the first edition on sound training guidelines, programs, sport physiology, nutrition, equipment technology, and injury prevention.

Much new information on training programs, nutritional supplementation, and training technology has evolved since the first edition, warranting the publication of this second edition. Also, many cyclists have asked for input on winning strategies and tactics used, by the top cyclists, that can be used to improve race performance.

I have responded to these concerns and others, updating and revamping much of this second edition. I have revised the content to include new scientific research and the experiences and knowledge of elite-level coaches and cyclists whom I am in contact with on a continuing basis. I hope that their ideas about training, racing, and sport science give you a better understanding of endurance cycling and improved performance.

Serious Cycling bridges the gap between scientific observation and cycling performance. The great body of knowledge about the science of cycling lies unused by most cyclists. Trial and error may go a long way, but who knows the potential of a cyclist armed with the knowledge of a thousand dedicated scientists? Knowledge is strong medicine.

Although many books have been written on cycling, few report cutting-edge data in the depth and manner that will improve performance. Improving performance is not a primary goal for many scientists, but it may be one of the most important contributions they can make. My primary goal for this book is to interpret complex information on physiology, biomechanics, nutrition, injury, and training, and to make it understandable to all cyclists.

Serious Cycling provides the basis for a better understanding of the scientific preparation for cycling for all cyclists, whether they are top-level racers or dedicated enthusiasts with a passion for riding. Drawing together the latest research in cycling science and training theory, I have created a framework of training principles for improved performance. The text provides a basis for understanding cycling research, so you can use these discoveries to improve your fitness and excellence in the sport.

In chapters 1 through 3, I use physiological training principles and real-world experiences as the basis for designing endurance-training workouts. These guidelines are especially suited for road racers, but I also include tempo-training regimens (that time trialists will value) and sprint workouts for road cyclists (who often find that the race comes down to a mad dash for the tape). Whatever your cycling goals, you're bound to benefit from several of these workouts and this scientific information.

Chapter 4 discusses many off-bike and off-season training modes and explains how to use equipment such as power meters and heart rate monitors to gauge what is happening in your body while you work out. In chapter 5, I show you how to prevent injuries and illness, as well as how to care for yourself during periods of hard training and racing.

Chapters 6 through 8 will give you clear guidelines on how to fuel yourself properly to train and compete on a daily basis. I also discuss key areas of sport nutrition and recovery and cover how macronutrients and supplements can help you train hard and recover more effectively.

Chapters 9 through 11 show you how to put it all together, outline yearlong training programs for serious cyclists, and explain how not to overtrain to reach your goals. Whether you're a junior competitor, a senior-level competitor, a college student, or a working person who loves nothing more than to cycle like a pro, these chapters provide a program that's right for you.

But cycling performance doesn't come exclusively from the power of your lungs and legs and proper nutrition. Successful cycling also takes proper positioning on the bike, biomechanics, and attention to race tactics and strategies. Chapters 12 to 14 represent much of the best and most current cycling-specific information available. You'll learn ways to make yourself and your bike work with, not against, each other. Finally, you'll learn how to read a race properly and apply tactics and race strategy to ensure your success in racing or other endurance events.

This information does little good unless you remain committed to your cycling. Whether you plan to race or you ride "just" to keep in top shape, you need to stay with your program. Commitment combined with correct technique and smart training equals cycling success. I urge you to commit to your sport by using this four-step process:

1. *Know yourself.* Acknowledge your strengths and weaknesses. If you are a poor sprinter, are you willing to spend time on the track to improve your speed? What keeps you going when the times are tough?

2. *Set goals and targets.* What do you want to achieve during this season and the next? How will you get there?

3. *Be tough on yourself.* What are you willing to give up to become a better cyclist? Will you go out on those long rides in the middle of winter? If you get dropped, do you chase until you get back to the pack?

4. *Have a plan.* Do you have a yearlong training schedule designed to let you peak for the events that are most important to you? Do you have specific goals for each training ride? Do you keep a training diary? Know where you are going and how to get there.

We all have surprising athletic potential; it waits only for us to understand our bodies, coax our strengths, and meet the special needs that result. If this book offers you inspiration, the empirical basis for making sound training decisions, or the wherewithal to implement the four-step process that enhances your commitment to cycling, it serves its purpose.

No other book has been so usable by cyclists and has sparked so much debate on ideas about training, racing, and sport science. By studying this text, both the experienced cyclist and the cycling enthusiast can gain valuable information on how to improve performance. The information provided in the following chapters will challenge you to create your own training programs, combining your own experiences and intuition with the guidance provided here to help you reach your goals.

Work your hardest, cycle your best, and enjoy the ride.

ACKNOWLEDGMENTS

I am indebted to many people for the information, ideas, and concepts that make up this book. First, I would like to express my appreciation to the athletes who have worked with me over the past 25 years and to the sport science and cycling researchers who have shared their information. I particularly want to thank Dave Costill, who first showed me the way of sport science; Chester Kyle, who is always a source of assistance; and Peter VanHandle, who was always there to help not only cyclists but all athletes trying to improve their performance. To the many coaches, especially Eddy Borysewicz and Chris Carmichael who helped me better understand the sport, my thanks. I also must acknowledge the editors who have helped me and improved my writing to where it is understandable. To Kathleen, my wife, I owe the greatest debt. She has unselfishly provided the encouragement and support that have allowed me to devote an excessive amount of time to work and to writing.

PART I

Hard-Core Training

Competitive road cycling is more demanding physiologically and psychologically than any sport I know. Criteriums can be up to 50 miles, calling upon a cyclist for stamina, strategy, and bursts of all-out speed. Cycling's premier event, the Tour de France, is a three-week grind that tests and punishes—and sometimes even rewards—cyclists for their endurance, determination, and time-trialing strength. Cycling may even require you to race city-to-city in weather that reaches all extremes and on terrain that sometimes takes you above the clouds. No wonder aficionados call it the king of sports. No wonder its champions are epic figures.

Champions adopt training procedures that match racing situations as closely as possible, procedures that simulate the exertion of the long-distance ride ending in a breakaway that spends the cyclist's reserves. These sessions also test a rider's knowledge of tactics and strategies, mastery of skills, and courage.

A systematic approach to training is one of the most important factors in becoming a successful cyclist. Greg LeMond, three-time winner of the Tour de France, once said, "Training is what a cyclist does most of the time. Even the professional European cyclist who races up to 100 times per year does a lot of training. And a European professional who wants to be successful needs to know how and when to train to win races." Because there is so much more training than racing in amateur cycling, it is important for the serious amateur cyclist to not only know how to train, but to know why certain types of training should be in the program.

The first part of this book will focus on basic principles and the physiology of training for the serious cyclist. I have gathered much of this information from top cyclists and coaches in the sport whom I have had the honor to work with over the past 20 years. This section also will present information on how to prevent injuries while training and racing to ensure a successful progression of training through the season and your career.

By training hard, learning smart strategies, building the right psychological frame of mind, and staying injury-free, you can improve your racing performance. Part I will give you the scientific and practical knowledge that will guide you in making the right training choices to become the best cyclist you can be.

1

BUILDING A MILEAGE BASE

© Michael Steele/EMPICS

Any professional cyclist will tell you that to be successful at road cycling, you need to build up your weekly mileage to develop a good endurance base. "Building my endurance base by putting in the miles was one of the first things I learned in my cycling career; that set the basis for my continued development in the sport," says Lance Armstrong, winner of the Tour de France. How many miles do you need to ride every week? It depends on the time of the season; your goals, ability, and schedule; and, in some cases, which cyclists and coaches you listen to.

Endurance training is the basic training that allows you to feel comfortable on the bike for longer periods without pushing yourself to exhaustion. You achieve this slow buildup of stamina by increasing aerobic fitness. You must habitually stress the aerobic energy system by staying on the bike longer and longer. After a while, the system acclimates itself to working more efficiently for longer periods.

Contrary to popular belief, endurance training is not used specifically to increase maximal aerobic capacity. The intensity of the effort is probably too low to have much effect on your body's maximal ability to transport oxygen to working muscles, referred to as maximal oxygen consumption. One of the greatest disservices perpetuated on endurance cyclists was the concept of long, slow distance training, which implied that extensive training with high mileage and low effort could improve aerobic capacity and allow cyclists to race effectively at shorter distances, such as criteriums. Long, easy rides provide a base of endurance that you can sharpen for races with speed work and intervals.

If you do only endurance training, you will not possess the speed to race criteriums, chase down breakaways, or sprint to the end. Endurance workouts are aerobic because they are conducted at a pace below the point at which lactic acid begins to accumulate in the blood, a sign that you are starting to use a significant amount of anaerobic metabolism to produce energy.

The purpose of the endurance ride is not only to stress the aerobic system but also to give you the experience of being on the bicycle for a long time and to increase your ability to burn fat as fuel. Mileage helps your body adapt to the extended hours of sitting in the saddle during long road races in ways only your posterior will appreciate.

Generally, the maximum time spent on the bicycle will be 90 minutes to 3 hours per day for juniors and women and 4 to 6 hours per day for senior male amateurs and professionals. Rides should be conducted at a reasonably comfortable pace; you should be able to carry on a conversation with teammates while riding. However, if you incorporate sprints or intervals into these rides, conversation will turn intermittently into heavy breathing.

The Physiology of Endurance

Endurance cycling stimulates primarily slow-twitch (type I) muscle fibers because they are more responsive to the lower intensity than fast-twitch (type II) fibers. The adaptations of the muscle cells and the cardiovascular system that occur with endurance training allow each slow-twitch fiber to work at lower intensities with less fatigability.

In research with trained cyclists at the University of Texas, Ed Coyle has shown slow-twitch fibers to be more efficient in converting chemical energy within the muscle into the mechanical work of pedaling. Thus, fewer muscle fibers are needed to maintain a given pace, or those that are activated do not need to work as hard as before. This helps improve cycling economy because less muscle activity is involved (and less oxygen is needed) for pedaling. Cyclists perceive this, often remarking that they feel smoother and are pedaling in circles and not in squares.

Work completed by Dr. David Costill and coworkers at Ball State University has shown that when national-class cyclists significantly increase their mileage, they often see little change in maximal oxygen consumption ($\dot{V}O_2$max). Costill's work shows that the muscle fibers are becoming more economical, which causes improved performance.

Costill's work also has shown that endurance training helps cyclists better utilize stored carbohydrate (glycogen) in their muscles and liver, which can be converted rapidly to simple glucose as it is needed during exercise. Glycogen is the preferred fuel for muscles during cycling, but glycogen stores can become depleted within 90 minutes of riding at a moderate to high intensity. A well-trained cyclist can store 400 to 500 grams (1,600 to 2,000 calories) of carbohydrate. Depleting this supply often is referred to as "bonking" or "hitting the wall." Therefore, cyclists have learned to eat and drink more carbohydrates during long road races (more on this in chapter 6), or they use more of their fat stores for fuel.

Endurance cycling also teaches your body to burn other types of fuel along with stored glycogen, stretching the duration of your reserves from 90 minutes to 2 hours or more. Top professional road riders are probably so efficient in metabolizing fats and glycogen throughout a road race, because of the many miles they put in during training and racing, that they probably rarely deplete their glycogen stores. Simply stated, endurance training teaches your body to be more efficient, sparing glycogen and burning larger stores of fat.

Some cyclists refer to endurance training in the early season as base training. During this time they also are improving ligament and tendon strength, which will prepare their bodies for harder sessions of intervals and sprints. During the racing season your program should include endurance rides as well as tempo and speed work and races. The faster-paced miles put a lot of stress on your body; slower miles on the bike allow you to recover from hard efforts and build up your body for even more hard efforts. Putting miles on the bike builds your foundation in the early season, and the physiological experience of those miles is used during the season to help maintain fitness. Endurance training is a must for all cyclists because it

- increases the potential to store carbohydrates within the muscles and liver;
- improves your respiratory system, allowing more oxygen to be delivered to the working muscles;
- increases the pumping efficiency of your heart so you can pump more blood per minute to the working muscles;
- helps your thermoregulatory system by increasing blood flow to the skin while cycling;
- brings about increased neuromuscular efficiency of pedaling technique;
- increases your ability to burn more fat during long road races; and
- improves the endurance of your cycling muscles by increasing the number of mitochondria, the subcellular structures in your muscles that produce aerobic energy.

Cycling Muscles

Being successful in training depends largely on how your muscles adapt to produce the energy and force needed to turn the pedals. Technological advances have made it possible for researchers to obtain samples of muscle tissue from cyclists before, during, and after exercise, allowing them to study the makeup of muscles and gauge the effects of exercise and training.

To perform a muscle biopsy, a doctor uses a needle 3 to 5 millimeters in diameter. The subject is given a local anesthetic, and the doctor makes a small incision into the muscle being studied. Because muscle tissue has no pain receptors, the feeling is usually described only as "weird." The needle extracts 20 to 40 milligrams of muscle, which is enough for several biochemical tests including fiber typing.

Muscle contains bundles of fibers (cells), all of which function basically the same way—when stimulated, they contract to maximal tension. Nevertheless, muscle fibers do differ, and the difference is important to cyclists.

Muscle Fiber Types

Certain muscle fibers are able to contract repeatedly without much fatigue. This is type I or slow-twitch (ST) fiber (figure 1.1). ST fibers have a high content of myoglobin (an oxygen-storing protein) and enzymes that favor aerobic energy production. ST fiber has a high aerobic capacity, which means that it can produce energy for a long time when sufficient oxygen is available.

The other major type of muscle fiber, type II or fast-twitch (FT) fiber, has a lower aerobic capacity but a high anaerobic capacity, meaning it can produce energy without oxygen. This fiber is normally found in high percentages in sprint and power athletes. FT fibers (figure 1.1) can be further broken down into type IIA and type IIB fibers. Type IIA fibers are generally a bit more aerobic than type IIB fibers.

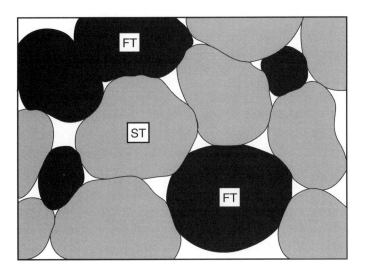

Figure 1.1   Slow- and fast-twitch muscle fibers intermingle in a cross-section of human muscle.

From Training for Cross-Country Ski Racing: A Physiological Guide for Athletes and Coaches (p. 11) by B.J. Sharkey, 1984, Champaign, IL: Human Kinetics. Copyright 1984 by Brian J. Sharkey. Reprinted by permission.

ST and FT fibers have different capacities for breaking down glycogen (stored carbohydrate) and accumulating lactic acid. That is, they have different aerobic and anaerobic capacities. ST fibers are superior in producing energy aerobically. FT fibers have a higher anaerobic capacity: they can perform short-term, very intense work when sufficient oxygen is not available.

This isn't the whole story, however. There is a spectrum of aerobic and anaerobic potential within ST and FT fibers. One person's FT fibers, especially if he has more type IIA fibers, may have a greater aerobic capacity than another person's. But within an individual, ST fibers usually will have a higher aerobic capacity than FT fibers. The reverse is true for anaerobic capacity.

Muscle Fiber Composition

Slow-twitch muscle fibers are more responsive to the lower intensity of endurance cycling. Work completed by Ed Coyle and others from the University of Texas found that, in addition to needing a high maximal oxygen consumption for success in competition, elite national-class road cyclists (group 1) possessed a higher percentage of ST fibers and a greater amount of capillaries supplying oxygen to the muscles than did a group of good state-class cyclists (group 2). Actual 40-kilometer time-trial performance also correlated highly with average power output during a one-hour laboratory performance test.

When you train better, you become a better rider. You have to push yourself to the limit—that's what makes the top riders. Some people can't do it, but that's what makes the good ones and the great ones.

Sean Kelly, known as the King of the Classics for his 193 race wins

What factors allowed group 1 to produce more force and perform better in competition? This is an interesting question because it begins to specifically and directly explain the superior performance of elite national-class cyclists. It is likely there is no single factor but numerous factors that may vary in magnitude from one cyclist to another. Coyle thinks that cyclists with a high percentage of ST fibers have a distinct advantage because at the same level of energy expenditure (oxygen consumption) their muscles produce more force and power.

It also appears that the thigh muscles of the cyclists in group 1 were less fatigable than those in group 2; this allowed group 1 cyclists to maintain higher intensities and to continually push the pedals with more force. As mentioned, group 1 possessed more capillaries around each muscle fiber; these capillaries serve to flush lactic acid away from the exercising muscle, thereby reducing fatigue.

So, a high percentage of FT fibers may be a must for a sprinter or a kilometer rider who must accelerate with big gears at slow speeds, and too many ST fibers may be a disadvantage for a road racer in certain races. Even though a composition of 60 to 80 percent ST fiber is ideal for endurance and muscular efficiency, the road racer will have a hard time chasing down breakaways and sprinting at the finish and may have to stick to time trials or stage races to be successful.

EFFECT OF WEIGHT ON THE ENERGY COST OF BICYCLING

For years cyclists have been spending hundreds of dollars to reduce the weight of their bicycles. Even Armstrong switches to his light carbon fiber frame with super-light wheels to reduce the overall weight of his bicycle during mountain stages of the Tour de France. The logic is that a lighter bike will have faster acceleration and lower rolling resistance and will require less effort on a climb. In simple mechanical terms, it takes more energy to average the same speed with additional weight. It's valid thinking, provided that frame, crank arm, and wheel stiffness can be maintained with a lighter machine. Here are some tips and information to consider if you are going to choose lightweight components and bikes to improve your performance.

The ability to accelerate quickly—whether starting, coming out of turns, or chasing down another rider—is critically important to racing cyclists. Adding weight to a bicycle will reduce the rate of acceleration, but by how much depends in part on where the weight is located. Reducing so-called rotating weight, for example, is generally more important to performance than taking the same amount of weight off the frame or another static component.

Additional weight slows you down when you are climbing. The energy you need to move a weight up a hill increases in proportion to the weight being moved—in other words, the weight of you and your bicycle. Less weight on the bicycle means less weight to drag up the hill.

In addition, extra weight causes a greater deformation of the sidewalls and tire tread, thus increasing rolling resistance. Rolling resistance increases in direct proportion to the weight that the wheel supports and is equal to .3 to .5 percent of the load on the wheel. Rolling resistance can be reduced by carrying lighter loads on the wheel and using larger-diameter wheels with smoother and thinner treads and stronger sidewalls.

Having light rotating components is even more important. To accelerate a wheel or pedal-and-shoe system, you need the kinetic energy of rotation as well as the kinetic energy of linear motion. For example, if the weight is mostly concentrated in the wheel's rim and tire, you will need almost twice the energy to accelerate as for a nonrotating weight. In other words, 1 pound added to a wheel or pedal-and-shoe system is equivalent to nearly 2 pounds on the bicycle frame.

Work that I completed with Ned Frederick of Exerter Research has shown that the addition of 250 grams to a pedal-and-shoe system, or 500 grams total for both feet (about the difference between the lightest and heaviest pedal-and-shoe systems on the market), would require an additional power output of 1.3 percent of rotational power at constant speeds on a level road. Climbing and accelerating would add about another .4 percent. The effect on rolling resistance would be about .07 percent. This means that the net effect of all factors of a realistic increase of 250 grams on each leg would be to increase the power required by a cyclist by approximately 1.5 to 1.7 percent. The

(continued)

increase could be significant in a long road race of 100 to 125 miles, with several hills and a sprint at the end. We estimated that 1.3 percent more oxygen would be needed for 200 watts of work (approximately 24 to 25 kilometers per hour) when an additional 125 grams are added to each pedal-and-shoe system (250 grams total).

The number of companies selling titanium replacement components is staggering. Cyclists are looking for ways to reduce energy cost or are foregoing purchasing new bikes in favor of lightening the bicycles they already own. Titanium parts can cost significantly more than standard components, from as little as $0.35 to over $1 per gram. Changing from a traditional turbo-style saddle, weighing over 375 grams, to a lightweight saddle, weighing a mere 210 grams, costs $0.35 per gram. Switching from a standard steel-bottom bracket (210 to 270 grams) to a 139-gram titanium-bottom bracket will cost you about $1.04 per gram. Upgrading from a 600-gram clipless pedal-and-cleat system to the Speedplay X/1 pedal-and-cleat system (224 grams) will cost you $1.33 per gram. Similar "savings" can be found in skewers, stems, seat posts, tires, rims, hubs, spokes, and bolts. The cost is high, but remember, for every pound of weight saved, that next hill will not seem as difficult to climb.

Increased weight retards cycling performance far less than aerodynamic drag does. Thus, aerodynamic handlebars and disk wheels, for example, which increase weight but reduce wind drag, may be more beneficial in a 100-mile competition than an ultralight frame and wheels. Fortunately, lightweight disk and tri-spoke wheels can be built with the same shape and rigidity as the heavy disk wheels of a few years ago. There is no reason for a heavier frame or components unless stability and handling cannot be maintained otherwise.

Endurance Training Guidelines

As a general rule, the longest of these endurance sessions should be no more than 20 to 25 percent greater than the distance at which you intend to compete. You may need to adjust the distance and effort for environmental (wind or temperature) conditions so that the effort is not too intense. Your heart rate intensity should be 60 to 80 percent of your maximum.

At the lower intensities, you should be able to carry on a conversation. It would be interesting to see a study that shows the maximum intensity that would still permit conversation. In the absence of a friend (and if you do not wish to be caught talking to yourself), your pulse rate is another good judge. Maintaining a pulse rate of 65 to 70 percent of your maximum heart rate is sufficient to produce the desired effects. This is where a heart rate monitor may be helpful in keeping you from going too hard up a hill or from riding with a group that wants to go faster. A pulse rate of closer to 75 percent will produce similar effects if you have less time to train.

Riding for shorter durations, as little as 30 minutes, at the same effort or pace (or at less than 65 percent of your maximum heart rate) serves as a recovery session or a warm-up but does little for overall conditioning. Although various names are applied to this training, it is essentially active recovery. It is too low an intensity and volume for long-term training changes in a serious athlete and is used to help recover from previous intense training or races or to prepare for future races.

Beginning cyclists often want to know at what speed they should ride during endurance training. Speed is not the important consideration; it is the intensity of effort and the time on the bike that are important. Remember, speed depends on the terrain you are riding and on environmental conditions. If it is very hot and windy, your miles per hour may be reduced. Also, these average speeds are easier to maintain if you're riding in a group of five to eight cyclists.

One of the more enjoyable ways to get in your endurance rides is to join the local cycling club on its weekend ride. This will give you an opportunity to ride with other cyclists and to share your knowledge with up-and-comers.

Average cyclists who try to copy the high mileage of professional or elite amateur cyclists may actually spend significantly more time than their mentors on the road. Be cautious when comparing your mileage to other cyclists'. The slower you ride (compared to cyclists of better ability), the more you should consider time, not mileage, in setting your weekly and monthly training goals. Some cyclists prefer to record hours and minutes in their diaries because this more accurately represents their training. That makes sense for that group of cyclists, but in this book we will report training programs in miles because we are looking at a total training program of endurance, tempo, and speed.

Increasing Mileage

Don't continuously increase your mileage. Every few weeks, level off your mileage before adding more to your program. Occasionally, when you reach a level you are comfortable with, such as 200 to 250 miles per week, stay there for several weeks. These periodic plateaus help you regenerate physically and mentally before the next mileage increase. These plateaus may last several months and are determined by age, ability and past training, and competition goals. Periods of steady mileage, or even decreased mileage, will help you recover or get physically stronger. You do not have to increase mileage every week or, for that matter, several weeks.

Determine the upper limit to the number of miles you can handle, mentally and physically, at this stage in your competitive career. If you are not careful and do not set realistic goals, you may become overtrained or experience an overuse injury. Don't compare your program to a cyclist you read about in a popular magazine. After several years of cycling, you may know that your upper limit is about 200 miles per week. However, the next year, because of a different off-season training program and/or increased experience, you may be able to safely handle 225 miles per week, mileage that would have been too much to handle previously. Table 1.1 lists some factors to consider in planning your endurance-based mileage program.

TABLE 1.1 Factors That Affect Endurance Miles	
You may find it difficult to keep up your mileage if you . . .	Reduce training mileage if you . . .
• work during the day and are running out of daylight in the morning or evenings	• are recovering from an injury
• are carrying a few extra pounds	• are racing often
• ride mostly by yourself	• are tapering for a race
• live in a hilly area	• are adding speed work to your program
• live in a climate that is either too cold or too hot several months of the year	• feel fatigued
• don't have a coach, team, or family to support you	• have reached the off-season

Year-Round Training

During the off-season and early season, many cyclists refer to endurance training as base building or the foundation phase that will allow for longer and harder training as the season progresses. During this time, almost all your miles or time on the bike should be spent on endurance rides in smaller gears. You should be spinning, with your revolutions per minute in the 90-plus range.

As you firm up your early-season training base, you can add speed work, intervals, hill training, and race-pace work to your program. This is covered in later chapters. You can add long intervals and long, gradual climbs to your program as well as a few jumps and short sprints.

During the peak racing season, make sure to include one long ride each week. Avoid the temptation to do one every day, or you will get exhausted and your speed will suffer. Instead, ride once a week for as many hours as your longest race or stage in an upcoming race. Getting ready for a 75-mile road race? About 3 1/2 to 4 hours will do.

You will have to eat often on your long rides. Don't make the mistake of riding 3 to 5 hours with only two bottles of water. By the end, you will be seeing stars and pedaling in squares, classic symptoms of the "bonk" or "hitting the wall." Carry plenty of food and drink with you, or, if need be, stop at a convenience store to stock up.

TIPS FOR MANAGING MILEAGE

Many of the cyclists I have worked with have found that by applying these simple rules to their training programs, they can safely manage their mileage or time on the bicycle:

- If you are injured or sick for several days or weeks, don't try to make up the mileage. Gradually build back up over a period of weeks and get back up to your mileage over time.

- Measure your training in miles or time. If you do not know the distance you are riding, purchase a cyclocomputer. If you are riding for time, use a watch.

- Some cyclists have more energy if they alternate long weeks with short weeks (for example, 200-250-200-250 for an average of 225 miles per week for the month). By setting monthly goals, you can be more flexible with your training mileage.

- Never be a slave to your training program or diary. If you become ill or have to work late, do not try to make up excessive mileage on the last day of the week. Remember, your success in competition will come from a proper blend of training, mileage, and rest, not by how many miles you record in your diary.

Skip Hamilton, an accomplished master's cyclist and a coach at the Connie Carpenter–Davis Phinney training camps, has these recommendations for increasing your mileage or time on the bike: "Early in the season do not increase your time on the bike or miles covered by more than 20 to 25 percent from one week to the next. For example, if you have been training for 10 hours a week, then the next week should be in the 10- to 12-hour range. In fact, you should never increase your time by more than 3 hours per week."

Hamilton gives this advice to many of the cyclists he works with who are in their early years of training: "It takes several weeks to adapt, but it may take several months to adjust." He is cautioning his riders to not make too many large jumps in their training programs; he wants their bodies to have time to adjust gradually to the increasing stress.

The Final Spin

The endurance phase of training is intended for the optimal development of your slow-twitch muscle fibers. Endurance training stimulates increased efficiency of these fibers, improves oxygen delivery, increases the number of mitochondria, and improves fat metabolism. This is the foundation on which all future training and performances are based. Prepare well and you should find the season a success. Neglect this foundation and you will lack the stamina for more intense training and competition as the season progresses.

Peter Snell is one of the greatest middle-distance runners of all time. He trained with the great running coach Arthur Lydiard, who is a proponent of large volumes of endurance training. Snell once said, "What people didn't understand about Lydiard's program was that it wasn't the high mileage that made the runners great. What made his runners great was the training they were able to do because they had done the mileage."

Look at endurance and base training as a multiseason progression. Think of your gains as cumulative: the more years you spend at it, the better you will be. With proper endurance training, you can reap bigger benefits over a longer period of time.

DEVELOPING SPEED AND SPRINT POWER

© Nancy C. Ross

Racing not only requires great endurance to remain a contender over several hours of competition, it also often requires a high-speed sprint at the end. Being able to sprint at the end of a road race or criterium is crucial to your cycling success.

Road races typically run up to 100 miles for amateurs and 125 to 160 miles for professionals. Often the finishes are attacked at higher speeds. Typically, 10 to 15 miles from the finish, teams will begin to drive up the pace to discourage breakaway attempts and to set up their designated sprinters. It is not uncommon for the finishing group to hit speeds of more than 40 mph in the final mile—and everyone is still waiting to sprint.

There are many ways to improve your speed and sprinting ability. If you're like professional cyclists Mario Cipollini and Erik Zabel, winner of many sprint competitions at the Tour de France, you are constantly searching for more speed, always squeezing a little more out of your body, your bike, and your training course. Later I will describe some workouts that you can insert into your training to help you ride faster. First, let's review the physiological characteristics of speed so that you can create methods for increasing your own cycling speed and sprinting ability.

The Physiology of Speed

Speed training is not interval training. Interval training develops anaerobic and aerobic capacity through work periods of approximately 30 seconds to several minutes followed by recovery periods of one half to two times the length of the interval. This type of riding plays an important part in riding fast, but it is very different from speed, or sprint, training.

Speed training is used to develop quickness and explosive power and involves short, intense periods of 5 to 30 seconds, with heart rates reaching 95 to 100 percent of maximum during the longer sprints. Speed, power, and acceleration are the key elements, not heart rate. It is important that a long recovery period (2 to 5 minutes) follow such sprints to allow for a total rebuilding of adenosine triphosphate (the muscles' ultimate energy source) and to ensure a quality workout.

Your total speed includes reaction time and movement time. Reaction time (the time from the stimulus—such as an opponent's jump—until the beginning of your sprint) is a function of the nervous system. You can't change the speed of your nerve transmissions. Thus, any major improvement in reaction must be achieved by increasing your response to the stimulus and by repeating the appropriate responses, reducing the time it will take your brain to process the information. Use jumping drills and group sprints to improve your reaction time.

Movement time (the interval from the beginning to the end of the movement) often will decrease (improve) with appropriate strength and sprint training. The key to your success in sprinting lies in the specificity of your training. Specificity applies to the rate of movement and the resistance employed, which means that your training should simulate the competition as closely as possible. If you want to be successful at sprinting, then you need to sprint-train in several situations: in a group, up a hill, out of a corner, and at the end of several hours on the bicycle.

To be a pure sprinter like Zabel, you may need to have a high percentage (over 50 percent) of type II (fast-twitch) fibers. But don't feel like you will never win a race if this isn't the case. Although you may never be as fast as Marti Nothstein, Olympic gold medalist in the match sprints, or Mario Cipollini, you can improve your reaction and movement times by practicing the drills in this chapter.

But first let's discuss the principle of power. Power equals work divided by time or the rate of doing work. Work equals force times distance. Power combines a cyclist's strength (force put into the pedals) and velocity (distance divided by time). For example, suppose you cycle at a power output of 500 watts (power) for 10 seconds. You have done a certain amount of work in that time. Because power is the rate of doing work, you produce twice the power if you do the same amount of work in 5 seconds. You also can produce twice the power by doubling the force you exert over the 10 seconds. In other words, power is not only a measure of how much force you exert, but also of how quickly you exert it. Later in the chapter you will find examples of how to increase your power by sprinting uphill, by sprinting in large gears, and by using high-speed repetitions in weight training.

Who Needs Speed Work?

Endurance training gives you base mileage that will get you to the finish line comfortably. Eventually, you will enter harder and faster races, and you will begin to struggle to finish well and stay with the group. You need to consider sprint or speed work if you

- lack the strength to sprint strongly at the end of a race or to attack during a race,
- need to improve your high-speed racing coordination,
- get dropped in the first few miles of a criterium because the pace feels too hard,
- need to peak for a key race or series of races,
- need to improve your ability to generate power while riding the hills, or
- feel it is difficult to hold a fast pace during a race.

Bernard Hinault, five-time winner of the Tour de France, once said, "If there is one area where experience counts, it's in the sprint. The best school is the mistakes you make as you begin your career. It's best to commit them when you're young. You should try your luck even if you're not particularly gifted, in order to learn."

Sprints should be part of your program at least once a week after you have a good endurance base, from early season until the cool weather. Many cyclists that I have worked with on the National Cycling Team over the years will not do any speed work until they have 1,000 to 1,200 miles in their legs. Generally, 95 to 97 percent of your overall training will be endurance and tempo training, and only 3 to 5 percent will be speed work.

Do not add a lot of speed work to your program until you have raced for about one year, have completed a few races of varying distances, and have a good base of endurance miles. Your body needs to be ready to take on the extra load of speed or sprint training.

Speed training may be part of a short-distance ride (60 to 90 minutes) or may be part of a warm-up for an interval session.

Body Position

Body position on the bike, especially arm position, is important when working on your jump. Your arms counteract the strong forces being generated by your legs, hips, and back. Most sprinters prefer to sprint with their arms flexed. If you use this style, keep the angle of your elbows constant during the jump and acceleration phases of the sprint. This allows your body to remain stable as your hips are brought up and forward with greater ease. Your wrists should be on the outside of the bars on the drops, not bent toward the inside. This allows you to bend the elbows to the outside so that you can maintain your weight over the pedals better and remain more stable if you get bumped by another rider during the sprint.

Your hips should be aligned vertically over your front foot as the forward crank approaches horizontal. This will allow you to use your body weight during the power phase (downstroke) of pedaling. Remember to keep your head up and in a comfortable position.

When you accelerate or sprint using a big gear, learn to use your arms in a manner coordinated with the rest of your body. Pull against the left part of the bar when the left foot pushes down on the pedal. At the same time, apply enough counterforce with your right arm to keep from turning the front wheel. As the right leg begins its downward stroke, the process is reversed.

Roger Young, a former Olympian and coach to many top track cyclists, reminds his athletes of these key points for a sprint that is initiated at a very slow speed: "At the start, you should drive up and out of the saddle, hips forward and as square as possible, arms bent slightly, and act as if you are running on the pedals. Gradually, as you pick up speed, your shoulders should go forward and down as your elbows and hips bend. When you reach your top rpm, the hips and shoulders begin to come back, and you should make a smooth transition into the saddle" (see figure 2.1).

Figure 2.1 A cyclist sprints using Roger Young's key points.

Learn to keep your leg speed high; work on letting it reach 110 to 120-plus revolutions per minute. In some sprints, it may help you reach top-end speed if you concentrate on pedaling faster instead of harder. Let the bicycle move slightly from side to side as you power it forward.

Sprints With Snap and Power

Davis Phinney, the first American to win a stage in the Tour de France, once described sprinting as a combination of snap and power—power being the ability to push low gears quickly, and snap being leg speed and the ability to pedal smoothly in high gear.

I'm fascinated by the sprinters. They suffer so much during the race just to get to the finish, they hang on for dear life in the climbs, but then in the final kilometers they are transformed and do amazing things. Seeing them suffer throughout the race only to be reborn in the final is something for fascination.

Miguel Indurain, five-time Tour de France winner, two-time Tour of Italy winner

While training in Boulder, Colorado, Phinney often found short, steep rolling hills on which to practice sprinting. To work on power, he rode halfway up the hill, then shifted into a larger gear and sprinted over the top. It was a sprint that developed pure explosive power and strength. He never did this form of training alone because riding with one or two other cyclists made for better competition and pushed him to ride harder.

Phinney developed snap by sprinting down long hills. In the middle of the descent, the group would jump and then sit down and continue to sprint, the cyclists trying to spin as fast as they could. Not only did this help cyclists develop snap and speed, it also trained them to develop a smooth pedaling motion.

Gearing practice should coincide with your fitness and time training in the competitive season. Remember, you are trying to achieve maximal effort, not just mash big gears. Early in the season use smaller gears; then, when in peak form, use 53×15 to 53×13 gearing. Experiment with gears to find the best combination for fast acceleration and top-end speed. Juniors and some women may have to modify their gear selection, depending on their strength.

Jumps

You can increase reaction time on group rides by sprinting for the city limit or other specific road signs. The designated sprinter in the group decides when to initiate the sprint. The others respond and chase until the initial rider is caught or ends the effort. Take turns initiating the sprint and vary the distance from 100 to 300 meters.

Another possibility is to have someone act as a coach and follow the training group in a car or on a motorcycle. Occasionally while the group is riding at training pace, the coach will beep the horn and everyone will sprint until they hear the next beep. The coach can vary the distance and decide whether the sprint starts uphill or downhill.

Sprint Drills

The following drills will force you to learn to sprint in various gears, uphill, downhill, into the wind, with the wind at your back, and at various positions in the group. Get off the saddle, charge down the road as you build speed and cadence, then sit down and increase your revolutions. Stay low on the bicycle and reasonably smooth; a lot of erratic movement on the bike is unsafe and will slow you down.

- **Sprints in progressively lower gears.** After a good warm-up, complete two sprints of 200 to 250 meters, one sprint of 300 to 350 meters, and one or two sprints of 200 to 250 meters. Rest for 5 to 10 minutes between sprints, or until your heart rate returns to about 60 percent of maximum, while riding in an easy gear before you start another set. Use the first 50 to 100 meters to get up to speed and then ride all-out until the finish. As the season progresses, gradually increase the longest sprint from 300 to 500 meters.

- **Declining time sprints.** After a good warm-up, start with a sprint of 60 seconds, then 50 seconds, 40, 30, and 20. Allow your heart rate to return to below 60 percent before beginning the next sprint. Finish with two to four sprints of 30 seconds.

- **Race sprints.** While riding with several teammates (six at the most), try to replicate sprints you have seen in race videos or from past race experiences. One rider should attack at a certain place or at a particular speed, and then everyone goes from there. The person who is selected to jump also decides how long the sprint should last. These sprints can be completed during the last few hours of longer road rides.

- **Ins and outs.** Connie Carpenter-Phinney, 1984 Los Angeles Olympic road champion, has cyclists at her training camps practice sprinting while getting in and out of the saddle. Start by rising out of the saddle in a low gear for 10 pedal revolutions and then sit back down, sprinting for another 10 revolutions. Repeat these sprints three times, jumping out of the saddle and then sitting back down. You will sprint 30 revolutions in the saddle and 30 revolutions out of the saddle, for a distance of about 400 yards. These sprints are best done with the wind at your back or on a slight downhill. This drill works your ability to sprint and accelerate several times during a longer sprint. This often happens when riders keep jumping in the final kilometers of a race.

• **Motorcycle sprints.** This excellent sprint teaches you how to attack while riding in a group at high speeds as if you were in a team lead-out at the end of a race. While riding behind a motorcycle at 28 to 33 mph, practice jumping around the motorcycle and try to pass or "slingshot" around the driver. This replicates trying to attack opponents while they are racing full-speed. Motorcycle sprints should be conducted only with an experienced coach driving the motorcycle.

• **Hill sprints.** On a hill of 5 to 9 percent grade, find a spot where it will take 20 to 25 seconds to reach the top. From this spot, initiate each sprint with a jump of 7 to 10 pedal strokes and then return to the saddle and go all-out to the top; you may get out of the saddle again for the last 10 yards. Then turn around and pedal easily down the hill. Do not begin another sprint until your heart rate drops below 60 percent of maximum. Keep the bicycle as straight as possible and ride to the top in as straight a line as possible. Use a 39 × 17 gear for the first sprint, 39 × 16 for the second sprint, 39 × 15 for the third, and 39 × 14 for the fourth. If you feel really strong, go for a fifth sprint in a 39 × 13 gear.

THE ELEMENT OF SURPRISE

At one of his Carmichael Training Camps for cyclists, Chris Carmichael, Lance Armstrong's coach, gave the following advice to help cyclists surprise their opponents and cause them to lose their advantage in a road race or criterium: "This may sound simple, but in practice many less-experienced cyclists do not take full advantage of this strategy. One of the most common racing mistakes is enabling your opponents to predict your attacks."

Here are his guidelines for attacking opponents in a race: Attack opponents from behind. Try dropping back a few yards and then take a run at the riders just in front of you. By the time you pass them, you are traveling 2 to 3 mph faster and are at a decided advantage. Remember to attack your opponents in an area of the course, or time in the race, where they are least likely to expect an attack. You need to gamble a little in order to win races.

Carmichael gave the following example of how to use this tactic: In a flat, long road race, it may seem predictable that the race comes down to a field sprint or a small breakaway in the closing miles. This race development benefits the strong sprinter. If you are not a strong sprinter, you might try a breakaway with about 10 miles to go in the hope of holding out until the end.

Start your sprint by coming off the saddle as your pedal goes past the 12 o'clock position. It doesn't matter which foot you start with, though it probably will feel most natural to start with your strong foot. Increase pedal resistance. Shift as soon as you feel minimal pedal resistance. If you find you have to shift within the first 5 seconds of your sprint, you've lost momentum too soon and should have started your sprint in a higher gear.

The timing of shifts depends on terrain and wind conditions. If you're starting your sprint downhill or with a strong tailwind, you won't have to wait 5 seconds.

Experiment with accelerations by using different gears for varying terrain and wind conditions.

Carmichael also gave these guidelines for sprinting at the end of a race and for how much work you should do in a breakaway: Study the last 500 yards of a race. Try to pick a landmark in that last 500 yards, knowing that from that landmark, if you were to take a straight shot for the finish, you could continue to accelerate all the way. If you're in a group and there is a strong crosswind, stay on the downwind side of the group to begin your jump.

While riding in a breakaway, remember that all the energy you expend should benefit you so that you reach the finish area with strength to spare for the sprint. Ask yourself, "Am I the driving force in the break?" If the answer is yes, then chances are someone in the break is trying to level the playing field and get you to take the brunt of the work. The break should not live or die by your work. Try taking shorter pulls and maintaining the same pace as the rider who just finished pulling. It is possible to save considerable energy during a long breakaway if you reduce the length of your pulls in the pace line.

Isolated Leg Training

For many years cyclists have found that isolated or one-leg training can improve all aspects of cycling fitness. It can increase leg strength and refine spinning so that you have the fluid pedal stroke of a professional rider. It can boost leg speed and endow you with enough power to sprint over steep hills or accelerate quickly in a sprint.

One-legged cycling makes you pedal in complete circles. During traditional two-legged cycling, the other leg can't help you through the dead spots on the back of the stroke. These are the places your leg makes the transition from pushing down to pulling up and from pulling up to going across the top.

To make it happen, you have to use the hip flexors on the front of your upper thigh and the hamstrings in back and use them much more than normal. Do it enough, and this rounder, more powerful stroke becomes ingrained. Put both feet on the pedals again, and you'll turn them better than ever.

Before you begin, warm up for 10 to 15 minutes with both legs. Isolated leg training can be done on the road or indoors on a wind or magnetic trainer. "On the road, hold your leg just to the side and back a bit. This position will feel too awkward for a few minutes," says Ed Pavelka, coauthor of *The Complete Book of Long Distance Cycling*. To create sufficient resistance, use your gear system or find terrain with a slight upward tilt. Stick to roads that are relatively free of traffic so that you're safe in this unusual position.

Indoors, you can put your foot on a stool, reach back and hang it on the trainer, or rest it on the down-tube bottle cage. Training indoors is good because you can fully concentrate on pedaling without worrying about cars on the road or obstacles on the trail.

Don't try to pedal at your normal cadence when doing this training. The idea is to work on smoothness, coordination, and power, not leg speed or cardiovascular fitness. You can even think of it as a form of weight training.

Concentrate on different parts of the pedal stroke. Focus on pushing down for 25 to 50 pedal strokes, then on pulling up for 25 to 50. Work on a smooth transition across the bottom from downstroke to upstroke. A cadence of 60 rpm or less helps you coordinate these movements.

Improvement in pedaling style is a slow process. You gradually get better over weeks or months. It's hard initially; you feel uncoordinated, and your muscles fatigue quickly because they're being used in unaccustomed ways. You thought your pedaling technique was pretty good? Now you know better. But after just a few one-leg sessions, you'll see dramatic improvement.

Adjust the gear recommendations if they're too hard or too easy. Simply mix some one-leg pedaling into your weekly program as necessary to cultivate your feel for a round pedal stroke. Tables 2.1 and 2.2 list two workouts recommended by Ed Pavelka. Anyone can use these workouts.

TABLE 2.1	Workout 1	
Gear	**Cadence (rpm)**	**Schedule**
39 × 17	40–60	2 min. with left leg
39 × 17	40–60	2 min. with right leg
39 × 17	80–100	2 min. with both legs, spinning easy
39 × 19	80–90	2 min. with left leg
39 × 19	80–90	2 min. with right leg
39 × 17	80–100	2 min. with both legs, spinning easy
Do two to three times.		

TABLE 2.2	Workout 2	
Gear	**Cadence (rpm)**	**Schedule**
39 × 17	80–100	3 min. with left leg
39 × 17	80–100	3 min. with right leg
53 × 13	40–60	3 min. with both legs, pedaling hard
39 × 19	80–100	3 min. with both legs, spinning easy
Do two to three times.		

Ergometer Speed Work

At the Olympic Training Center in Colorado Springs, permanent resident cyclists often have to conduct some of their winter sprint training sessions indoors because of the weather. Other cyclists like to do sprints on bicycle ergometers because they are able to accurately repeat the workloads from sprint to sprint and are able to measure increases in power.

Here is a workout often used for developing leg speed, power, and quick recovery. You will have to adjust the gearing and sets according to your age and level of fitness.

Warm up for 10 to 15 minutes, including three or four accelerations of about 15 seconds at the end of the warm-up. Complete the following ride in 10 minutes with no rest: Ride 1 minute in 39 × 17 gear at a cadence of 90 rpm. Gradually increase the gearing, keeping the same cadence, over the next 9 minutes, allowing your heart rate to reach 90 to 95 percent of maximum as you try to reach a 53 × 17 gear. Follow with 5 minutes of recovery in a moderate gear at a moderate cadence. Then complete the following 1-minute sprint five times: sprint 45 seconds in a 53 × 17 gear at a cadence of 90 rpm, then raise the cadence to 110 to 120 for about 15 seconds. Between each sprint, ride 1 minute in a moderate gear. Finish the workout with three 30-stroke sprints (53 × 17 gear) at a 110 to 120 cadence. Cool down for about 10 minutes.

High-Speed Spinning

You also can work on your pedaling coordination for high-speed sprinting on a wind or magnetic trainer. During this exercise you will be turning close to 140 rpm for the effort.

After warming up, make an all-out, 30-second effort. Rise out of the saddle to get on the gear, then sit. Recover completely by pedaling easy for 4 to 5 minutes. Limit your hardest gear to 53 × 16 or 53 × 15. The key is to work on high revolutions per minute and maintain them for the whole sprint. Do 10 of these, then cool down.

 ## The Final Spin

Remember that any cyclist, regardless of size and muscular strength, can become a good sprinter. Recall the 2000 Olympic road race, in which Jan Ullrich, a great all-around cyclist and time trialist, beat the other two riders in the breakaway in the final sprint for the gold medal. By working hard on his sprint in the spring and summer of 2000, he became an Olympic champion.

There are many physiological reasons why speed work is necessary to maximize your potential at any distance, from criteriums to long road races. During speed work, you train your body to recruit the muscles needed for fast riding. You also learn a sense of relaxation at race pace, which comes as a result of training your muscles to function at an accelerated pace.

During speed work your muscles also begin to accumulate lactic acid. Eventually, so much lactic acid builds up that your muscles begin to lose their ability to contract. That is why your muscles begin to lock up after about 60 seconds of maximal sprinting. Training, especially speed training, can modify this physiological effect. One of the adaptations to the workouts presented in this chapter is the ability of your muscles to buffer some or most of the lactic acid. You can sprint faster and for a longer time before lactic acid brings you to your knees.

Building power and speed into your cycling program is a good way to add variety to your workouts. And there is no reason to repeat the same speed work every week, because there are many options for getting the same job done. It is possible to get your body to move faster, and speed training is the answer. Just give it a try!

3

RAISING LACTATE THRESHOLD

If you were to train a couple of days a week for road racing or time trialing, it would be best to spend those days doing lactate threshold, or tempo, training. This intensity often is referred to as the point of pushing "hard" on the ride. It is the intensity that you can maintain during a long climb, a breakaway, or a time trial—in other words, a maximal, steady-state effort.

At this point, you are riding in the threshold between when the energy for muscular contraction is coming primarily from aerobic metabolism and when anaerobic metabolism begins to kick in at a higher rate. Once you pass the threshold, excessive amounts of lactic acid produced by the muscles begin to accumulate. Lactic acid begins to shut down the metabolic mechanisms within your muscle cells, and, because it is an acid, you experience that burning sensation in your muscles.

For most fit cyclists, this phenomenon occurs when they ride at an effort requiring 80 to 90 percent of maximum heart rate or maximal oxygen consumption ($\dot{V}O_2$max). Training in this zone allows you to increase the speed or effort that you can work at before you cross into the pain of lactic acid accumulation. Provided you have the proper aerobic base, built primarily from endurance work, this could be the level of training that has been missing from your program.

When you ride at this intensity, you will experience heavy breathing, tired muscles, and increased fatigue. When you train at or slightly below this effort, you will experience an effect that will allow you to sustain more work at higher intensities and at a lower heart rate. Of all athletes, competitive road cyclists have some of the highest $\dot{V}O_2$max values recorded. Some coaches and scientists claim that the fastest cyclists are those with the highest $\dot{V}O_2$max measures; others claim that the fastest cyclists are those whose lactate thresholds are at the highest percentage of their $\dot{V}O_2$max. Many coaches say the best athlete is one blessed with both a high $\dot{V}O_2$max and a high lactate threshold.

Even though many cyclists use lactate-threshold training in their programs, it is still a nebulous term. Ask any 10 scientists or coaches to define lactate threshold and you are likely to get 10 different answers. "The point is that we are defining a small range where an athlete can train and compete optimally," says J.T. Kearney, former sports physiologist at the Olympic Training Center. "And lactate threshold is a term used to define that range." Other terms, such as anaerobic threshold, maximal steady state effort, OBLA (onset of blood lactate accumulation), and heart rate deflection point, often are used in the literature. When you read other books or magazine articles, realize that all are talking about the same physiological phenomenon.

LACTATE THRESHOLD: A FITNESS PREDICTOR THAT WON'T MAX YOU OUT

Although most top endurance cyclists have high $\dot{V}O_2$ max values, and it is a good predictor of performance, coaches and scientists have begun to look at physiological tests that don't push cyclists completely to the maximum to determine fitness and economy of effort.

One submaximal test determines a rider's lactate threshold. Lactic acid is the by-product of anaerobic energy production (energy produced without oxygen). Because it is an acid, it begins to shut down the muscles' contractile mechanisms and may even cause a burning sensation. During exercise, a cyclist can perform up to a certain intensity without building up much lactic acid in the blood. When this intensity is exceeded, lactic acid levels in the muscles rise, and the muscles fatigue rapidly. The critical exercise intensity at which the contractile mechanisms begin to shut down is referred to as lactate threshold.

The best way to determine lactate threshold is for a cyclist to ride a stationary bicycle at a given intensity for four to five minutes in a laboratory. Then a small sample of blood is taken from the cyclist's fingertip to be analyzed for lactic acid. The workload (intensity) is increased slightly. This process is repeated for four to five workloads. When lactic acid values are plotted against oxygen consumption and heart rate, an upswing in the graph occurs. The cyclist then has a range of heart rates or power outputs corresponding to her lactate threshold use to guide training intensity. Most elite cyclists reach their lactate threshold at 85 to 90 percent of $\dot{V}O_2$ max, whereas untrained individuals reach theirs at 50 to 70 percent of $\dot{V}O_2$ max.

Figure 3.1 graphs a cyclist completing a test on a bicycle ergometer that progresses from an easy to a maximum workload. His lactate threshold is at about 90 percent of his maximum, and the curve plotting lactic acid shows a

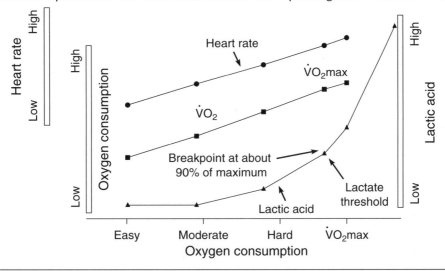

Figure 3.1   Physiological characteristics and the lactate threshold of a road cyclist.

(continued)

distinct break. At this point, the body begins to produce lactic acid excessively and/or has a hard time removing it from the muscles and blood. Being able to compete slightly below or at your lactate threshold for long periods of time is essential for successful performance. This is the intensity you need to hold in a 10- to 25-mile time trial or while going hard in a breakaway or on a long climb.

Lactic Acid—Is It the Bad Boy of Exercise?

Lactic acid results from the breakdown of glucose, the primary fuel for anaerobic work, in the absence of oxygen (glycolysis). Early work by scientists such as Dr. A.V. Hill from the Harvard Fatigue Laboratory theorized that lactic acid production during intense exercise was due to a lack of oxygen at the cellular level and was an indicator that anaerobic energy production had begun.

Today there is much evidence in the scientific literature showing that lactic acid is always being produced, even when you are at rest. A constant concentration of lactic acid in your bloodstream does not mean that no further lactic acid is being produced, only that it is being removed as fast as you are producing it. There also may be several reasons why lactic acid accumulates in your blood; insufficient oxygen may be only part of the story. We now know that glycolysis becomes very active during high-intensity exercise even when there is an adequate supply of oxygen being delivered to your muscles.

But when glycolysis becomes significant and not enough oxygen is supplied to your muscles, the amount of lactic acid formed becomes greater than what can be removed by your body, and the concentration begins to rise in your muscles and blood. High lactic acid concentrations inhibit your muscles' ability to contract properly, and you must either slow down or come to a complete stop. Although anaerobic energy production may not be significant during long road races, you must possess both the aerobic conditioning for prolonged energy production and the anaerobic conditioning necessary for shorter but more intense strategic efforts. For this reason, both energy systems must be trained to the fullest if you want to be successful.

The point at which lactic acid begins to rise in your blood depends on your $\dot{V}O_2$max and on your lactic threshold. This is the point at which lactic acid production exceeds removal and the effort becomes debilitating. At race pace, many competitive cyclists stay just below lactic threshold, which allows them to use both aerobic and anaerobic energy. An important part of training is to try to shift the lactic threshold so that it corresponds to a higher percentage of your maximal oxygen consumption.

Two basic strategies have been used to train this system. The first requires you to drive the production of lactic acid very high by completing relatively short but intense intervals of one to five minutes. Rests vary with the intensity and duration of the work; most coaches recommend a work-to-rest ratio of 1 to 2. For example, after completing a 90-second bout, you should rest for 180 seconds. Simply put, higher intensities produce larger amounts of lactic acid. During a specific training session you may complete several such intervals with several minutes of rest between each interval.

The second strategy is to work at a less intense level but increase the duration and shorten the rest intervals. The purpose is to sustain or tolerate the lactic acid for long periods of time. This method ensures that you will begin each work interval with a higher level of lactic acid because a decrease in the recovery interval reduces the time available for the removal of lactic acid. This means you will be able to train at increasing levels of lactic acid and thus gradually acclimate your body to the challenge of pushing through the fatigue associated with lactic acid buildup.

Training at Lactate Threshold

Training at lactate threshold is significant for several reasons. If everything else were equal, the higher your lactate threshold, the faster the pace or speed you could hold over long distances or steep climbs. Although success in road events is in part related to high maximal aerobic capacity and the ability to sprint, it also requires the cyclist to compete at a pace that is at a high percentage of her maximal capacity. Scientists often refer to this ability as meaning that a cyclist can effectively use a high percentage of maximal oxygen consumption for long periods while training or racing.

Training at or slightly below the lactate threshold is used to shift to the right the point at which lactate accumulates—that is, at a faster pace or a higher percentage of $\dot{V}O_2max$ (see figure 3.2). Everything else being equal, the higher the lactate threshold, the faster the pace that can be held over long distances.

The training programs listed in this chapter will help you raise your threshold from the 75 to 80 percent level to the 90 percent level of elite cyclists. This means that you will be able to ride at a pace closer to your maximal oxygen consumption. For example, you will be able to raise your speed in a time trial from 26 to 29 mph or your power output from 250 to 300 watts while time trialing. You also will be able to break away with fitter cyclists, climb hills better, and attack with more speed.

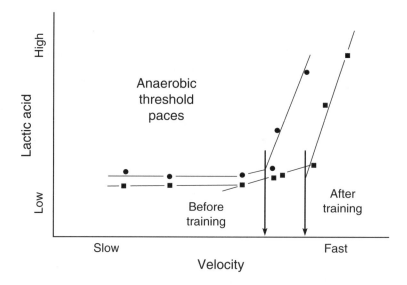

Figure 3.2 Training at lactate threshold will shift the threshold to the right, as shown on the curves above. A higher lactate threshold allows a cyclist to compete at higher intensities and/or speeds.

From "Science of Sport Training for Cycling: Part II" by Peter van Handel, 1991, Conditioning for Cycling, 1(2), p. 22. Copyright 1991 by the National Strength and Conditioning Association. Reprinted by permission.

Field Tests for Lactate Threshold

Identifying this pace without actually monitoring lactic acid levels in the blood may be difficult. Not many of us are able to be tested in laboratories and have our lactate thresholds determined by lactic acid measurements in relation to our intensity of effort. Here is a time trial test that you can use on the road to get a fair estimate of your lactate threshold based on heart rate and power output.

Rob Sleamaker, author of *Serious Training for Serious Athletes,* has developed a field test that predicts your lactate threshold using a time trial. You will need a heart rate monitor, a stopwatch, and a record sheet to record date, distance, time, and your average heart rate. Be sure to warm up properly before the test.

Start the stopwatch, or use a cyclocomputer with a stopwatch mode, as you begin the test. Perform a 10-mile time trial or long, moderately steep climb at the fastest pace you can sustain and at a steady effort with no loss of speed. Your heart rate should stabilize after about five minutes. Record your finishing time. Assume that the average heart rate you achieved and sustained is your lactate threshold. Make sure you complete a cool-down after this hard effort.

Complete this test every four to six weeks during the year. You can use this test in place of a scheduled interval, hill, or race-pace workout. Use the heart rate and pace-per-mile results to help you plan your workouts for the coming weeks.

As you become more fit, you will reach the point at which lactic acid accumulation becomes delayed or shifts to the right (see figure 3.2) and your lactate threshold coincides with a harder physical effort. Your lactate threshold will improve as your season progresses. Most elite athletes reach peaks in lactate threshold at about 85 to 90 percent of $\dot{V}O_2$max.

The heart rate or power you can maintain at this pace is indicative of your lactate threshold. Once again, it is important to consider environmental conditions because oxygen use, the level of lactic acid in the blood, and heart rate responses are markedly affected by wind and temperature.

An experienced cyclist learns to monitor lactate threshold by listening to specific physiological and psychological cues other than heart rate. Lance Armstrong describes his feelings this way: "You are usually at your lactate threshold heart rate when you are breathing hard and it is difficult to carry on a conversation with the other cyclists. In addition to heart rate and respiratory intensity, I try to monitor the feeling in my leg muscles and overall amount of effort."

Every year more cyclists use wireless heart rate monitors and power meters (more on both training tools in chapter 4) in conjunction with subjective measures to determine proper training intensity. A heart rate monitor and a power meter help you accurately determine your heart rate while you are riding.

Indoor Test to Determine Lactate Threshold

You also can complete lactate threshold testing on a magnetic trainer with your road bicycle. You must be able to accurately determine your power (watts) using a power meter (see chapter 4). You also should record your heart rate during the test.

During the test, you will gradually increase your speed or power output while staying seated on the bike. After a 10- to 15-minute warm-up, start the test by riding at about 100 watts for women or 120 watts for men. Every minute, increase the watts by 20. At the end of each minute, have an assistant record your watts and heart rate.

At some power output during the ride, you will reach lactate threshold as measured by your "ventilatory threshold." This is the point at which your breathing becomes labored and you start to feel the lactic acid begin to load up in your legs. Your breathing begins to rise exponentially because the lactic acid in your body is being broken down rapidly and converted to carbon monoxide that you have to exhale.

Continue to increase the workloads until you cannot hold the power output for 15 to 20 seconds. You will be able to ride at higher workloads, but your breathing will become excessively heavy.

Table 3.1 shows the results from an indoor test using power to determine lactate threshold. In this example, the athlete reached his threshold at a power output of 240 watts and a heart rate of 157. The cyclist can use this information and the information gained from the power outputs during the time trial test to fine-tune the heart rate and power output he will use in racing and training and increase his lactate threshold.

TABLE 3.1 Sample Results From an Indoor Lactate Threshold Test

Power (watts)	Heart rate	
120	119	
140	126	
160	134	
180	143	
200	148	
220	154	
240	157	Ventilatory threshold
260	162	
280	167	

CYCLING ECONOMY:
USING AEROBIC CAPACITY WISELY

Data for elite cyclists suggest that a high oxygen uptake and lactate threshold are required for successful competition at the national and international levels. But even though a high aerobic consumption and lactate threshold are necessary for success in road cycling, they are not the only determinants for success.

Economy to a cyclist is like economy to an automobile driver. Economy is the ability to do a certain amount of work using as little energy as possible. You want to conserve gas in your car. You want to use a low percentage of the $\dot{V}O_2$max in your body at a given cycling speed. Both examples represent economy.

"I would say that economy is an important determinant of success at the elite level of cycling," says Steve Johnson, PhD, exercise scientist for USA Cycling. "If two cyclists have similar $\dot{V}O_2$max profiles, the more economical cyclist will win more long-distance races. Even if a cyclist has a lower $\dot{V}O_2$max than many against whom he is racing, this cyclist can often defeat other cyclists because he may ride at a lower percentage of his maximum at any given speed."

An uneconomical cyclist may need to use 5 to 10 percent more energy than an economical cyclist to cycle at a given pace. This means that if the two cyclists have comparable $\dot{V}O_2$max values, the uneconomical cyclist will work closer to his maximal capacity than the economical cyclist. Because the physiological strain the body feels is directly related to the percentage of $\dot{V}O_2$max, the economical cyclist will have an advantage. In other words, he will be able to ride faster while experiencing less fatigue and conserving valuable muscle fuels at the same time.

Here is another example of the power of economy: Two cyclists with the same $\dot{V}O_2$max profiles enter a time trial. Cyclist A is more economical. Both ride at a high speed; however, to reach and maintain this speed, cyclist B must ride at a pace equal to 95 percent of her $\dot{V}O_2$max. Cyclist A, on the other hand, can ride at the same speed yet only be at 90 percent of her max. If cyclist A increases her effort to 95 percent, she would outride cyclist B and win.

Economy can be determined by measuring the amount of oxygen needed to perform at several submaximal intensities. To measure economy this way, ride a stationary bicycle for 5 to 10 minutes. Training, improved pedaling mechanics, and relaxation on the bike have been shown to improve economy. If economy really has improved after training, the oxygen cost for each intensity should be less.

Figure 3.3 shows the oxygen consumption at different workloads of two cyclists who have similar $\dot{V}O_2$max measurements. Cyclist A is more economical. At any workload she consumes less oxygen than cyclist B. At a workload of 300 watts, cyclist B uses about 70 ml/kg/min while cyclist A uses about 15 percent less. Cyclist A achieves a higher work output at her $\dot{V}O_2$max.

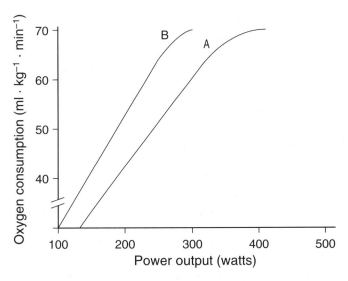

Figure 3.3 Economy curves for two cyclists.

(continued)

Tempo and interval training can improve your economy. The theory is that by practicing fast cycling you naturally become more economical. You have to be economical to ride at 30-plus miles per hour. Once you've trained your body to respond economically at these speeds, it most likely will do so at the slower speeds of distance cycling.

Another way to improve economy is through a biomechanical assessment. A film analysis of a cyclist riding often is used. From high-speed film, joint angles and forces can be calculated.

You also can improve economy by improving performance. First, improve pedaling mechanics. Learn to pedal smoothly and correctly so that your movements are more effective. In other words, improve the pedal stroke from top dead center all the way through the bottom, and learn how to spin instead of pushing big gears.

Other factors that waste energy without propelling the bicycle forward will affect economy. Fighting the bicycle, holding the handlebars too tightly, and riding in an unaerodynamic position affect economy. We'll get into the specifics of biomechanically correct riding technique in chapter 12.

The Right Dose of Lactate-Threshold Training

Lactate-threshold training can give you that extra boost to make those long climbs, breakaways, and time trials easier, but only after you have the proper base of endurance conditioning. If you do not have the proper aerobic conditioning, these workouts will tear you down rather than build you up.

"Many people think there's a secret to climbing. And there is: extremely high conditioning, low body fat and weight, and knowing how to pace yourself, especially on long climbs."

Greg LeMond, three-time Tour de France winner

Generally, lactate-threshold workouts take two forms: longer intervals and pace rides. Steady-paced threshold training often is referred to as tempo training; intermittent threshold training sometimes is referred to as tempo intervals or cruise intervals. Because work at this intensity is difficult to sustain, interval training is the best way to begin. Naturally, warm-up and cool-down rides should be included before and after each workout.

The following paragraphs describe several lactate-threshold workouts. If you're not already using lactate-threshold training, try adding a little to your weekly program. Start with one session per week, then gradually increase the intensity and length of these sessions (but not the frequency—once or twice a week is plenty), and continue your threshold training as you sharpen for big races. Time-trial times should come down and race performances should improve as your lactate threshold shifts to the right.

You do not have to limit yourself to one or two of the following workouts. Feel free to mix several of the workouts—variety will help make the intense efforts of threshold training more tolerable. Whatever you do, do it with commitment: intensity is the key to getting the most out of threshold training.

Threshold training is hard work and requires recovery, so be sure to spend a day of easy training after these workouts. You must occasionally train easy to give your harder sessions extra power and energy.

Long Intervals

These intervals are 5 to 12 minutes long. Start with shorter intervals; as you become more fit, lengthen the intervals. Gradually raise your heart rate to lactate-threshold level and maintain it until the end of the interval.

The rest intervals between the long intervals at lactate threshold should be two to five minutes long, or until your heart rate returns to about 120 beats per minute, although the length of recovery varies with the length and intensity of the interval. Ride easy until you feel you have recovered for the next interval.

Start with three or four intervals of up to five minutes. Then gradually increase the number of intervals (five is plenty), increasing the length of each interval until, after several months, you can complete two sets of five intervals. In the early part of the season use your small chain ring; once you are into heavy racing, use the big chain ring.

Timed-Distance Intervals

Mark off a known distance that will require about five to seven minutes to ride at your lactate-threshold heart rate. Then ride the distance and record your time and average heart rate. Come back to this test every few weeks. Your goal is to lower your time while not going over your lactate-threshold heart rate for extended periods during the ride.

Lactate Criss-Cross Training

Owen Anderson, editor of *Running Research News*, recommends the following workout to stimulate lactate-threshold training: You need a heart rate monitor with high and low alarms. Set the lower alarm about eight beats below your lactate-threshold heart rate and the upper alarm five to six beats above your lactate-threshold heart rate.

After a good warm-up, increase speed or intensity steadily until the upper alarm goes off, then gradually slow your pace until the lower alarm sounds. Travel back and forth between the upper and lower alarms, taking about two minutes to make each ascent and descent. Add length to each interval and repetitions to your workout as your fitness progresses during the season.

Fartlek

Fartlek is a Swedish term for speed play. Fartlek can be another form of lactate-threshold training. This less formal approach to long intervals is performed on a course that contains hills for work and downhills for active rest. Fartlek training can be performed with a small, well-matched group of cyclists. Cyclists should take turns leading up the hills setting the pace; the stronger riders can try to push the pace even harder when about half the hill is completed. Make sure that everyone recovers adequately on the down-hills. It is important to learn to go hard on all types of terrain. Fartlek is supposed to be unsystematic and spontaneous, a style of training that lets you tune into your power and rhythm.

Paced Training

This type of training calls for maintaining your riding pace or tempo for longer periods of time or distances. These longer tempo rides will help you measure your fitness, improve your pedaling technique while pushing larger gears, and keep you motivated. Most cyclists train on a known course that replicates a time-trial course or short, rolling road circuit. Using the same course will help you gauge your progress and keep you motivated as the season progresses.

Paced training is completed at a specific intensity (use a heart rate monitor and/or power meter), and the course should be 5 to 10 miles long. The major difference between paced training and long intervals is the length of the workout and the emphasis on maintaining the pace throughout the ride. As your lactate threshold goes up, your time for the course will come down. Remember to take into account wind, temperature, and equipment when riding the set course. Paced training is great for working on your racing technique and for testing your time-trial fitness.

Anaerobic Training: Training Above Lactate Threshold

Occasionally you will be called on for short efforts that exceed your lactate threshold. Attacks lasting a few minutes; starts of criteriums; short, steep climbs; and efforts to close a gap require you to work anaerobically for a few minutes. Training above lactate threshold enhances your muscles' ability to produce adenosine triphosphate (ATP). This type of training involves mostly type II (fast-twitch) muscle fibers. The prescription to improve your anaerobic capacity is relatively simple: work at a higher intensity (90 to 95 percent of your maximum heart rate) for a short duration, take an active rest of easy riding, and do another repeat of the interval. The primary method of anaerobic training is interval training.

Most cyclists and coaches find that six to eight weeks of high-intensity work of this nature before the peak of the season is adequate. Most cyclists cannot tolerate more than one or two sessions per week. Be sure to count short time trials as tough sessions.

Hill Intervals

Complete these intervals up a moderately steep hill. Gradually pick up your speed as you enter the hill, then shift to a larger gear and "jump" until you reach maximum speed. Hold it for no more than one minute. At the top of the hill, turn and ride easy down the hill until your heart rate returns to below 60 percent of maximum, and repeat three to eight times. These intervals should be done early in the week and not until late spring, after you have established a good base of endurance work and some lactate-threshold training.

Medium Intervals

Work intervals on flat roads and hill intervals that last one to two minutes at 90 to 95 percent of maximum heart rate will overload your anaerobic capacity. This leads to the increased capacity of the anaerobic system to tolerate more lactic acid and produce more ATP through glycolysis (the production of ATP with carbohydrate only and without oxygen). A session of 8 to 10 intervals with recovery rides of twice the time of the work intervals make for a hard training session.

Bridging Power Intervals

Tom Ehrhard, a USA Cycling elite-level coach, occasionally has his athletes train above lactate threshold to help train them for bridging situations such as bridging up to a breakaway. This is a heart rate or power output that is halfway between lactate threshold and $\dot{V}O_2$max heart rate or power output. During a training session you may want to try one to three intervals of three to five minutes at this intensity with about five minutes of easy riding between repeats.

 ***The Final Spin***

Having a high $\dot{V}O_2$max is not the only key to success in cycling. All other variables being equal, a cyclist who can maintain a pace requiring 80 to 90 percent of his maximum capacity of 70 ml of oxygen is far better off in a race than a cyclist who has a maximal oxygen consumption of 75 ml but who can only sustain a lactate-threshold pace of 75 percent. This shows the importance of knowing not only your $\dot{V}O_2$max but also your lactate threshold.

Training at lactate threshold is the most effective way to induce a shift to the right in the lactic acid curve (figure 3.1, page 29!). After proper training, the shift occurs at a faster speed and a higher percentage of maximal aerobic capacity.

Training too far below lactate threshold does not stimulate the anaerobic systems for lactic acid production within the muscle. You are basically training your aerobic energy system. On the other hand, too intense a pace will rapidly produce lactic acid, which will accumulate, resulting in early fatigue and a reduction in work intensity.

The benefits of training to increase lactate threshold and anaerobic power are primarily for cyclists who are interested in high-performance training. If you just want to improve your fitness, you probably do not need to spend much time training at these intensities. If, however, your goal is to win races and perform well in time trials, you need to spend one or two workouts a week training at lactate threshold.

4

ENHANCING CYCLING STRENGTH

© Jon Buckle/EMPICS

Perhaps one of the most important investments you can make to improve your cycling is to spend time developing a stronger body and investigating supplemental equipment and techniques to improve your fitness and performance. Resistance training, cross-training, indoor training, and heart rate and power monitors are just some of the tools you can add to your training arsenal. Training with free weights or machines and using plyometrics provide multiconditioning effects and help reduce injuries.

Cyclists who have worked all spring and summer on their bicycles will find cross-training a good change of pace during the off-season. Cross-training is a nice mental break and gives you something different to look forward to. For example, cyclists who cross-country ski look forward to snow-covered trails because they know that they will soon be gliding across them.

All cyclists can benefit from using a heart rate monitor and power meter during training and competition. Training with these monitors is like having a portable, full-time coach attached to your body. A heart rate monitor, power meter, and cyclocomputer serve as excellent motivators and take the guesswork out of evaluating your performance and adjusting your training program.

This chapter presents a menu of different modes of exercise that you can use year-round for improved performance. These training modes and various types of on-the-bike training can be knit together to form a yearly training program (see chapter 9).

Resistance Training

Successful cycling requires a combination of muscular endurance, strength, and power. The particular cycling discipline you are training for determines which of these attributes you should emphasize in training. A road race requires mostly muscular endurance, but you also will need power to climb steep hills and sprint at the end. An explosive sprint during a match sprint requires strength and power. Because of this, resistance training with free weights and/or machines has always been part of a good training program.

Recently resistance training has attracted the interest of middle-distance and distance athletes in many sports. Are resistance training and aerobic conditioning compatible during the same conditioning period? Will resistance training provide the necessary strength, power, suppleness, stamina, and potential?

Only in the past few years have researchers and coaches begun to investigate these issues. Several recently published studies and books have shown that strength training can increase leg strength and time-to-exhaustion during cycling without increasing maximal oxygen consumption. There is also evidence that increased strength reduces an endurance athlete's incidence of injury.

Robert Hickson and others from his laboratory at the University of Illinois at Chicago studied the impact of heavy-resistance training on leg strength in eight runners and cyclists who had been training for several years. Strength training was performed 3 days a week for 10 weeks while the subjects continued their normal endurance training. After 10 weeks, leg strength had increased by an average of 30 percent. Maximal oxygen consumption did not increase, which would have indicated increased maximal aerobic capacity, but time-to-exhaustion at maximal work rates increased by 13 percent in the running group and 11 percent in the cycling group.

Data do not demonstrate any negative performance effects from adding heavy-resistance training to ongoing endurance training. The authors concluded that certain types of endurance performance, particularly those requiring fast-twitch fiber recruitment (for example, the ability to chase down a break), can be improved by supplementing training with resistance training.

Recently, a group of researchers from the University of Maryland completed a study investigating the effects of resistance training on lactate threshold and endurance performance. The researchers randomly assigned 18 healthy males either to a group that engaged in resistance training for 12 weeks or to a control group. After 12 weeks, despite no changes in maximal oxygen consumption, there was a 33 percent increase in cycling time-to-exhaustion at 75 percent peak oxygen consumption in the strength-trained group. The improved endurance performance was associated with a 12 percent increase in lactate threshold.

Steve Fleck, PhD, author of *Designing Resistance Training Programs,* says of this study, "A higher lactate threshold and endurance time-to-exhaustion means that an athlete can ride at a higher intensity before fatigue sets in and causes a reduction in cycling speed. Their findings indicate that resistance training improved endurance performance independently of changes in oxygen consumption. This improvement appears to be related to increases in lactate threshold and increased leg strength." Put simply, endurance training and resistance training are not mutually exclusive. Both may be needed for improved performance.

If resistance training can improve performance, then how much time should be devoted to it? Remember that any supplemental training, whether it's resistance training or some other activity, is only an aid to improve cycling, not a substitute for riding, and should not be overdone. During any week of training, cycling should be the major component. But as you will see later in this chapter, resistance training of varying amounts of time and intensity needs to be part of your overall cycling program.

When designing a resistance program to fulfill your individual needs, keep these points in mind: First, track specialists need more power and strength than do longer-distance cyclists. Second, you need to identify your individual weaknesses and strengths and put an emphasis on developing muscle groups that need increased strength and power. Do maintenance work for muscles that are already well-conditioned. Third, resistance training should receive more emphasis during the off-season, when higher-volume training (more reps or sets) is done.

Resistance training offers the additional benefit of reducing injuries by helping to strengthen the muscles, tendons, and ligaments around the foot, ankle, knee, and hips. Thus, a strength program of moderate resistance and 12 to 15 repetitions per exercise that emphasizes injury prevention may be appropriate for distance cyclists and not adversely affect their endurance performance.

Program Planning

When you design a strength-training program for yourself, have specific goals in mind. Consider the needs and energy demands of the different events; the prescribed exercises should increase the realization of your potential. Exercise prescription for resistance training demands considerable thought, planning, evaluation, and organization. The key motivating factor to your participation in a strength and conditioning program will be improved performance.

Your first emphasis should be on proper planning. As with road training, you should develop strength training within your yearly training program. The various parts of the resistance-training program are matched against periods of the cycling season and shown in table 4.1. (For more information about dividing the cycling season into specific periods, please see chapter 9.)

The transitional phase of the resistance program begins with the end of the competitive season and is designed to help you reduce time on the bicycle while your body adjusts to new stresses. These exercises are done with a minimum of equipment. Body resistance can be used for some, avoiding the common problem of using too much weight too soon. Actual workout time should be short: 15 to 20 repetitions of each exercise for one to three sets. The training can be done two or three days a week as you gradually taper your miles on the bike and let your body get adequate rest.

The foundation phase begins after the muscles have been properly prepared. Begin using slightly heavier resistance while decreasing the number of repetitions. This phase is geared toward allowing the muscles to grow. Harvey Newton, former strength training consultant to the U.S. Cycling Team, commented on the concern many cyclists have that they may add too much muscle mass to their bodies. According to Newton, resistance training "does not mean that body weight will increase; in fact, body composition may change—body fat will decrease, while some muscle growth takes place—while body weight remains constant. By working the muscles more intensely and allowing some growth, the body will be properly prepared for the next phase."

TABLE 4.1 Strength Training Program Phases

Road cycling season*

	Transition	General preparation phase I	General preparation phase II	Specialization	Competition
Months	Oct.	Nov. to Dec.	Dec. to Jan.	Jan. to Feb.	Mar. to racing season
Number of weeks	4	4 to 6	4 to 6	4 to 6	4+
Resistance training phase	Transitional	Foundation	Basic strength	Power	Peaking
Purpose	Adjust to strength training	Build muscle tissue	Gain strength	Build explosive power	Maintain strength
Sets	1 to 3	3 to 4	5 to 7	5 to 6	1 to 3
Repetitions	15 to 20	8 to 12	1 to 6	1 to 15	6 to 10
Exercises	General in nature: circuits, body weight as resistance, etc.	4 to 6, specific muscle groups: quads/glutes, biceps, triceps, abdominals, back, deltoids, gastrocnemius	3 to 5, combined muscle groups: concentrate on weak areas	3 to 4, muscle groups specific to cycling: partial squats, lunges, rowing	Work on 1 to 3 weak areas not directly strengthened while riding
Intensity	Minimum	Moderate	Heavy (80 to 100% of maximum capacity)	Moderate	Light
Days per week	2 to 3	3	3	2 to 3	1 to 2

* This season assumes the rider trains and rides in the Northern Hemisphere.

From "Strength Training for Cycling" by H. Newton. In *Science of Cycling* (p. 24) by E.R. Burke (ed.), 1986, Champaign, IL: Human Kinetics. Copyright 1986 by Edmund Burke. Adapted by permission.

The basic-strength phase is geared toward increasing the strength of individual muscle groups and using these groups in a coordinated effort. Weight is increased as repetitions are decreased. The exercises may change during this phase in order to test your body's ability to move more effectively in a unified effort and to allow for variation in training. Increasing your strength quickly is quite easy; the real benefit comes from converting strength gains into power.

Power is the ability to use force in an explosive fashion. Increased power allows a sprinter to jump more quickly and a road cyclist to bridge gaps more quickly, and to do this repeatedly if necessary. Therefore, in the power phase, resistance is reduced, perhaps along with the number of strength-training sessions each week, to allow for more training on the bike. Exercises are all done in an explosive manner, using timing devices where appropriate.

As the power phase ends, you need to decide how much, if any, maintenance training you will do. This is the peaking phase. Because you will be racing on a regular basis, reduce the amount, duration, and intensity of strength work. Continuing to train weak areas not normally stressed on the bike is often a good idea. This can be done with simple exercises using body weight. This additional work will allow you to maintain your newfound strength so that the next transitional phase begins with a level of strength higher than the previous year's.

Cycling-Specific Exercises

Table 4.2 lists exercises you can do during the various phases of your resistance-training program. These are only meant as examples; you may add other exercises that you are already doing to the list. For example, to prepare your lower back musculature, you could begin the transitional phase with back extensions, isolating the muscles but not using any large resistance. During the foundation phase, you could employ stiff-legged dead lifts or "good mornings." Once your muscles have been properly prepared, you could add power cleans and high pulls during the basic-strength and power phases. For peaking, you could again employ back extensions. Use your imagination to design specific exercises, or consult other books on resistance training. It is beyond the scope of this book to outline every movement that could be of use. Rather, a few basic exercises are shown here. It is always a good idea to consult a knowledgeable coach who is familiar with resistance training.

Begin and end each resistance-training session with some stretching and aerobic exercise to warm up and cool down. As an additional cool-down, you also should ride a bicycle, a wind-load simulator, or a stationary bicycle for 5 to 10 minutes to help loosen your muscles in a familiar fashion. You want to maintain your smooth pedaling style.

Always keep safety a top priority. Use spotters on certain exercises, such as squats, and use collars on all barbells and dumbbells. Wear proper shoes when lifting heavy weights. Shoes should have firm soles and the heel should be designed to prevent instability or imbalance.

TABLE 4.2	Suggested Strength Training Exercises per Phase		
Phase	**Day 1**	**Day 2**	**Day 3**
Transition	Trunk curl Dips Leg extension/leg curl Pull-ups Back extension **or** General circuit	Twist/side bend Leg press Lat pull-down Hanging leg raise Press **or** General circuit	Trunk curl Lunges Calf raise (single leg) Back extension Upright rowing **or** General circuit
Foundation	Squats Straight-arm pullover Trunk curl Calf raise Dips Back extension Pull-ups	Dumbbell press Hanging leg raise Good morning Leg press Trunk curl Bent-over rowing	Squats Bent-arm pullover Trunk curl Stiff-legged dead lift Pull-ups Calf raise Dips
Basic strength	Push press Power clean Squats Trunk curl Calf raise	Bench press High pulls Barbell twist (one end weight) Partial squats	Power clean Speed squats Incline press Rowing
Power	Power clean Dips Heavy partial squats Trunk curl Bent-over rowing	High pulls Push press Squats Trunk curl	Power clean Pull-ups Heavy partial squats Trunk curl
Peak	Back extension Trunk curl Squats Dips Pull-ups	Partial squats Dips Pull-ups Calf raise	

From "Strength Training for Cycling" by H. Newton. In *Science of Cycling* (p. 27) by E. R. Burke (ed.), 1986, Champaign, IL; Human Kinetics. Copyright 1986 by Edmund Burke. Adapted by permission.

Trunk Curls

Your lower legs can be in a straight or crossed position above your body or on a bench (see photo). When the feet are not braced, only the abdominal muscles are used, not the thigh and hip muscles. Slowly contract your abdominal muscles, placing your chin on your chest and attempting to touch your elbows to your knees. The actual movement should be about six to eight inches.

Dips

From a fully extended arm position, lower your body by bending your elbows. After lowering your body as far as possible, push back up to a locked-arm position.

If you are too weak to push back to the original position, perform only the first part of the exercise. Take about six seconds to lower your body, resisting the weight of your body and gravity all the way. Then use a bench or chair to return to the original position and repeat. After several weeks, you will be able to perform the complete exercise. This technique also can be used to modify pull-ups.

Back Extensions

Although a padded apparatus is pre-ferred, you may, with assistance, perform this exercise off the edge of a table or chair. From the position shown, slowly contract your lower back muscles until your trunk is parallel to the ground. There is no need to rise any higher. You can keep your back flat throughout the entire exercise or begin with your back rounded and finish with it flat. As you become stronger, you may hold additional weight behind your head during this exercise.

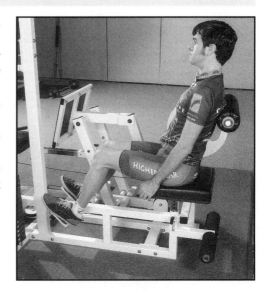

Leg Presses

Various leg press machines are available (slanted, horizontal, or vertical). Regardless of the machine, bend your knees to the desired level and return them to a locked position.

Lunges

Stand with your feet shoulder-width apart, torso erect, arms straight down, head up, and eyes straight ahead, as shown in photo A. With a firm grip on the dumbbells, step forward and sink down, as shown in photo B. Return to the original position, then repeat with the other leg. Very little weight is needed for this exercise to be effective. You can adjust the depth of your movement to mirror the knee flexion that matches pedaling.

a

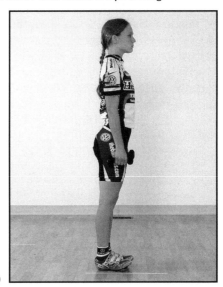

b

Upright Row

Assume the position shown in photo A by gripping the bar with your hands shoulder-width apart (or slightly less). Using your trapezius muscle, biceps, and middle deltoid, raise the weight to the level of your sternum, as shown in photo B. Your elbows should rise to a point beside the top of your head.

a

b

Squats

Squats are the base for any resistance-training program. They may be done throughout the training cycle; simply adjust the depth, intensity, and speed to match the phase of your program. The normal starting position is shown in photo A. The bar is on the trapezius and shoulders. (Use a towel or pad as a cushion if you need to.) Keep your feet hip-width apart and your toes pointed slightly out or straight ahead. Throughout the movement, keep your back flat and make sure the bar remains over your feet. Control your descent, taking one to three seconds. Be sure not to bounce on recovery.

You can use full squats (photo B) during the foundation phase of your resistance-training program. For full squats, lower yourself until your knees are fully bent. As you increase the weight, you can adjust the level of your squat so that at your lowest point only the tops of your thighs are parallel to the floor. The partial squat—in which you lower yourself only a few inches—can be used during any phase of your program, but it works best in the basic-strength phase. You may use a lot of weight as long as your trunk—your abdominal and lower back muscles—is strong enough to allow you to maintain proper position.

During the power phase of your program, you may try speed squats, in which you descend normally but rise as quickly as possible. Have someone time your ascent, starting a stopwatch as soon as you begin your upward movement and stopping it when your knees are straight. Strive to improve your ascent time for given weights. Keeping each squat under one second at a weight that is 80 to 85 percent of the total weight you can squat will help recruit fast-twitch muscle fibers. For lighter weights, set faster goals. Keep a record of your repetitions, times, and weights.

a

b

Straight-Arm Pullovers

Use a light weight (15- to 20-pound barbell or dumbbell). Start in the position shown in photo A and inhale deeply while lowering the weight (photo B). Exhale as you return the weight to the original position. You can use this exercise to help you regain your breath after a round of squats. The amount of weight is not important. This is a breathing exercise.

a

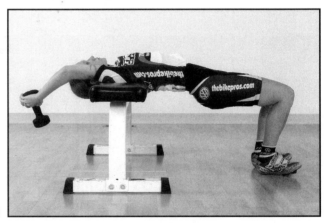

b

Good Mornings

The motion of this exercise resembles the old-fashioned custom of gentlemen bowing to wish people "good morning." Start with the bar on your shoulders (photo A), then flex your knees slightly while bending forward (photo B). Your lower back may be rounded or flat. Return to the original position to complete one repetition. Use light to moderate weights only. This exercise can be stressful if too much weight is used.

a

b

Bent-Over Row

Keep your knees fully flexed and your back mostly flat. Draw the weight up to your chest or abdominal area using your arms, shoulders, and the latissiumus muscles of your back. Do not allow the bar to drop as you return to the starting position. A variation of the exercise would be to lean your chest against an incline and use two dumbbells.

a

b

Calf Raises

For this exercise, you may use a barbell across your shoulders, hold a dumbbell in one hand (for exercising one calf at a time), or have a partner help you with the "donkey raise" (see photo). Put a board under your toes and stretch your calf muscles to the position shown, then raise your heels. Keep your knees straight. Do 15 to 30 repetitions.

Bent-Arm Pullovers

Place a bar on your chest (photo A) and inhale as you pass it over your face until it rests near the ground (photo B). Exhale as you return the weight to your chest. Use much less weight than in the straight-arm pullover.

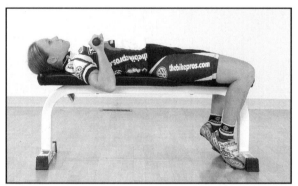

a

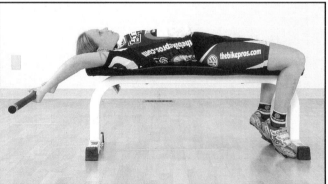

b

Stiff-Legged Dead Lifts

Even though this is called a stiff-legged dead lift, keep your knees slightly bent. Start in the position shown in photo A. Round your back and lower the weight, as shown in photo B. Performing this exercise on the floor limits your range of motion. Using a bench will allow a maximum stretch of your back and hamstring muscles.

a

b

Push Presses

This also can be called a "cheat press." Use your legs to start the bar's movement, but recruit your triceps and deltoids to finish the lockout phase. Hold the bar as shown in photo A, letting it rest on your front deltoids. Bend your knees a few inches. Then combine leg and arm thrust to get the bar over your head (photo B), rising up on your toes. Complete the lockout with your feet flat on the floor. Do not allow yourself to bend backward. Return to the original position for the next repetition.

a

b

Heavy Partial Squats

Begin from the position shown in the photo, with the bar resting on pins in a power rack. Keep your back flat and rise as quickly as possible. All cyclists should be able to work up to the 300- to 800-pound range.

Power Cleans

This is an excellent exercise for the basic-strength and power phases of your program. Start with your feet flat, about hip-width apart, and your knees over your toes (photo A). Use your legs and hips to raise the bar to knee level. Keep your arms straight and your back flat at this point. After the bar passes your knees, bend your ankles and knees and place the bar on your thighs above your knees. Jump up forcefully as you quickly raise the bar. Slightly dip your knees and rest the bar on your shoulders (photo B). This exercise uses the bigger muscles of your body and helps you develop a quick, explosive movement. It should take you one second to pull and place the bar on your shoulders.

a   b

High Pulls

Be sure that your back is flat and your hips do not lift too quickly when you do this exercise. This exercise uses the same technique as the power clean, except you can use a heavier weight since you do not pull the weight all the way to the shoulders. Start in the position shown in photo A and lift the bar to about waist high, as shown in photo B.

a

b

Barbell Twists

This exercise uses a rotational movement to work your muscles. Use your oblique muscles and the muscles of the abdominal wall to help rotate your body weight from side to side (see photos A and B). Do not use your arm muscles. Be sure to keep your hips stable.

a   b

From "Strength Training for Cycling" by H. Newton. In *Science of Cycling* (pp. 28–45) by E.R. Burke (ed.), 1986, Champaign, IL: Human Kinetics. Copyright 1986 by Edmund Burke. Adapted by permission.

Plyometrics for Power

One problem for many cyclists is the inability to fully use their muscular strength in explosive-type actions, such as sprinting up a short hill or accelerating at the start of a sprint. What they need is a training procedure that increases power, the ability to generate force quickly. In addition to the power phase of your resistance-training program, a training modality known as plyometrics emphasizes the explosive-reactive power of training.

Plyometrics often is called jump training. Plyometric exercises are jumps that are designed to contract muscles in a specific way. Concentric muscle contractions, which shorten muscles, are more forceful when they are preceded by eccentric muscle contractions, which lengthen muscles. When you land from a jump during a plyometric exercise, your thigh muscles tense while lengthening (an eccentric contraction). This eccentric contraction puts those muscles in a stretched position prior to jumping again (i.e., a prestretched position). When you leap from this prestretched position, you are taking advantage of both the elastic and the contractile components of your muscle tissue as well as something called the stretch reflex to generate a more powerful concentric contraction.

To picture the elastic property of a muscle, think of a rubber band and how it responds to being stretched. When you increase the stretch on the band, both the tension in the band and the velocity of shortening when you let it go increase. Similarly, when you stretch the elastic component of a muscle, you develop tension because of the muscle's elastic resistance to the stretch. When this tension is released, it aids the resulting muscle contraction.

When muscles lengthen quickly, the stretch reflex (also known as the myotactic reflex) is invoked and causes the muscle to contract. Inducing the stretch reflex in conjunction with the voluntary muscle contraction results in a more vigorous concentric contraction. Both the elastic component and the stretch reflex contribute to the total force generated in concentric contraction.

In a plyometric exercise such as stadium hops (see page 64), the rapid stretching (loading) of the muscles activates their stretch receptors and sends a very strong stimulus by way of the spinal cord to the muscles, causing them to contract powerfully. In sports, plyometrics can be used to improve the leg muscles' force and speed of contraction.

Good morale in cycling comes from good legs.

Sean Yates, British professional cyclist and Tour de France stage winner

An excellent book offering elementary drills is *Jumping Into Plyometrics* (2nd ed.) by Dr. Donald Chu. This section describes a few drills, taken from Dr. Chu's text, that are specific to cycling. Plyometrics should be initiated in the later part of the transition phase and can be continued into the power phase of your resistance-training program.

Like other exercises, plyometrics can lead to poor results if not used properly. Indeed, symptoms of tendinitis and synovitis, particularly of the knee, can result from too much plyometric training. Your fitness level and experience determine the frequency and duration of your plyometric training session. Stronger athletes can train more often and include more jumps in their routines, but even the most experienced individual should perform no more than two sessions a week, with a maximum of 60 to 80 jumps per session. You should have a sound conditioning base and have incorporated stretching into your program before engaging in plyometrics.

Split Squat With Cycle

No equipment is needed. Begin by standing upright. Spread your feet far apart, front to back, and bend your front leg 90 degrees at the hip and 90 degrees at the knee (see photo A). Jump up, switching leg positions in the air—the front leg kicks to the back position and the back leg bends up and comes through to the front (photo B). While bringing your back leg through, try to flex your knee so that it comes close to the buttock. Land in the split-squat position (photo C) and jump again immediately.

a   b   c

Alternating Push-Off

Use a box 6 to 12 inches high. Stand on the ground and place one foot on the box, heel close to the closest edge (photo A). Push off of the foot on the box to gain as much height as possible by extending through the entire leg and foot. Use a double-arm swing for height and balance (photo B). Land with feet reversed (photo C); the box foot lands a split second before the ground foot.

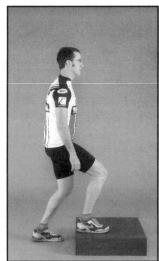

a   b   c

Squat Depth Jump

Use a box 12 to 42 inches high. Stand on the box in a quarter to half squat, toes close to the edge (photo A). Step off the box and land in a 90-degree squat position (photo B). Explode up out of the squat and land solidly in a squat (photo C). For added difficulty, land on a second box of equal height after doing the jump.

a   b   c

Single-Leg Push-Off

Use a box 6 to 12 inches high. Stand on the ground and place one foot on the box, heel close to the closest edge (photo A). Push off the foot on top of the box to gain as much height as possible by extending through the entire leg and foot. Use a double-arm swing for height and balance (photo B). Land with the same foot on top of the box (photo C) and push off again.

a   b   c

Stadium Hops

This exercise is best accomplished on bleachers or stadium steps. Stand in a quarter squat at the bottom of the stairs with hands on hips or back of neck and feet shoulder-width apart (photo A). Jump to the first step (photo B) and continue up for 10 or more jumps (photo C). Make landings light and quick; movements should be continuous up the stairs without pauses. As you gain fitness and power, you should be able to take two steps at a time.

a   b   c

From *Jumping Into Plyometrics* (2nd ed.) by D.A. Chu (pp. 84, 100, 104, 105, and 114), 1998, Champaign, IL: Human Kinetics. Copyright 1998 by Donald A. Chu. Adapted by permission.

Indoor Cycling

The biggest problems with cycling in the winter are early sunsets and foul weather. For most of us, who must juggle training with real-world schedules, indoor cycling on a wind or magnetic trainer is the only real choice. Coaches such as Arnie Baker, MD, author of *Smart Cycling*, incorporate indoor cycling into their athletes' off-season training by using either these trainers or rollers. Baker's athletes enjoy working out at home because it gives them time to concentrate on specific exercises to improve their cycling performance. He has his athletes use indoor training during the season as well because he likes to accurately control the workload from one session to another during certain workouts. This can be done easily on indoor trainers.

Before you complain about indoor cycling as a boring alternative to "real" cycling, acknowledge some specific benefits. The controlled environment of a trainer allows you to isolate and concentrate on specific areas of cycling fitness and technique.

Rollers

Rollers consist of three round cylinders mounted on bearings and fixed to a frame. A belt connects one of the rear cylinders to the front cylinder to keep the front wheel spinning at the same speed. Rollers sharpen your bike-handling ability because you must rely on skillful steering and balance. They teach you to work on smooth, fast spinning but offer little resistance unless you add a fan or magnetic unit. It takes weeks to be able to ride on rollers and feel relaxed enough to lift your hands off the handlebars. Once you get past the first learning stages, the bike-handling skills you obtain will make you a more confident and successful cyclist.

Magnetic and Wind Trainers

Magnetic, or mag, trainers have powerful magnets and a nonconductive disk that produces resistance and dissipates energy as heat. Performance mag trainers have six resistance settings (low to high) and are controlled by a bar-mounted lever. Wind, or turbo, trainers have two fans with slotted blades that churn the air.

A wind trainer's greatest advantage is that it closely mimics the resistance you experience on the road—it increases resistance exponentially. If you increase your speed on the wind trainer from 15 to 30 mph, you need to increase power output by a factor of about 8. The disadvantages of wind trainers are the noise generated by the fans and the lack of resistance adjustment.

With mag trainers, resistance increases in direct proportion to speed, which is less realistic, but they do provide enough resistance to elevate heart rate. Several magnetic training units incorporate a small, precisely weighted flywheel that creates a slight coasting sensation and helps you pedal through the dead spots in your stroke for a more realistic road feel. An advantage of mag trainers over wind trainers is that they are much quieter to use.

What Bike Should You Use?

Use an old bike. Enormous pressures are generated on the bicycle when it doesn't move freely beneath you. The bike you use on the trainer will become wet with sweat and rusted; the headset, with the bike always "going" straight ahead, will get grooved. For these and many other good reasons, don't use an expensive bike on your stationary trainer. Any old or used bike will do; just make sure it is set up identically to your regular bike.

You might consider changing your rear cogs for indoor cycling, however. The setup that has worked best for most of my riders is a 12-13-14-15-16-17-20-28. The closely spaced high gears allow you to precisely tune the hard efforts. The large 28-cog allows you to work on spin and leg speed without muscle strength or aerobic capacity limiting the drill.

Finally, specific workout plans demand a cadence-equipped computer, which allows you to precisely tune your efforts, see your progress, and record your improvement. A heart rate monitor and/or power meter also provide important feedback about your workout.

Improving Your Riding Technique

Surprisingly, working on an indoor trainer can lead to rapid improvements in riding technique. The isolated environment allows you to concentrate on specific skills without distraction. Spinning, the ability to maintain a high cadence with a continuous application of power, can be improved simply by listening to the trainer's noise. If you hear a steady "whoosh" on the downstroke, you are not pedaling properly. Concentrate on pedaling in circles. This will help you begin the power stroke earlier at the top and pull your foot across the bottom of the stroke. After a while, you will develop a longer and smoother delivery of power to the pedals.

Another exercise on a trainer that has dramatic results is one-legged cycling (see chapter 2). Most cyclists are not symmetrical in the application of power to the pedals, favoring one leg over the other, and exert more force on the pedal with this leg. The result is asymmetrical pedaling, which leads to loss of power.

To alleviate this problem, try this exercise: Place one foot on a 16- to 18-inch box. With the other leg, force yourself to pedal smooth circles for 5 to 10 minutes. This technique will improve your ability to apply power over a longer portion of the crank circle because you do not have the inertial support of the other leg. After several weeks of alternating work with both legs, slip the trainer into a very low gear and, using both legs, attempt to pedal with a smooth application of power. This is what professional cyclists refer to as pedaling with suppleness.

Indoor Workouts

As with any workout, spend a few minutes warming up and cooling down before and after each session on the bicycle. Cycling indoors is quite different from cycling outdoors. Indoors if you don't have a cooling system, you will be overheated within five minutes. It is easy to forget how the wind keeps us cool. Use a fan or ride in the coolest part of your house. Try riding in an unheated garage, where it is cooler than a house but where you do not have to fight the cold winds of winter. Remember to fill your water bottle before you start your workout.

Cycling to music is a personal choice. Make a couple of training tapes of your favorite songs (preferably songs with a strong beat) and put on your headphones. Use a cyclocomputer to monitor your progress.

Chris Carmichael, coach to Lance Armstrong and other professional cyclists, recommends not spending more than two hours at a time on the trainer. He has seen many inexperienced riders spend a great deal of time on stationary trainers, peak too soon in the season, and then fade by midseason.

If you want to emerge in February or March in the best early-season shape of your life, here is the indoor-cycling program for you. Each workout is designed to provide variety, build the cycling muscles, and train your body's different energy systems.

- For general conditioning, find a resistance-and-gear combination that elevates your heart rate into your training zone. After you warm up, raise your cadence to 85 to 100 rpm, maintaining your heart rate at no more than 85 percent of your maximum.

- For climbing strength and to become accustomed to pushing larger gears, put the bike into a low gear or, on a trainer, increase to the resistance that forces you to drop your cadence about 15 rpm. Maintain this cadence for a few minutes and repeat several times during a training session. Many find it helpful to place a 4-by-4-inch block under the front wheel to simulate riding up a hill. Vary the ride by occasionally getting out of the saddle and pedaling at 50 to 60 rpm. Gradually build up to 10 minutes while riding out of the saddle.

- For speed work and to work on your anaerobic capacity, intervals on a trainer are just the answer. You can structure interval programs similar to those you use on the road. The key is to remember to not overwork.

You can perform the following technique-specific workouts on trainers. You also can perform variations of these workouts on indoor stair-climbers and rowers.

- **Hard–easy intervals.** Start with a 10-minute hard effort followed by 2 minutes of easy spinning for recovery. The next interval should be 8 minutes hard, 2 minutes easy. Each hard interval decreases by 2 minutes but increases slightly in intensity. The easy 2-minute interval remains the same. The workout ends when you reach 2 minutes hard and 2 minutes easy.

- **Ladder drill.** Ride progressively harder gears. Start in a relatively low gear and ride for one to two minutes (keeping the same cadence), then shift to the next-higher gear, and to the next, and so forth. When you're finished with the highest gear you plan to ride, ride back "down the ladder." Usually, riding up four or five gears is sufficient for a good workout.

- **Ladder drill variations.** There are dozens of variations for the ladder drill (e.g., hard gear, easy gear, back to hard, up two gears, down one). You also can vary the cadence, increasing it to 110 or 120 rpm, but always keep it above 80.

- **Speed intervals.** To develop speed, throw in some intervals: 10 to 12 all-out, 15-second pedaling sprints, alternating with 45 seconds of easy pedaling.

- **Power intervals.** To develop power, try three to six repetitions of three minutes at 90 rpm in a big gear, with three minutes of low-gear spinning between efforts.

- **Zone workout.** Here's a good workout when you want to do an endurance ride at a specific heart rate zone. For example, if you want to work out between 75 and 80 percent of your maximum for a good aerobic workout, follow this plan:
    1. Warm up for about 5 minutes, starting with low to moderate gears, and gradually raise your revolutions per minute or gearing until your heart rate is 75 percent of your maximum.
    2. For the next 30 minutes, keep your heart rate within the 75 to 80 percent target zone. That's the range you calculated before getting on the bike. The challenge of this workout is to keep your heart rate there. If it rises above or falls below this zone, decrease or increase your effort.
    3. Cool down for 5 to 10 minutes until your heart rate is below 110.

A final tip: Ride your trainer only every other day. Otherwise, you're likely to get stale. On days you don't ride, get your aerobic workout by rowing or stepping. You also can row or lift weights the same day you ride.

Going for a Spin

Occasionally training on an indoor training bike can take the boredom out of the usual indoor cycling workout, especially when completed in a class situation. Spinning instructor Johnny G. recommends the following type of program for those who wish to purchase an indoor bike for home use, or even if you are using an indoor wind load trainer. Make a tape of five invigorating songs, then try this program. If you do not have a spinning bike, you still can attempt the jumps, although this may be unsteady on a wind load simulator. After the fourth session, you'll be able to mix it up with intervals, add resistance, stand, and sit. Find a workout that is hard and varied, then work to get better at it.

- **First workout:** Ride at a steady pace that varies with the music and throw in a few jumps.

- **Second workout:** Repeat the first workout, this time adding more jumping, climbing-out-of-the-saddle, and sprinting segments.

- **Third workout:** Warm up and gradually increase the tempo during the first song. Increase your heart rate to about 80 to 90 percent during the second and fourth songs while adding a few jumps and climbing segments. Recover during the third song, and gradually get your recovering heart rate down to about 65 percent during the fifth song.

- **Fourth workout:** Gradually increase your heart rate during the first song, then do three songs hard, increasing the resistance with each song (80 to 95 percent maximum heart rate). Begin your cool-down with the fifth song.

INDOOR JAM SESSION

I have to admit I was very skeptical when I first heard about "Spinning," a class in which an instructor leads a group of exercisers on stationary bicycles through a vigorous indoor workout.

Granted, the thought of training indoors on a stationary bicycle sounds boring, but the workout changes constantly. Spinning keeps your mind engaged while offering the variety of any challenging outdoor workout—an excellent indoor training program for competitive cyclists.

Imagine: You close your eyes, focusing on the imaginary road, determined to make this unforgiving climb. You challenge yourself constantly, increasing your resistance. The hill gets harder and harder, and you can do only one pedal stroke at a time. Your heart pumps fast; you feel a little thirsty but the rhythm of the music is riveting as it pulsates in your ears. You move side to side; there is no stopping on this hill. Soon, you reach the crest of the imaginary hill.

From the start of each 40-minute workout, music synchronizes the group and sets the tone for a great workout. "Spinning is an aerobic and power workout combined into one that combines fast, smooth pedaling and out-of-the-saddle riding along with visualization techniques," according to Johnny G., the eclectic developer of the Spinning workout program. Johnny may be known to many as a successful finisher of the Race Across America in under 10 days.

Competitive cyclists will appreciate that most indoor cycling bikes have a fixed gear attached to a heavy flywheel, a combination that encourages a smooth and powerful round pedal stroke. A knob mounted behind the stem adjusts resistance throughout the workout session to simulate intervals, hills, and sprints. Big gear mashers can dial in a heavy resistance, or you can work on your high cadence training by decreasing the resistance and increasing revolutions per minute.

"The essence of spinning is fluidity," Johnny says. "Spinning is when you can revolve the pedals at a high speed while staying in the saddle or while standing. An efficient spin is achieved when your legs are pushing and pulling the pedals in a complete circular motion and the body is not hopping all around the bike."

My introduction to Spinning came at a Schwinn sales meeting in Vail, Colorado, with Johnny leading the session. The warm-up was at a steady pace with my Polar heart rate monitor reading about 60 percent of my maximum heart rate. Then the ride started; Johnny had us increase the resistance on the bikes while increasing our revolutions per minute. Then I pedaled while standing out of the saddle. I alternated my body position from a rocking side-to-side position to a crouched position with my butt over the saddle. Next, we pedaled sitting down, with increased resistance as if climbing a hill in a seated

(continued)

position (heart rate about 85 percent of maximum). Then we pedaled while "jumping," four counts up, four counts down, and so on. We never stopped pedaling throughout the 40-minute workout. When finished, I was exhausted but exhilarated. The information from my heart rate monitor showed that my heart rate ranged from 65 to 93 percent of maximum, similar to what I would have experienced on the road.

During the session, Johnny encouraged us with his underlying philosophy that a strong mind builds a strong body, and his classes exist to firm up that connection. While the workout may sound like another boring indoor stationary bike session, Johnny's direction helped all of us to banish the universal temptation of zoning out while riding, and he helped us tune into the rhythms of the music and the mind and the bike.

Part yoga. Part Tour de France. An indoor training adjunct to your winter training program.

Cross-Training

In many parts of the world, late November through March is considered downtime for many outdoor activities. Cyclists may turn to weight training and wind trainers as their sole forms of conditioning. But with all the new and wonderful winter sporting gear available at reasonable prices, there is no longer any reason to stay indoors. In winter the outdoors and backcountry are beautiful, and cyclists are increasingly discovering the thrills and benefits of training outside. New ultralight skis and snowshoes make the mountains and woods more accessible. Instead of plodding along with heavy gear, you can do what you wanted to do all along—make outdoor exercise a four-season sport.

Skinny Skis, Big Legs

Jan Ullrich, Tony Rominger, and Allison Dunlap are just a few of the cyclists who have found that cross-country skiing provides an excellent complement to a year-round cycling program. For cyclists, cross-country skiing is an opportunity to work not only the lower body but also the upper body and torso, which get rather minimal use during cycling. In addition to building upper body and leg power, cross-country skiing is a great way for cyclists to maintain a high level of aerobic conditioning.

Another advantage to cross-country skiing is psychological. Most of us get stale doing the same activity day in and day out. Skiing can be a break in the routine: a chance to do something different, at a different pace, and with different people. For cyclists, skiing in the quiet of the forest is a welcome change from working out indoors or dodging cars on snow-packed roads.

Virtually all ski racers use the skating technique rather than the traditional diagonal stride. Skate skiing requires you to push off the inside edges of your skis. Your skis are no longer confined to tracks; you use the better part of a wide path. Once you learn the technique, you can travel at a rapid clip and get a great workout. You can experience the power and endurance required to get up a hill and then the excitement of descending and carrying all that speed around the turns. Technique and style are important to success in both cycling and skiing.

Don't plan to use skiing as a complete replacement for conditioning. You still need to be on the bike and in the weight room. Once you are comfortable on skis and if there's reliable snow cover, you can take a short break from cycling and ski every day. If you can only ski on groomed trails on the weekends, then add one or two sessions a week on roller skis.

Chris Carmichael gives these guidelines for training in winter: He suggests skiing about two days a week, a day of endurance training and a day of anaerobic-threshold training, in which your heart rate stays at anaerobic-threshold level or slightly higher for 30 to 90 minutes. The rest of the time, ride either indoors or on the road.

If you live in snow country, consider skiing about three days a week, taking road rides twice a week, and mountain biking twice a week. Use the road rides for steady endurance work and the mountain biking for climbing. Four or more rides a week maintains aerobic endurance, and skiing, though hard work, is a refreshing change. Skate skiing rests your mind, works your cardiovascular system hard, and allows you to approach spring with increased energy.

Snowshoeing 101

If you don't have the time to learn the technique of mastering cross-country skiing, then I have the activity for you. It will develop strength, power, and aerobic capacity. If you can walk, you can snowshoe.

The combination of physical exertion and fun has Skip Hamilton recommending snowshoeing to many cyclists. The accomplished mountain biker and personal coach to top riders on the mountain-bike circuit is a veteran snowshoer. "For cross-training in winter," says Hamilton, "snowshoeing is an excellent training option. You use many of the same muscles as in cycling; it's a great aerobic workout and does not subject one to the injuries of running."

Compared to road running, running in snowshoes involves lower knee carriage, shorter strides, and harder arm pumping. The lower body range of motion is similar to that used in cycling.

If you have never snowshoed, find a trail with packed snow or loose snow that is only a few inches deep. Keep your strides compact and in a few outings you will develop a natural rhythm and will be able to cover terrain not accessible on skis. Frozen and snow-covered lakes become huge, flat highways for speed work and intervals. Ski areas and hills become playgrounds and offer lung-searing vertical climbs and downhills.

Some snowshoers use poles when the snow is deep or the terrain uneven. Poles can be a hindrance to running, but for steep ascents, poles may provide that extra thrust. The claw on the sole of the shoe provides traction for climbing, so you can attack the steepest hills with only your cardiovascular system as your limiting factor. Your quadriceps will feel as if you are riding up a steep hill during a power workout.

You can rent snowshoes from outdoor shops and Nordic centers, where they should be able to help you select a suitable pair. Day rentals generally cost $10 to $15 plus deposit. If you choose to buy them, snowshoes are moderately expensive, from $160 for the training models to over $200 for racing shoes. One pair should last the average snowshoer several seasons.

Imagine yourself surrounded by snowfields and snow-covered hills. You are about to attempt a grueling workout. But with your feet strapped to snowshoes, this won't be an ordinary winter workout. You're partaking in one of the hottest winter cross-training sports: snowshoeing.

In-Line Skating

Skating offers another excellent outdoor, off-season activity for cyclists who do not have access to snow. Until recently, "blading" was only for kids or for recreation when you visited Venice, California. But now droves of athletes—including runners, cross-country skiers, and cyclists—cross-train on blades because the motion works both the upper and the lower body. In-line skating uses the quadriceps and gluteal muscles to provide the extra lower-body workout that cyclists need in the off-season. In addition to giving your cycling muscles a good workout, in-line skating allows you to train away from the bicycle for a psychological recharge.

In-line skating is every bit as good for developing your quads, glutes, and hamstrings as cross-country skiing and snowshoeing. Now the message is out, and more cyclists are taking up in-line skating. But before you join them, there are several things to consider to ensure an effective and safe workout.

Three main components determine the performance of in-line skates: boots, bearings, and wheels. The fit of the boot is critical. Buy skates that are fairly snug. Your toes should just touch the tip when you're standing up. Most in-line skates come in unisex sizes and run wider than what most women are used to. Get fitted properly and consider adding insoles to accommodate narrow heels or flat feet.

Beginners and individuals who want more resistance should consider using wheels with lower precision bearings, "lower rebound" polyurethane wheels with hubless construction, or wheels of a smaller diameter. If you purchase skates from a quality dealer, you can tailor the wheel/hub combinations to your specific requirements. I recently switched to Rollerblade Max-Trainer wheels for greater resistance and aerobic benefits. For racing, you'll want high-precision bearings and quality wheels.

Sooner or later you will fall, and on a hard surface. Most beginners put out their hands to break their falls, and as a result some fracture their wrists. I recommend wearing wrist guards. Knee and elbow pads, to help prevent abrasions, and a helmet also may be prudent.

In addition, skating places less impact on the musculoskeletal system than running does and may reduce the risk of injury to hip, knee, and foot joints. In-line skating also develops the hip and knee extensor (thigh) muscles better than running does. Though in-line skating may not be the perfect imitation of cycling (nothing is), it can be a great training tool if used properly.

Cardiovascular Training

Control of your training is critical to peak performance. Through the systematic use of heart rate monitors, many athletes have scientifically monitored their training to progress more rapidly or to a higher level. Lance Armstrong, Mari Holden, and George Hincape are just a few of the athletes who have experienced the benefits of training and competing with heart rate monitors. In this portion of the chapter, you will learn key information on how to use heart rate monitoring to help you ride and train at your optimal heart rate.

The cyclocomputer also has become a necessary accessory for the competitive cyclist and the multisport athlete. Along with heart rate, measurements such as current speed, cadence, elapsed time, and trip distance allow you to quantitatively measure and track your performance. A heart rate monitor and a cyclocomputer are performance monitoring tools for the serious cyclist.

Your Heart Rate

All of the control and monitoring you could ever want is contained in an instrument built into your body: your heart. The heart is an amazingly sophisticated organ that reflects every change in your physical and mental state. The heart adjusts heart rate and contraction force automatically to respond to the demands put on it during exercise. Your heart can tell you how hard your body is working with remarkable accuracy. The heart is your built-in monitor, telling you when to pick up the pace or when to slow down.

You need to be aware of three different heart rates: resting, maximum, and exercising heart rate. Resting and exercising heart rates are good indicators of fitness and capacity for exercise. Maximum heart rate is probably not a good fitness indicator since it varies quite a bit with age.

Your can find your resting heart rate just after you awaken in the morning. The better condition you are in, the lower your resting heart rate will be. Some athletes sleep with their monitors on and record their heart rates during sleep. True resting heart rate is obtained about one hour before your normal wake-up time. Some mornings your resting heart rate may be higher; this may be a sign of overtraining, lack of rest, or emotional stress.

Maximum heart rate is the highest number of beats your heart attains when you exercise at maximum effort. The standard method of estimating your maximum heart rate is to subtract your age from 220 for males or from 226 for females. However, for trained cyclists there may be a more accurate method.

I have determined that the average heart rate during a 5-km time trial is approximately 95 percent of a person's maximum heart rate. Use your heart rate monitor during an all-out effort of 5 km and determine your average heart rate at the midpoint of the ride. This is your exercising heart rate. A heart rate monitor with a memory function and a cyclocomputer will come in handy. Manually plot your heart rate against your time and speed on a graph. You'll see that your heart rate levels off in the midportion of the ride. This corresponding heart rate is your average heart rate. Multiply that number by 105 percent to arrive at your maximum heart rate.

Another method is to record your heart rate several times when you are putting out a maximum effort. Sally Edwards, in her book *The Heart Rate Monitor Book*, suggests finding a long hill or series of hills and, after warming up, hitting the bottom of the hill relatively fast. Work the hill extremely hard until your heart rate reading no longer rises and you approach exhaustion. This number is your maximum heart rate.

Cardiovascular Monitoring During Training

Medical authorities use the term target heart rate to prescribe the amount of cardiovascular exercise sufficient to achieve fitness without exceeding safe limits. This target zone is the level of activity that produces a heart rate of 70 to 85 percent of maximum heart rate. In other words, you can use your own heart rate to gauge how much exercise your body needs for optimum fitness.

A heart rate monitor and a cyclocomputer have a place in all aspects of your training and competition. First let's look at how they will help you gauge and adjust your cycling workouts.

- **Resting heart rate.** Strap your heart rate monitor on at night, and the next morning you'll have a good baseline to go by. Use this number to monitor your body for signs of overtraining or incomplete recovery. Any major deviation from the norm may indicate that you need extra rest.

- **Easy days.** Many cyclists are more likely to exercise too hard than to undertrain. They believe the more and harder they train, the faster and longer they will ride in competition. This is true to a point, but you can overtrain, which will ultimately lead to diminished performances rather than success. On days when you know you should be taking it easy after a previous hard interval or distance workout, use your heart rate monitor and cyclocomputer to hold yourself back. Many cyclists like to work at a heart rate of 25 percent lower than their lactate-threshold heart rate.

• **Hard days.** A heart rate monitor also can prevent you from training too hard on your hard days. On long climbs, if your heart is working too hard, the heart rate monitor will beep, telling you to slow down and return to your ideal heart rate range. This only works if your monitor has a high and low alarm system. You also can track your speed and cadence to monitor your effort.

• **Intervals.** You can get the most from interval training by using your heart rate monitor to help you recover properly between intervals. After riding for several minutes you may feel it is time to start the next interval, but your heart may not have recovered enough. A heart rate monitor tells you exactly when your heart rate has slowed to the proper level of recovery so that you can begin your next interval. If you do intervals without adequate recovery in between, you will notice a drop in your speed and cadence and you will benefit less from the workout.

• **Comeback from injury.** If you have been off the bike because of injury or illness, the monitor can help you gradually work your way back to fitness. A heart rate monitor and a cyclocomputer help keep highly motivated cyclists from overdoing too soon.

• **Postexercise recovery.** One of the best indicators of fitness is the ability to recover and return to normal heart rates following exercise. Routinely record your heart rate at one, two, and five minutes after exercise. As the weeks pass, you will see a more rapid return to your resting heart rate. Then, if you notice an unusual rate of recovery, such as your heart rate staying elevated longer than normal, you might conclude that your training effort was more intense than you had planned, and you can adjust your next workout accordingly

• **Cycling cadence.** In most situations, you will want to pedal around 90 or more revolutions per minute. As a general rule, higher revolutions per minute emphasize leg speed and lower revolutions per minute emphasize leg strength. Ideally, you want a blend of leg speed and leg strength; 90 to 100 rpm is the best compromise. During sprinting your cadence may climb above 120, and during climbing it may drop as low as 75. Use your cyclocomputer to monitor your cadence in various training situations of sprinting, climbing, and time trialing.

• **Cycling efficiency.** Find a hill about one mile long and mark the beginning and the end. Ride the hill in your normal riding position and gearing. Time yourself and record your cadence and heart rate during the whole effort. Ride the section again and again using different techniques: use a bigger gear, pedal at a higher or lower cadence, climb in and out of the saddle. Through this process you will determine the most efficient technique for climbing (the fastest method at the same energy expenditure). The same procedure can be used for time-trial training.

Cardiovascular Monitoring During Competition

A heart rate monitor and a cyclocomputer are also valuable tools to use during competition. During a race, the monitor can be used to judge when you should push and when you shouldn't.

• **Racing.** During time trials, breakaways, or hill climbs, use a heart rate monitor to determine if you are going into anaerobic debt or a cyclocomputer to monitor when your cadence is too low. For example, by not pushing too hard you may be able to save yourself from "blowing up" on a climb, which will enable you to catch the group on the descent. Remember, though, that during a race you will be able to push yourself a little harder because of the release of adrenaline and "race psych" factors that in practice can affect your sustainable heart rate.

• **Before the race.** Before important races, wear your monitor from the time you get up until the race is over. Just wearing a monitor will probably remind you to relax, and it will give you feedback about how uptight you're getting. You have limited energy, so it's best to use it for racing, not for worrying about the race before it happens.

• **Time trials.** In the past, a cyclist measured the intensity of competition by the time or speed it took to cover a familiar course; for example, 25 miles in 64 minutes, or about 2 minutes and 34 seconds per mile. But on a given day many environmental and physiological variables can affect the speed of a particular time trial. Temperature, wind, humidity, altitude, and terrain vary from course to course and affect intensity. A heart rate monitor allows you to measure intensity by monitoring heart rate along with speed, distance, time, and cadence. By riding at your lactate threshold you will finish the event with maximum effort and not "blow up" by riding too fast.

• **Race feedback.** Use your monitor to collect data when you are racing to help you improve training sessions. If you get dropped in breakaways, design your interval training to incorporate longer intervals at higher heart rate intensities. If you get beat in the sprint, check your cadence and speed and see if you can turn over the big gears for a short burst of energy output.

REVOLUTIONIZE TRAINING WITH A POWER METER

Chris Carmichael

Two-time Ironman Hawaii World Champion Peter Reid made good use of his power meter during his preparation for winning the Hawaiian Ironman. As power-measuring devices become more affordable and user-friendly, it is important to investigate why and how this new technology can help make you a better cyclist.

Just as portable heart rate monitors changed training methods, power meters are pushing the theories and methodology of endurance training into new territory. The biofeedback that power meters provide brings amazing clarity to training, if the information is interpreted well.

Speed, perceived effort, and heart rate are very useful for gaining insight into a person's training, but variables associated with those measures lead to ambiguous results. Power is a more concrete, objective way of looking at a person's training. More specifically, the amount of power an athlete produces at given heart rates provides a very clear picture of her current state of fitness. Just like heart rate values, power outputs cannot be compared between individuals but can be effectively used to chart one's own progress. And progress is the desired end result of any training program.

Power equates to the amount of work you produce in a given period of time. Riding a bicycle up a specific hill always requires the same amount of total work. When you produce that work at a faster rate, you are producing more power. Conversely, a cyclist producing more power over a given distance will cover that distance at a faster rate.

Current bicycle-mounted power meters measure the strain a rider puts on the crank, rear wheel, or chain and translate that into watts. Watching your wattage during the course of a ride is not very useful. Wattage fluctuates quickly and often; heart rate is a much better gauge of workload during a workout.

Power becomes useful when you are sitting in your living room after the workout. I recommend purchasing a power meter that can be downloaded to your home computer. Downloadable power meters help you see how your power output changes with your heart rate, speed, and cadence during the course of a single ride, a few weeks, or several months.

I started working with Peter Reid in June 2000 with the goal of improving his performance on the bike leg of the Ironman. He started working with a power meter so that I could get more precise information on his training. We started loading his training program with long intervals near his lactate-threshold heart rate to increase the amount of power he could produce for sustained periods of time. During the rides, Reid concentrated on keeping his heart rate and cadence within specified ranges; I did not want him to consciously try keeping his wattage constant.

(continued)

After a few weeks, I compared the computer files from those workouts and was pleased to see the results I expected. His heart rate and cadence ranges remained generally constant, but his average power output for 20-minute efforts increased by over 9 percent. When dealing with world-class athletes, 9 percent is an astronomical increase in performance. A few weeks later, Reid won Ironman Canada, an important event in his preparation for Ironman Hawaii, which he also won. Increasing sustainable power output at lactate threshold is very important for improving time-trial performance.

The intensity level for these workouts is critical. They must be done very close to an athlete's lactate-threshold heart rate, but not above that heart rate. You want to ride at the highest sustainable workload possible without accumulating lactic acid, which will force you to slow down.

One way to keep the intensity high enough without overloading the muscles is to keep the cadence for lactate-threshold workouts above 90 rpm. The higher cadence shifts some of the stress of the effort from the legs to the cardiovascular system. A highly aerobic engine can handle the extra stress better than the muscles can because accumulated lactic acid is more detrimental to performance than breathing faster is.

Power meters are like any other piece of training equipment: the information you gather can be useful or useless, depending on what you do with it.

Power outputs start falling when athletes get tired, but power meters still provide useful information for short-burst on-the-bike resistance workouts in which a heart rate monitor is generally irrelevant. When you use a power meter, you can view the power output of each interval during the rest periods between them. When power output starts falling rapidly during successive intervals, it is time to stop and go home; you're too tired to put forth a full effort and are therefore just wasting energy.

Information is power, and right now power is the newest form of information. Advances in technology have moved power monitoring from the lab to the road, track, and trail. What was previously only available to world-class athletes is now available to anyone interested in efficiently improving his fitness and performance. Use it wisely.

Why Power and Heart Rate Training?

Blending heart rate with power makes for a more comprehensive and effective system of monitoring your training and racing program. In cycling, power is expressed as "watts." You can increase power by increasing your cadence, increasing the gear, or by pushing harder on the pedals while riding your bike.

In terms of useful information, power is much more valuable than speed and distance. Speed variations are difficult to evaluate. In fact, maintaining a certain average speed may be an inefficient use of energy, especially if you don't know the power required to maintain that speed. The power calculation provides an accurate picture of how efficiently your body is performing. Whether racing or training, you can compare one ride to another using power as the basis. Within any given ride you can easily evaluate performance based on power output. At any point in the ride you can know if you are performing at, below, or above previous best performance.

Focus on power for intervals, hill training, sprint-power training, and all anaerobic workouts. Through the use of a heart rate–power system, you will see significant improvement in race performance when you begin training with power. Heart rate is best used for steady-state training, particularly that done below the lactate threshold. It is especially effective during long, aerobic rides and for recovery workouts. Applying each of these intensity monitoring systems has the potential to dramatically improve training and racing.

Training With Power and Heart Rate

How does the added element of power monitoring play into training? Power output does not replace heart rate measurement but is intended to be used in conjunction with it. The main benefit is that it allows you to actually measure workload rather than make a guess at it based on heart rate, which can be affected by temperature (heat or cold) and other factors.

One can now base workouts on power levels and heart rate zones. If you are making the same power at a lower heart rate than during previous efforts over the same terrain, you can measurably tell that your fitness has improved. Likewise, if you're making less power at the same or higher heart rate, it is a sign that you are losing fitness. Your heart rate is higher than normal, but you can't ride at your target power output? Incomplete recovery from previous workouts is likely to blame. Also, you can monitor recovery time from an effort of a certain intensity, like during intervals. Equal power output (intensity) followed by a more quickly dropping heart rate shows improved fitness. Combine this information with distance, speed, cadence, and other cycle computer information and you have a complete training monitor.

Critical Power Zones

Joe Friel, coach and author of *The Cyclist's Training Bible*, has shown that any given individual time-trial duration has a maximal effort associated with it. This effort can be expressed as average power or "critical power" for a specific effort. Friel often uses an example of a cyclist riding a 20-km time trial that takes 30 minutes to complete; average power output is 320 watts. From this example we can say that the rider's 30-minute critical power is 320 watts. The same test can be completed for efforts lasting 60 seconds and 60 minutes, and beyond.

In order to express this critical power as a narrow training zone, Friel suggests adding and subtracting 5 percent of 320 watts, or 16 watts. So the resulting training zone is 304 to 336 watts. This zone is called "CP30," the critical power for 30 minutes. In the same manner, he points out that zones may be created for other durations that have physiological significance.

The zones that Friel is now using for riders training with power are based on 12 seconds (CP0.2), 1 minute (CP1), 6 minutes (CP6), 12 minutes (CP12), 30 minutes (CP30), 60 minutes (CP60), 90 minutes (CP90), and 180 minutes (CP180). Friel suggests that these power zones require regular testing, but not for each of the durations. To avoid all of the suffering of the 60-, 90- and 180-minute durations, create a graph with power on the vertical axis and each of the durations on the horizontal axis. Then plot your critical powers for all durations through 30 minutes. Extending the average slope of the line from the 6-, 12-, and 30-minute out to the 60-, 90-, and 180-minute points will provide an estimate of the power of your longer-duration rides.

Power-Based Workouts

Once you have found your critical power zones doing time trials, how do you use this information? The following power-based workouts are based on Joe Friel's critical power measurements and suggest how you can do them using critical power zones. You also can combine them with training programs from earlier chapters to improve your endurance, sprint, and lactate-threshold performance.

• **Active recovery.** During your easy days, or days when you want to go out early in the season to build up your base miles, ride steadily in the small chain ring at a lower power output than CP180.

• **Extensive aerobic endurance.** Do a steady paced ride at CP180 on a flat to gently rolling course.

• **Intensive aerobic endurance (tempo).** Do a steady ride at CP90 for 20 to 60 minutes.

• **Lactate-threshold endurance.** Do a steady ride at CP60 for 20 to 40 minutes.

• **Lactate-threshold power.** Do three to five cruise intervals of 6 to 12 minutes each at CP30 with 2- to 3-minute recovery periods between efforts.

• **Hill strength.** On a hill that takes 1 to 3 minutes to climb, do repeats totaling 10 to 30 minutes of climbing time at CP6. Cadence is in the range of 50 to 60 rpm for those with healthy knees. Recover for 2 to 6 minutes after each repeat. You also may do this sitting up into the wind if no hills are available.

- **Aerobic capacity.** Complete four to six intervals of 3- to 5-minute duration at CP6. The recoveries are initially as long as the intervals but get shorter as the season progresses. Cadence should be kept high.

- **Anaerobic endurance.** Do three sets of three to five, 30- to 45-second repetitions at CP1 with recoveries that are a quarter as long (8 to 11 seconds). Recover for 5 minutes after each set. Talk about suffering! This is a very hard workout. Start with the low ends of the options.

- **Sprint power.** On a flat road or short hill do 10 to 12 pedal-revolution (each leg) jumps at CP0.2. Use a high cadence. Do three to five sets of five of these jumps within a workout. Recover for 1 minute between jumps and 5 minutes between sets.

FAST DECISIONS

Manufacturers have made many claims that their cycling equipment or how the equipment positions you on the bike will make you go faster during competition. Regardless of such claims, you need to examine the efficiency of your cycling using various equipment options. A cyclocomputer, power meter, and heart rate monitor can help you. Here are some ideas.

- **Equipment.** Use your power meter to evaluate new handlebars, wheels, or tires. Keeping the same power, ride a known loop with different pieces of equipment and review your heart rate. This method will give you an idea of which pieces of equipment are faster for the same energy output.

- **Position.** You can spend a lot of time working to achieve a more aerodynamic position on the bike. You need feedback on how subtle changes will improve speed without increasing energy cost. A heart rate monitor and a power meter will help you find a good, all-around aerodynamic position that is both efficient and comfortable. Though a position may be more aerodynamic, it may restrict your breathing or increase your energy cost because it requires more use of your back to support your position. Ride a familiar course and check out various positions against power, cadence, and heart rate. The more aerodynamic positions will allow you to ride faster laps at a constant heart rate and power output.

Test a position change only after you have had sufficient practice in the new position. Testing too soon probably will net a slower performance. If after several weeks you see a significant increase in speed without a rise in heart rate, you know you are on track to a faster position.

The Final Spin

Until a few years ago, training to be a cyclist was relatively simple. To improve, you hopped on your bike and headed for the road. To develop speed, you rode hard. To build endurance, you rode farther. During the off-season, you took about eight weeks off to help your body recover. Simple stuff.

Well, times have changed. Off-season training and conditioning is very important to overall conditioning and injury prevention. After a short break at the end of the season, think about integrating some cross-training into your cycling skill work to increase your strength, endurance, and speed. Many top riders say their cycling performance has improved dramatically with a winter training schedule that combines resistance training with other activities, such as cross-country skiing or in-line skating.

In addition to supplemental training, the times have brought heart rate monitors, power meters, cyclocomputers, and, consequently, high-tech biofeedback training to all cyclists. These tools have allowed cyclists to develop sophisticated training programs, the likes of which were un-heard of just 10 years ago. We have seen the benefits of being able to accurately monitor training power, time, speed, distance, and cadence during training and racing. A monitor takes much of the guesswork out of training intensity and serves as an excellent motivator. It's like having your own personal coach. Monitor your performance during your next workout or race and receive the encouraging personal feedback that you are indeed improving physiologically.

Heart rate monitors, power meters, resistance-training equipment, and in-line skates are tools you might expect only elite cyclists to use, but now this equipment is within reach of almost everyone. When you have the chance to use these tools, you'll probably wonder how you ever did any serious exercise without them. The answer is simple: You probably didn't.

STAYING HEALTHY AND INJURY-FREE

Few cyclists get through their careers without falling off their bikes and getting "road rash." They also risk fractures, contusions, sprains, and a variety of overuse injuries, though many of these injuries are preventable through skillful riding, correct positioning on the bike, and bicycle maintenance.

Some cyclists are challenged by health conditions such as asthma or diabetes. All of us fall prey to illnesses, such as colds and flus, which we may or may not be able to ride through. And we all encounter environmental conditions that can be hazardous to our health.

This chapter will focus first on injuries. Bicycling injuries can be classified by the mechanisms that cause them. Some are caused by crashing, others by overuse and errors in training. We will explore the injuries that you'll most likely experience and how they may be prevented and treated. Later, we will talk about the possibilities of riding through some illnesses and adverse environmental conditions.

Finally, we will see how stretching can be used to help prevent many of the overuse injuries caused by cycling and how it can make your time on the bike more comfortable.

Crash-Related Injuries

Two studies in the medical literature have reported on the type and number of injuries experienced by competitive cyclists while racing and training. Both papers point to abrasions as the number-one injury experienced by cyclists.

One study reported on the more than 600 participants in the Idaho Women's Challenge bicycle stage race. Of all the injuries the cyclists experienced in the race, over 72 percent were abrasions. Drs. Michael Gibson and Richard King, physicians for the race, reported contusions and lacerations as the second and third most experienced injuries in the race. Most of the athletes returned to competition the day after being treated in the mobile clinic after the race.

A second study by Thomas Bohlman in *Physician and Sportsmedicine* reported that most of the superficial injuries he observed were abrasions and that 65 percent of the abrasions were minor and occurred at the hip, elbow, and knee. In fact, 20 percent of all abrasions were to the hip, the first impact point in most injuries. The abrasions occurred in falls caused mostly by flat tires or colliding with other cyclists.

Both studies reported that the incidence of head injuries was reduced with the use of approved helmets. Each year in the Women's Idaho Challenge, crashes result in many broken helmets, but only two serious head injuries have occurred in the eight years of the race when the data have been collected. Although Bohlman's study was completed before helmets were required in bicycle racing, he still showed that a helmet may have helped prevent head injuries.

Preventing Crash-Related Injuries

Not knowing how to elude dangerous situations and making tactical errors are leading factors in cycling accidents. Exhaustion, leading to poor concentration and slow reflexes, also plays an important role. This particularly applies to riding in large packs. Here are some points to remember to help prevent serious crash-related injuries:

- Experienced cyclists practice tumbling exercises in the off-season. When they fall, they try to roll with the fall, protecting the head with the arms, so the impact will be taken on the back and shoulders.

- Always wear gloves while cycling to protect the palms of your hands when you fall with your hands outstretched.

- Except in extremely hot weather, wear two layers of clothing on your upper body. In a fall, the outer layer will slide over the inner layer, protecting your skin from greater abrasions by dissipating some of the friction.

Riding in a pack, knowing how to fall, keeping your bicycle in top mechanical condition, and—most importantly—wearing your helmet will reduce the frequency and severity of crash-related injuries. The notion that the effort spent preventing injuries is more rewarding than the energy spent curing them makes good sense, and not just for cyclists.

The problem is that you can be wounded mentally as well as physically after a bad crash.

Marco Pantani, winner of both the Tour de France and the Tour of Italy

Why Wear a Helmet?

More and more cyclists are wisely buying bicycle helmets to protect their most valuable asset—their brains. If you are one of the few still not convinced you need a helmet, consider the following:

- When you crash, you are likely to land on your shoulders and head because in most circumstances, the top tube and handlebars will trap your legs. Many people think they will be able to tuck their heads and roll, but unless you practice this maneuver a lot, do not expect to do it instinctively.

- A drop of only one or two feet at very slow speeds can cause serious brain damage. Broken bones will heal; a scrambled brain will not. Your brain, the most important part of your body, is very sensitive to impact even at slow speeds.

- You will crash on your bicycle. The odds are that it will happen, and the more you ride your bike, the sooner it will happen.

- Helmets are needed even in quiet, rural areas. Car-bike collisions cause only 12 percent of all casualties to cyclists; other dangers are still present on every ride you take.
- On any ride you take you may catch a wheel in a crack, skid on gravel, hit a pothole or drain grate, or collide with another bike, vehicle, or dog.

Even careful cyclists crash—every 4,500 miles on the average. Nobody expects to fall, but in time, you will crash, too. When you do, it is essential to have proper head protection; 75 percent of the more than 1,400 annual deaths from bicycle accidents in the United States are due to head injury. Road rash and broken bones heal; major injuries to the brain may not. There are other benefits to wearing a helmet:

- **Visibility.** You are easier to see with a colorful headpiece on, especially at dusk, in rain or fog, or after dark. Putting retroreflective trim tape on the helmet or wearing a neon helmet cover makes you even more visible.
- **Image**. When you wear a helmet, motorists expect you to ride correctly because you look like you know what you are doing.
- **Climate protection.** A helmet will help keep your head dry in rain or snow. If you do have to cycle in bad weather, a helmet will make your riding much more enjoyable.
- **Emergency data.** Write your name, address, phone number, and any medical condition on a piece of tape inside your helmet. This will save you from transferring this information from jersey pocket to jersey pocket.

Pick a helmet that looks good on you. If you don't like the way it fits, the color, or the shape, you probably will not wear it. With the variety of colors, shapes, and designs available, there is no reason for not wearing a helmet. No cyclist I know has ever regretted buying a helmet, but several crash victims I know have regretted not having one on.

"Never in any professional cyclist's mind are thoughts of what the consequences would be to have an accident at speeds of more than 60 mph. A professional knows there will be no mistake, no crash."

Eric Heiden, former U.S. road champion, winner of five Olympic speed-skating medals

Hot Heads

Many cyclists wonder if wearing helmets can lead to overheating. Several years ago, Dr. Carl Gisolfi conducted a study at the University of Iowa to answer this question. For two hours, cyclists rode a bicycle ergometer in an environmental chamber at about 70 percent of their maximums. In two trials, the cyclists wore either no helmet or a hard-shell helmet in over 90-degree Fahrenheit temperatures. Head, skin, and rectal temperatures were recorded at regular intervals. Results showed no statistical differences in external or internal body heat, heart rate, or sweat production between the two rides. The participants described the exercise as similar to a 50-mile race. None of them felt the helmets caused them to overheat.

Remember, though, you must train in your helmet in order to acclimate yourself to the heat. Otherwise you'll experience discomfort during races or long tours. You must adapt to the helmet in training, not just put it on for an event.

Road Rash

You're on a fast descent and as you corner, your wheels slip out from under you. Several layers of skin are left on the asphalt. Abrasions, the most common cycling injury, are wounds that break the skin's protective barrier, damaging the soft tissue underneath and opening the way for invading bacteria.

If not taken care of properly, what may seem an insignificant injury can lead to infection and fever. Complications from abrasions, the result of improper and delayed wound care and management, can result in several days off your bike. All abrasions, even the most superficial, must be considered potential contaminations and must be cleansed and dressed properly.

First Aid for Road Rash

Numerous products and treatments are available to protect you from infection, promote healing, and permit you to resume cycling and exercise as soon as possible after an accident. The following wound-care regimen outlines how to use the several products available at your local drugstore to care for abrasions:

First, clean the wound thoroughly. Several products are available to supplement or substitute for soap and water. Hydrogen peroxide, an old standby, not only cleans but also kills germs. Any visible foreign particles should be cleaned from the wound.

After cleaning the wound, apply dressings in order to

- protect the wound from germs and infection;
- provide a moist environment to speed healing;
- provide pressure and compression to the wound (this limits or reduces swelling while increasing drainage);
- protect the wound from further injury that might cause pain or disrupt the healing process; and
- prevent movement of the wound that might interfere with healing, especially on arms and legs.

Many athletes use a topical antibiotic ointment and a nonadhering dressing. These ointments are a shotgun approach to the prevention of infection in abrasions. They contain two or three different antibiotics, each effective against a different range of bacteria, to make sure nothing grows in the wound except skin.

Cover the antibiotic ointment with a nonadhering dressing and hold it in place by tape or a "fishnet" sleeve. This sleeve (a tubular netting) holds the dressing in place but still allows free range of movement. The netting also will not cause excessive heat buildup in hot weather. If your local drugstore does not carry these products, inquire at a medical supply company.

High-Tech Dressing for Abrasions

Welcome to the world of high-tech first aid and semipermeable dressings, made of hydrogel (a 96-percent water substance) wrapped in a porous plastic. These dressings are available under the brand names Second Skin, DuoDerm, Tegaderm, Bioclusive, and Op-Site. They encourage a moist wound environment in which scab development is inhibited and epidermal (skin) cells form rapidly. Several clinical studies have shown that when these products are applied to a clean wound and changes in dressing are made at 24-hour intervals or as needed, most abrasions heal in four to eight days.

As with using antibiotic ointments, you should monitor the wound and change the dressing when it appears to be dirty or no longer adheres properly. Once again, tape or fishnet can be used to hold the semipermeable dressing in place. Removal should be done carefully to eliminate potential reinjury of the newly formed skin. The wound can be rinsed with saline or clean, cool water, but it is not necessary to remove all traces of the dressing material.

These procedures should suffice in most cases. If a fever develops and the wound feels warm to the touch, or the borders turn pinkish or red, consult a physician to check for infection. By using proper cleaning and wound management, you can take care of the most common cycling injury.

Body Damage

If injury results from a hard fall, you may want to reduce potential swelling by cooling the injured area as quickly as possible. Applying a cold compress immediately can reduce swelling and inflammation, minimize pain, and reduce bleeding under the skin, which causes bruising. For best results, apply cold before swelling occurs. Getting the ice on quickly can make a big difference. Most of us do not carry ice to events, and if we do, it usually has melted by the time we need it for emergencies. Now there is help, however— instant cold packs are available from several manufacturers.

Cold packs contain an inner bag of blue liquid that, when broken and mixed with water crystals, sets up a chemical reaction to produce instant cold. Carry one in your race-day accessories bag or waist pack with your other first-aid equipment and you have the equivalent of an ice pack, even when you are miles from an ice cooler.

The ice pack should be applied after a wound is cleaned and dressed and the dressing held in place with a compression or stretch-type bandage (this type of wrap will provide compression, which will reduce the swelling).

Overuse Injuries

Crashing results in some gory, dramatic, traumatic, and painful injuries. No matter what, you can't prepare for every accident; that's why they're called accidents. But the prevention of a second type of injury is almost totally under your control. These are injuries that result from training and riding poorly or training and riding too much. Saddle sores, painful joints, muscle soreness, and burnout result from the use and abuse that serious cyclists commonly inflict upon themselves. These injuries creep up on you much more slowly than that irresponsible cyclist who causes the peleton to crash, but these delayed-onset injuries may be as painful as crash-related mishaps and, worse, can keep you off the bike every bit as long.

Injuries may be a fact of life for you as a serious cyclist, but that doesn't mean you have to put up with more than your fair share of them. Being in condition, maintaining a correct position on the bike, and wearing protective clothing will prevent many overuse injuries and illnesses.

Saddle Soreness

During one of his Tour de France rides, Greg LeMond was forced to adjust his riding style (and not enter any races after the Tour) because of saddle sores. What is a saddle sore? It's a crotch infection that usually starts as a small pimple. In most cases, a saddle sore's life span is just a few days, but during this time it may become hard, red, inflamed, and painful. In some cases, the infection doesn't disappear; it spreads to adjacent tissue and creates larger sores, boils, or cysts that affect more tissue and may even require surgery. It can happen to the best of cyclists.

To prevent saddle sores, you need to keep the part of your anatomy that everything in cycling "hinges on"—the groin area—clean and as free from friction as possible. Saddle sores usually occur from irritation or chafing of the hair follicles. The predominant bacterial infection, staphylococcus, is forced into the skin by pressure or irritation from the saddle, and a saddle sore is born.

Because chafing and sweating are major causes of saddle sores, every effort should be made to minimize them. First, dress right. To control chafing and cushion your posterior, wear chamois- or synthetic-lined cycling shorts. Keep the chamois material soft by rubbing in a washable lubricant such as A&D Ointment or Chamois Butt'r before every ride. Wash the shorts often. In fact, buy two or more pairs so that you always have a fresh pair.

Many companies offer more high-tech and synthetic liners. You will hear terms such as Suedemark (Hind), Microsuede (Cannondale), and Ultrasuede (Pearl Izumi), among others. Combined with other fabrics (for example, terry or polypropylene) they create a viable combination of performance, durability, and ease of care. Pearl Izumi and Hind also offer shorts designed especially for women, with better fit and chamois design.

Second, wash regularly with an antibacterial soap. Steward Pharmaceutical's Hibiclens and Purdue Frederic's Betadine Surgical Scrub work well and are available at drugstores without a prescription. Regular use of these products will reduce bacterial growth and the chance of infection. Ordinary soap will not work as well because it does not contain any antibacterial agents. After your shower, use talcum powder or baby powder to control moisture.

Third, experiment with different saddles. There are many saddle brands and configurations on the market, in gel, leather, and nylon. Find one that fits you best, one that is wide enough to let the bones of your rear end (ischial tuberosities) make proper contact with the rear of the saddle but is not too wide. A wide saddle will cause chafing, which could lead to bacterial infection. A good saddle should be stable enough to keep your body still, yet flexible enough to absorb large road shocks.

If early symptoms of saddle sores occur, such as redness or soreness, consider changing your saddle. You may have to try several types to find one that is comfortable for you. As with running shoes, some brands of saddles will fit you better than others. Sitting farther back on the saddle will distribute more surface area over the saddle, and lowering your handlebars a little will help reduce the pressure on your seat by shifting more weight to your arms and hands.

Fourth, ride smart. Stand up on the bike periodically and stretch out the posterior muscles for 15 to 20 seconds every half hour. It's also wise to rise out of the saddle to go over railroad tracks and rough patches.

If all else fails and you still develop a saddle sore, don't cover it with salves or ointments because they have a tendency to keep the bacteria alive. Use the antiseptic Hibiclens and take a few days off the bike.

A stubborn sore can be helped by what's known generically as a "drawing salve," made to bring a boil to maturity so that it will drain. Check with your doctor or pharmacist for availability. It's applied to the sore, then covered with an adhesive bandage. You should see results in a couple of days. Drawing salve can be combined with an over-the-counter product called Boil Ease, which contains a topical painkiller that may reduce discomfort enough to let you continue riding. In fact, saddle pressure combined with the effect of a drawing salve can help a sore discharge. You'll pull off your shorts and the bandage to find a bit of a mess, but the pressure will be gone and the sore will start healing.

Another effective product is Bag Balm, particularly for raw areas caused by chafing. Available at pharmacies and veterinary stores, Bag Balm was developed "to soothe a milk cow's irritated teats." I'm not kidding. It works for irritated bike riders, too. In fact, dermatologist Bernard Burton, MD, says, "When it's applied after your shower, it will usually clear up the problem overnight." Be careful, though, until you learn how your body responds to this product. Some riders who have tried using Bag Balm as a daily crotch lubricant report an adverse skin reaction.

If quick treatment doesn't result in a quick cure, consult your physician or a dermatologist. They may recommend a broad-base oral antibiotic, such as erythromycin, or topical antibiotics.

Like all great cyclists, you will have to deal with saddle sores sometime, but cleanliness, proper clothing and equipment, and skin care may be all that is needed to keep you in the race and not on the sidelines sitting uncomfortably in a comfortable chair.

REDUCING SADDLE PAIN

There are two basic types of saddle pain. The first is the result of the pressure against the tender skin covering the ends of the pelvic bones that rest on the saddle—your sit bones. The problem is usually most severe on early-season rides because your skin has softened over the winter. If you are using a top-quality saddle and you're riding regularly, the problem normally diminishes with more exposure to the saddle.

The second source of pain comes from your position on the bike. Saddle position is of importance. If your saddle is too high, your hips will rock with each pedal stroke and subsequent chafing will occur. If the saddle is too low, you will tend to slide forward toward the saddle nose, putting more pressure on the crotch area. Again, insure that you have the proper position set up on the bike, with proper saddle height and tilt.

Eliminating posterior pain begins with selecting the proper saddle. In most circumstances, the narrowest saddles are for competitive cyclists who lean forward much of the time; their body weight is much further forward onto a narrow part of their crotch. Long-distance cyclists prefer to sit more upright. They need support further back where the ischial tuberosities (sitting bones) put more weight on the saddle. Hence, they require a little wider saddle. Remember, saddles, like stems and handlebars, can be exchanged for better fit and comfort.

When speaking of saddle comfort, remember that posteriors come in all shapes and sizes. Women's pelvic structures are different than men's, and women generally prefer a wider saddle. This is because their ischial tuberosities are about a half-inch wider. Therefore, many manufacturers produce saddles that are about a half-inch wider and slightly shorter for women.

In recent years, several saddle manufacturers have tried many avenues to improve the pain-preventing qualities of their products. There are combinations of closed-cell foams, gel, air, titanium rails, viscous liquids, and anatomical cutouts to improve rider comfort.

(continued)

The newest design in saddles deals with the padding materials or areas of the saddle being removed to relieve pressure on the crotch area. The common, anatomically sculptured foams are being replaced with new densities and types of cushioning. A firmer saddle shell with stiffer padding or gel insert padding material or a strategically positioned cutout will be more desirable for longer rides. If you continue to have problems with discomfort and soreness because of pressure, the new polymer-gel saddles may be your salvation. They act to distribute the weight over a larger area and absorb road vibration.

Almost every male rider has experienced the feeling of numb genitals at some time during his riding career. You may experience this problem if you are using a saddle that is too narrow, you're on a saddle that is adjusted with the tip too far up or down, you do not rise off the saddle when hitting large bumps, or you are not riding in cycling shorts or tights. Also, the problem may come from using an inferior saddle on long rides.

Sometimes, you still may experience numb genitals in spite of proper equipment and technique. Although the condition is usually temporary, more and more cases of numbness lasting for weeks at a time are being reported. If you suffer from the problem on a regular basis, first double-check your riding position and experiment with different saddles. If the problem persists, try to make a habit of regularly standing up while riding to restore circulation. The period of time devoted to standing while riding does not need to be long, but you should stand up for a short period of time at regular intervals beginning at the start of the ride. Don't wait until the numbness begins. For best results, get into a routine. For example, you may want to stand after each turn in the front of the pack, or on every hill, or at every stop sign.

If the problem has not resolved itself with the above equipment changes and changes in your riding style, then it is time to seek medical advice.

Back Pain

Your workouts were going great until you decided to train for your first long stage race. You had been putting in 150 to 200 miles per week. This mileage made you feel good, kept your weight down, and gave you defined calves and rock-hard quads. When you decided to train for the stage race, though, things started to fall apart.

Maybe you were too eager, or maybe it was the excessive mileage or the hard intervals that led to your injury. Could it have been the hill work or an improper position on the bike? It started as a dull ache in your lower back, but not in any one place you could put your finger on exactly. Soon, riding your bike any distance was painful, and it began to bother you even as you sat at your desk.

Most low-back discomfort is not serious and reflects only minor injury, caused by overexertion or an improper position on the bike. Pain occurs when specific nerve endings are abnormally stimulated to send messages up the spinal cord to the brain. Because the bones, discs, ligaments, and muscles of your back are supplied by many nerve endings, various and often interrelated conditions can cause back pain. Frequently, the muscles, receiving your brain's message of pain, try to protect your back and go into spasm to hold your back immobile and quiet. In addition to the most common causes—improper positioning and physical overuse—the stress, fatigue, and anxieties of daily life can significantly increase low-back pain.

Before we go too far, let me point out that cycling is good exercise for your back when you ride correctly. The exercise of cycling supplies blood and nutrients to the muscles, discs, and ligaments of the back. But, as with all exercise, it must be performed properly and in moderation.

Although the muscles of the back may not be directly involved in pedaling, they help stabilize your body on the bike and increase the energy transfer from the hip and leg muscles to the pedals. The primary muscle groups of the lower back and trunk that affect cycling are the latissimus dorsi, the erector spinae, and the external obliques. The muscles of the upper back used in cycling are the trapezium, the teres major and minor, and the infraspinatus. In order to get the most from these muscle groups, you must be set up properly on the bike. Proper positioning will ensure that you use the large muscles of your trunk to your advantage.

Most back problems arise from riding in a position that is too low or from excessive time with your hands on the drops of the bars. Dropped handlebars give you the advantage of being able to switch hand positions during long rides. Change positions among the drops, the brake levers, and the tops every few miles or as the terrain warrants. Most of the time your hands should be on the tops of the bars. Changing hand positions will allow you to use your back muscles differently, stretch your muscles, and vary the flexion of your back while you are riding.

Take advantage of your dropped handlebars to gain the most power and leverage from your back muscles. During a long climb, ride seated with your hands on the tops of the bars, a position that facilitates breathing under a heavy workload. Slide slightly back in the saddle and use your lower and upper back muscles to put more power into each pedal stroke, which also allows you to use larger gears. Periodically on longer and steeper climbs, get out of the saddle, wrap your hands around the brake hoods, and use your arms, body weight, and back muscles to turn the pedals over. This will use the back muscles a little bit differently and stretch them out so that they do not become too stiff or fatigued on the long climb. Even on flat ground, getting out of the saddle occasionally relieves stiffness and lets you stretch the back and leg muscles.

Some other simple precautions will reduce your risk of back pain caused by cycling. Do not make any abrupt changes in your training program, position, equipment, or the terrain on which you train. Increase mileage, speed, and gearing gradually. If you add a hilly route to your program, take it easy the first few times and let your body get used to the stresses of hill climbing. Let your back muscles gradually adapt to the increased workload. The same goes for time trialing. Increase your distance and intensity gradually.

Make stretching a part of your program and add specific exercises to your routine if you experience pain or stiffness in your lower back. Tight back muscles limit your range of motion and make you more prone to pulls and strains. Strengthen your abdominal muscles; weak abdominals allow the lower back to curve inward, increasing the strain on the muscles, ligaments, and discs of the lower back. By strengthening and stretching your torso— back and front—you will improve your overall fitness and performance.

If you experience back pain that does not subside after stretching or correcting your bike position, slow down and take one to two weeks off the bike. It is time to seek the advice and care of a sports medicine specialist. Most specialists will first prescribe a program of rest, stretching, and abdominal exercises. If the suspected cause of the back pain is bone related—such as compression, spondylolysis, spondylolisthesis, or a herniated disc—more extensive and prolonged methods of treatment will be prescribed.

Finally, before riding in cold or cool weather, make sure your jersey or warm-up top is long enough in the back to cover you fully. Keeping your lower-back area warm will make you less susceptible to muscle or ligament strains. As is true of most cycling injuries, preventing back injuries is preferable to experiencing and treating them and is certainly more conducive to a longer and less painful cycling career.

Muscle Soreness

"My legs and shoulders feel so heavy that I have a hard time lifting them. I'm going to take the day off." These are common words after early-season intervals or a hard session in the weight room. Why? What makes muscles sore and stiff? How could your body let you down like this? You, who worked out in the gym several hours each week and had plenty of miles in your legs, who up to this point believed your body could take any punishment, should not feel any pain. Whatever you did, you did too much, too soon. Now it's the day after, and you have an athletic hangover. You are experiencing muscle soreness.

Causes of postexercise soreness vary from the overuse of large muscle groups to minor strains in individual muscle fibers. Despite what your high school coach may have told you, the culprit is not lactic acid. Lactic acid buildup has been blamed for prolonged muscle fatigue and discomfort, but this concept is not widely accepted today.

Lactic acid is produced during intense exercise when the oxygen demands of the muscle fibers increase beyond what the blood is capable of delivering. To produce the energy it needs, the body begins another process that works in the absence of oxygen. Lactic acid, a by-product of this process, locks up your muscles and, because it is an acid, causes that burning sensation.

But lactic acid is completely washed out of your muscles 30 to 60 minutes after you finish riding. Muscle soreness does not show up until 24 to 36 hours later, so scientists have been racking their brains to come up with another explanation. The most popular theory today is that when you overdo your cycling, skiing, or weight workouts, you cause microtrauma to the muscle fibers, localized damage to the muscle-fiber membranes and contractile elements.

Over 24 hours, the damaged muscle becomes swollen and sore. Chemical irritants are released from the damaged muscle fibers, which stimulate pain receptors in the muscle. In addition, your workout increased the blood flow to the worked muscle, causing it to swell and exert enough pressure to stimulate pain receptors. Instead of having free-moving muscle fibers the next morning, you have fibers that are fatigued and swollen and have microscopic tears.

Whatever the precise mechanism, current scientific research points toward muscle damage as the culprit of muscle soreness. The nerves in your muscles perceive this abnormal state and send messages of pain to your brain when you start to move around the next morning. By moving the sore muscles, you gradually begin to restore them to a normal state, but you will not be able to exercise to your full potential because the damaged muscles have lost some strength.

Typical recommendations for short-term treatments include stretching, applying sports balms or creams, submerging in a hot tub, or spending time in a sauna. Some athletes also use aspirin and anti-inflammatory medication to reduce the pain and swelling.

The cure for chronic muscle soreness is relatively simple. Gradually increasing the strength and endurance of your muscles, and stretching and warming up properly before engaging in activity, will prevent your muscles from getting as sore. Cycling, running, and swimming call upon muscles not used regularly in daily life. It all comes down to specificity of training, in which your muscles, tendons, and ligaments adapt to a particular sport, activity, or movement pattern over a period of time.

In addition, as we grow older our muscles and surrounding tissues have less elasticity, so we tend to feel soreness and tightness more quickly than we did in high school. An individual who stays in shape throughout the year should be able to exercise with minimal muscular soreness even when he reaches his 30s and 40s. After a hard day on the bike or in the weight room, he may feel somewhat stiff, but after a little stretching and warm-up activity this feeling should go away.

Sore muscles are usually damaged muscles. As with any injury, sore muscles must be given time to heal. This may mean a few days of easy cycling or other light activity before you can begin to push harder again. But don't go too hard or too fast because you'll wind up back on the sidelines. Remember, the best way to prevent or reduce muscle damage is prior physical conditioning.

Knee Pain

Knee pain is one of the most common overuse injuries that cyclists experience. Johan Museeuw and Gianni Bungo are just two of the cyclists who have come close to having their careers end because of knee problems.

Andy Pruitt, EdD, PA, who has treated some of the top cyclists in the world, says that "anterior knee problems—specifically, chondromalacia and patella tendinitis—were the most common problems found in 63 percent of the 134 cyclists I studied several years ago. Medial knee injuries were diagnosed in 21 percent of the cyclists and accounted for the second-largest type of overuse injury." He reported that training modification, rest, ice, massage, and bicycle-position correction effectively improved symptoms in 75 percent of those treated. Also, the work showed that most injuries occurred predominantly in the preseason and race season, the time of year when cyclists' mileage is high, they are pushing large gears, and they may not wear cold-weather clothing when they should.

Thomas Dickson, MD, a former team physician for the U.S. Cycling Team at several world championships, states that "many cyclists often make the mistake of keeping their saddles too low and, secondly, many people ride in too high a gear. By riding along in a high gear with a low saddle position, the cyclist is unnecessarily increasing the force across the kneecap at the top of the pedal stroke." On the other hand, a saddle that is too high causes excessive extension of the knee and undue strain of the tendons and ligaments in the back of the knee. Ride only gears that you are comfortable with, and be sure you have properly fit the bike to your measurements, as discussed in chapter 12.

How the foot is positioned on the pedal also can affect the pressure on the knee. The use of clipless pedals, which allow the foot to "float" a few degrees during the pedal stroke, reduces stress on the knee's ligaments. Remember to have someone experienced check your initial cleat alignment on the pedal. Visit your local bike shop or work with an experienced coach to adjust your cleats properly.

Wearing warm clothing during cold weather also helps protect the knees. Wear tights when the temperature is below 60 degrees Fahrenheit. In inclement weather, wear tights that have a windproof material over the front of the legs. And during the spring or while riding in the mountains, when and where the weather can change rapidly, carry leg warmers with you on the bike.

Hot Feet

If you experience "hot feet," that numbness or burning sensation in the balls of your feet, there are several remedies to consider. First, check to make sure the forefoot of the shoe is wide enough to accommodate your foot. You also may consider inserting a thin replacement insole in your shoe. Several compaines make replacement insoles, which are available at most bicycle and sporting goods shops. If you still have problems, you might try using a leather-soled shoe with an insole; this combination attenuates road shock better than nylon or Lexan.

The type of shoe closure you decide upon also may add to your cycling comfort. You have a choice of Velcro closures, laces, or a combination of both. Recently, ski-binding-type closures have been added to several brands of shoes. Velcro closures are popular among triathletes because Velcro makes the shoes easier to get in and out of in the transition area. The other advantage of Velcro closures is that the tension can be easily adjusted during long rides, which is important when your feet swell after about 50 miles of riding on a hot day.

Sore Hands

The ulnar nerve is the major nerve of the lower arm. Descending along the inside of the forearm, it enters the hand on the palm side. Stress on this nerve causes numbness in your hand, weakness in your grip, and loss of muscular control in your fourth and fifth fingers.

Every time you ride a bike, road or trail vibrations are transmitted through the bike to your body. Not wearing gloves or wearing worn-out gloves, using inferior bar grips, riding rough trails, and riding in an incorrect position can lead to ulnar neuropathy, or deadening of the ulnar nerve. Adjusting the handlebars to allow proper weight distribution, using quality handlebar grips, and wearing padded gloves help prevent or decrease pain and discomfort. Ignoring continued pressure and vibration in the palms can lead to permanent nerve damage.

Until recently, if a cyclist needed some cushioning to alleviate sore hands, she looked for a pair of gloves with a thicker layer of foam padding or she added more handlebar padding to her bike. This may have contributed to loss of road feel and interfered with shifting and braking. But now several manufacturers have stepped forward with the use of viscoelastic polymers, or "gels," offering cycling gloves with gel pads in the palms. The viscoelastic polymers absorb shocks and vibrations that are transferred through the handlebars to the hands, elbows, and shoulders. These materials add a protective layer of lifelike synthetic tissue that absorbs and evenly disperses handlebar pressures. In addition, gels will not compact over time, as foams do, and lose their ability to attenuate trail shock.

Environmental Conditions

Cycling is an outdoor sport; that's probably one of the things that draws you to it. Breaking away from the house, school, or office can bring a great sense of freedom. Taking that twisting road as fast as you can or climbing that hill is hot, demanding work. Still, you love it.

Let's face it, though: Sometimes the great outdoors can be a great pain. As fun as it is, there are challenges other than the road to overcome: heat and humidity, solar radiation, air pollution, and the thin air found at high altitudes.

Heat and Humidity

As the rains of spring fade into the hot, hazy days of summer, cyclists must adjust to riding in the heat. Excess heat can trouble any cyclist, whether beginner or experienced stage-race rider, causing problems from simple tiredness to heat exhaustion.

During cycling, heat produced by the working muscles exceeds heat released by the body, and body temperature rises. The rise in body temperature causes an increase in sweating and blood flow to the skin. Heat is removed by the evaporation of sweat from the skin.

The most efficient way to lose heat during cycling is through sweating with some convective heat loss. Convective heat loss is increased as the air temperature drops. On a long ride, a cyclist may incur sweat losses of 1/2 to 2 pounds per hour. Even under moderate weather conditions (65 to 79 degrees Fahrenheit, little cloud cover, and moderate humidity), there is the threat of heat stress. Water loss of this extent puts severe demands on the circulatory system, which is approximately 70 percent water. When water is removed from the blood, the blood's capacity to carry nutrients to the working muscles, as well as its ability to distribute heat to the skin to be vaporized as sweat, is reduced. When the cooling mechanism fails because of dehydration, the result is heat exhaustion or heatstroke.

Heat exhaustion is characterized by peripheral circulatory collapse. The cyclist becomes weak and fatigued and may faint. Headache and nausea are other symptoms. When heat exhaustion occurs, stop riding immediately and move to a cool and shaded area. If possible, begin drinking fluids and have someone put cold, wet towels over your body. Seek medical help if your condition does not improve fairly rapidly or if your symptoms get worse.

Heatstroke is caused by failure of the sweating mechanism. It is characterized by a rapidly increasing body temperature. The skin is dry, the body temperature is over 105 degrees Fahrenheit, and the pulse is rapid and weak. The cyclist may be unconscious. Treatment is immediate emergency care. Lower the body temperature to below 102 degrees as soon as possible using cold water. If the victim is conscious, he should be given cold fluids.

Immediately take the victim to the hospital and keep wetting all body surfaces on the way.

Ingesting fluids while cycling in the heat can help lower body temperature. Research completed on cyclists shows that rectal (core) temperatures were two degrees lower when cyclists drank fluids than when they did not. One cyclist's internal temperature reached 105.5 when he ran out of fluid, but leveled off at 103 when he drank fluids, during a two-hour ride at 75 percent of maximum in an environmental chamber.

Many cyclists will go on a 50-mile ride on a hot day with only two water bottles. In a ride of this distance, a cyclist may lose 6 to 8 pounds of water weight if he rides hard on a very hot day. Even if the cyclist drinks two bottles (approximately 40 ounces), this will only replace about 2 1/2 pounds of fluid. The advantages of drinking plenty of fluids are a lower core temperature and a delay of stress on the circulatory system, allowing the body to perform at its maximum.

In addition to drinking fluids, cyclists can acclimate to excessive heat and humidity by cycling at a moderate pace in a hot environment. Aim to ride 1 to 1 1/2 hours per day for 5 to 15 days before taking a long ride, entering a tour, or racing in hot and humid weather. The cyclist who has acclimated to the heat will be able to perform better because she has a lower internal temperature and heart rate, a better regulation of body temperature, and fewer heat-stress symptoms than a cyclist who has not. Exposure to heat without exercise results in only slight acclimatization. It is important for a cyclist who works out in air-conditioned places but is going to have to race in the heat, or for a cyclist who is heading to a warmer climate for the winter, to get some hot-weather training in as often as possible.

There are a number of other tricks you can use to prevent overheating. First, during periods of extreme heat and humidity, ride during the coolest part of the day. This may mean rising early and riding before you go to work or school. Second, if you are sensitive to heat, the hotter the day, the slower and shorter you should ride. Third, regardless of hydration and acclimatization, a cyclist can add to heat stress by wearing improper clothing. A light-colored jersey will help reflect the sun's rays, not absorb them like a dark jersey. A loose jersey of a breathable fabric will allow more sweat to evaporate. Never wear a long-sleeved jersey or tights in hot weather.

Fourth, keep track of your body weight; don't allow yourself to get into a state of chronic dehydration. This is especially important if you're training or riding a tour of several days in length in the summer. Weigh yourself each morning; if you are down two or three pounds from the day before, you have not rehydrated yourself properly. You should make an effort to drink plenty of fluids at meals and in the evening during hot weather.

Finally, reconsider what fluids you drink during cycling. As described in chapter 8, fluids ingested during cycling should contain 5 to 10 percent carbohydrate and small amounts of electrolytes. Such drinks will provide a source of fuel for the working muscles and will facilitate the absorption of water and glucose from the intestine. Find a sports drink on the market that tastes good to you when you are cycling and use it on rides lasting more than an hour. You will be surprised at how it will improve your performance and make the ride more enjoyable.

Although the summer sun can melt the asphalt, the properly prepared cyclist, armed with common sense and plenty of fluids, can ride all summer long without overheating.

Altitude

Above 6,000 feet, breathing is the limiting factor to performance. When you travel to the mountains, atmospheric pressure decreases and the air is thinner, so there's less oxygen available. You will notice that your breathing is faster and deeper, your heart rate is elevated, and at times you feel short of breath. These are the normal and helpful results of your body's attempt to get more oxygen to the working muscles.

You also may have a headache, experience a touch of nausea, or feel tired. About 15 percent of all cyclists have such symptoms, which usually go away in 24 to 48 hours. As your body works harder to get oxygen, you will lose more fluid than usual from the deeper breathing and from sweating, although often you won't notice this. It is important to maintain body fluids, so drink two or more times the amount of water or juices you would at sea level. Alcohol and caffeine have an extra impact at altitude, so consume them in moderation.

At this altitude the sun has more burning power. A bad sunburn can spoil your race, so use a protective sunscreen. It also can get cold very quickly at altitude, so while you're out training, in addition to extra fluids and sunscreen, be sure to carry a light jacket, tights, gloves, and a hat. Hypothermia (low body temperature) can come on rapidly if you are caught out in a rainstorm without proper protection at 6,000-plus feet, even during the summer.

Sleeping problems are the number-one complaint people have when they arrive at altitude. The lack of oxygen affects both sleep and arousal patterns, so your sleep tends to be lighter and you wake up a lot during the night. You also may experience a dry mouth while you're sleeping, so you may want to keep a glass of water by your bed at night.

How can you prepare for cycling at altitude? We know that the longer you can train at altitude, the better prepared you will be to race at altitude. Respiratory distress will go down, your body will begin to produce more red blood cells to help carry oxygen, and more changes will begin to take place at the cellular level. The whole effect is a more rapid and efficient movement of oxygen from the lungs to the tissues. The net effect of this acclimatization to high altitude is a gradual improvement in performance.

Two weeks to acclimate is best, but 7 to 10 days will do for some cyclists. A more realistic choice for some people is several weekend visits to altitude. This can be feasible if there are mountains not too far from where you live. Try to get into the 6,000- to 9,000-foot range. Your best bet is getting in several visits to altitude and then coming out 7 to 10 days before the race. If such acclimatization is not possible, then literally fly to your event as late as possible the day before the race, compete, and leave before the effects of altitude can take place.

Here are some additional tips to follow throughout your training at altitude and during your final stay before a race:

- Don't waste your first days loafing around. Light exercise stimulates breathing and circulation and speeds adjustment.
- Even if you are having trouble sleeping, try to get plenty of rest.
- Use a humidifier. Bring one with you or rent one while you are there.
- Eat smaller but more frequent meals because digestion can be more difficult at altitude. Eat plenty of carbohydrates, which you need for energy and recovery.
- Take deeper breaths as often as possible.
- Drink as much water as you can, but avoid alcohol for the first two or three days.
- Stop for short rest periods if your heart rate exceeds your target range for extended periods of time.
- Carry and drink more water during training than your thirst dictates. When you run, drink a little every 5 or 10 minutes.
- In the final days before the race, consume 60 to 70 percent of your calories in carbohydrates. This will ensure that your muscles are loaded with glycogen for race day.

Here are some additional things to remember on race day:

- Set out at a pace that does not allow for undue lactic acid accumulation. If your respiratory rate appears faster or your depth of breathing more labored than usual, chances are the pace is too intense.
- Accept fluids and food at the feed zones. Do not allow yourself to become dehydrated.
- Carry extra clothing. In the mountains the weather changes rapidly, the wind can dramatically reduce temperatures, and hypothermia can set in quickly.

With a better understanding of your responses to altitude and a well-thought-out training program, you can have an enjoyable experience training or competing at altitude.

Changing Environments

You have trained long and hard to reach your level of fitness. You have started traveling to races in various parts of the country and plan a trip to race internationally during the early season. Did you know that your fine edge can be quickly lost after traveling across as little as one time zone or that eating improperly in a foreign country can spell immediate disaster?

Two of the most common concerns of traveling (OK, besides airline meals) are jet lag and traveler's diarrhea. A cyclist who understands the problems of extended travel and how to avoid travel-related minor illnesses will be able to perform more effectively.

What Is Jet Lag?

Most plants and animals, including humans, have become synchronized with the 24-hour light-and-dark cycle. This is known as the circadian rhythm, from the Latin *circa dies*, meaning "about a day." Because our body rhythms are synchronized with this cycle, we sleep, work, and perform more effectively at certain times of the day than at others. Body temperature steadily drops early in the morning while we're sleeping and rises in the afternoon. Similarly, blood pressure and hormonal functions fluctuate according to a 24-hour cycle.

When the light-and-dark cycle is changed, the body rhythms become desynchronized, and an athlete may experience problems with sleep, digestion, alertness, performance, recovery, and temperament. In women, menstrual pain and dysfunction may occur.

Upsets in the body's circadian rhythm will occur after traveling quickly through several time zones. Generally, jet lag follows this pattern:

- 1 to 2 time zones crossed: little or no effect
- 3 to 6 time zones crossed: noticeable effect
- 7 to 10 time zones crossed: considerable effect
- 11 to 15 time zones crossed: marked effect

The following guidelines can help reduce the effects of extended air travel and the resulting changes in circadian rhythm:

Some cyclists like to take a very long ride just before a trip, knowing that they might be spending one or two days in transit and, hence, not be able to ride. That's a mistake. A trip through a number of time zones is a workout in itself. If it will be morning when you arrive at your destination, try to sleep on the plane; if it will be evening, try to avoid sleeping on the plane.

Before the trip, learn about the environment you'll be entering. Prepare for the weather conditions, customs, food, transportation, and so on. This may reduce some of the stress.

Try to change your sleeping schedule before the trip. For example, if you will be traveling to where the waking hours come earlier than what you are used to, go to bed earlier and get up earlier for several days. Before traveling to a time zone where the waking hours come later than you are used to, retire later and rise later. You will adapt somewhat to the time schedule at your destination.

Eat lightly during the trip, but drink plenty of fluids such as juice and water to avoid dehydration. Avoid alcohol and caffeine. Mild isometric exercises and walking around the cabin during the flight may relieve stiffness and boredom and help lessen fatigue.

If possible, schedule your arrival for the evening hours. Otherwise, a light ride after you arrive may help you get to sleep. During the first few days don't let the excitement of your new surroundings cause you to work too hard. Take it easy, or you may get worn down and increase your chances of becoming sick.

Adapting Your Diet

A major factor that influences your degree of impairment from jet lag is diet: the type of food you eat and the timing of your meals. Certain foods appear to help the body adjust more quickly to changes in circadian rhythms, and properly timing food intake also has been shown to facilitate adaptation after transmeridian flight.

According to Dr. Charles Ehret, one of the leading authorities on diet and jet lag, "Two of the major keys in combating jet lag lie in the storage organs for energy reserves of the body, including the muscles and the liver, and the body's natural production of glycogen, which, in a very real sense, is the fuel of the body." Alternating light and heavy meals before a flight continually empties the body's supply of glycogen and then replenishes it, allowing a person's circadian rhythms to quickly shift to a new time zone.

The condition of acute diarrhea has been most extensively studied in Americans visiting Mexico, where about 60 percent of travelers are affected. Known as "tourista" and "Montezuma's revenge" in Mexico, traveler's diarrhea can be just as common in the Mediterranean and Europe. Cyclists visiting Russia, where it's commonly known as "trotsky's," also have suffered it.

Contributory causes of the disease include changes in living habits, unusual foods or drinks, and viral or bacterial infections. But the major cause is the bacteria E. coli (Escherichia coli), which stimulates the intestine to hypersecrete fluid and electrolytes. E. coli can be picked up when you drink from mountain streams.

There are several ways to help prevent traveler's diarrhea. Drink only bottled water and use it for ice cubes, coffee, and brushing your teeth. Peel fruits and avoid leafy vegetables. Stay away from dairy products that have not been pasteurized.

Recently some physicians have been administering the antibiotic doxycycline (trade name, Vibramycin). Although this and other antibiotics reduce the incidence of diarrhea, there is concern that extended use of this drug might induce resistance to bacteria. It also can cause skin rashes in some people when they are exposed to strong sunlight.

Bismuth subsalicylate, known by the trade name Pepto-Bismol, also has been used to treat and prevent traveler's diarrhea. Its greatest benefit is that it is nearly nontoxic. In a recent study, preventive oral doses of Pepto-Bismol (two ounces taken several times a day) reduced the incidence of diarrhea by 50 percent. Whether the inconvenience of such a large dose is worth a 50 percent chance is a personal decision. In any case, the compound is safe and also can be used to help treat the disease once it has occurred. It may be wise to pack a bottle of diarrhea medicine when you travel to other countries, just in case. Remember, if you use antibiotics or other medication (e.g., Lomotil) for the prevention or relief of traveler's diarrhea, they should be taken only with a physician's advice.

If you get traveler's diarrhea, go on a liquid diet that includes fruit juices rich in potassium and add a pinch of salt. As symptoms subside, you can add bland foods such as bananas, rice, toast, and eggs. You should avoid dairy foods.

Personal Conditions

As if it weren't enough that you must guard against injuries and adverse environmental conditions, there are a number of non-cycling-related medical conditions, from the common cold to a chronic disease, with which you may have to cope.

Colds

Though it is relatively mild, the common cold is one of the most ubiquitous hazards known to humankind. It afflicts nearly everyone many times, and some more than others. Despite our occasional delusions of invincibility, even cyclists are susceptible to colds.

Viruses are the cause of the common cold. Incapable of living on their own, these small particles need the human body to survive. Viruses invade their host—you—through the lining of the nose and throat. At some point you may feel temporarily worse, suffering headaches and muscle aches, but these more severe symptoms usually are caused by a brief run of the virus through the body. Rarely does your temperature stay elevated for long.

The primary factor that makes a person susceptible to colds, and something we usually have little control over, is exposure. Exposure to a cold virus can occur simply by touching the hand of an infected person or any other contaminated surface. This is why individuals who live or work in crowded conditions are more susceptible to colds. Contrary to popular wisdom, there is absolutely no evidence that cold weather, dampness, or changes in temperature will lead to colds. The only reason for not cycling on a cold, damp day is that it is unpleasant.

The onset of a cold usually is announced by dryness or burning in the nose, then a watery nasal discharge appears. This is the point when treatments of nasal sprays, antihistamines, and decongestants usually begin. Despite relieving the symptoms, these drugs do nothing to the viral cause nor do they prevent further complications. In fact, most of the time they make you feel tired and lethargic.

The most effective treatment for a cold is to liquefy and warm your mucus so that it flows more freely and carries with it more of the virus as it leaves your body. One method of doing this is to take a shower or lie in a bath and breathe in warm, wet air. Drinking warm fluids also will help.

Adequate humidity in your living and working areas is quite important in cold prevention and treatment. To keep the relative humidity from dropping below 35 percent, a home humidifier is a good preventive investment. Cycling outdoors in the winter can aggravate dry airways because of the low humidity associated with lower temperatures. Wearing a face mask and drinking fluids will alleviate this problem.

A cold should not curtail your training. If a cold strikes, increase fluid intake, turn the humidifier on, and take aspirin to relieve your aches and pains. Unless there are complications, you should be able to maintain your cycling program. When symptoms progress to involve more body functions, special precautions are advised. Increased muscular pain, ear infections, a sore throat, and colored mucus are signals of complications. Medical assistance is required, and antibiotics will have to be used to fight the secondary bacterial infections. Curtail your training and rest.

The fever associated with these bacterial infections is your body's way of increasing metabolism so that your body will produce more antibodies to kill invading germs. Fever also may be beneficial because many germs that attack humans grow best at the body's normal temperature of 98.6 degrees Fahrenheit. They do not multiply at higher temperatures. Fever is the body's way of telling you that it is fighting bacterial infection, and you're better off resting, not cycling.

As soon as your temperature returns to normal, it is all right to resume your cycling program. However, you may be surprised to discover how quickly you lost your endurance. Studies on endurance athletes show that after 10 days of not exercising, they lose about 10 percent of their endurance. The results may be more devastating after a cold associated with fever. A study conducted in Sweden showed that colds associated with muscle aches and pains kept athletes from regaining their full capabilities for several weeks. It took this long for certain chemicals necessary for energy production to return to normal levels in the muscles.

Once the symptoms of the cold or infection subside, recovery is an individual matter. Remember, as long as no fever is present, it appears safe to cycle through a cold, taking care to ride within the limits of your energy and capability to stay warm. Gentle exercise tends to break up the congestion quicker than complete rest does. But keep the pace down to prevent coughing.

Colds with fever, and the flu, require more delicate care. A period of convalescence—first rest, then a gradual return to a full schedule—is a must. Don't ride with a fever. As a rule, take two days easy for each day of fever. For example, four days of fever would mean an additional eight days of recovery. You should avoid extended cycling that causes fatigue, or recurrence is a possibility.

Asthma

What is it like to ride with asthma? Alexi Grewal, former Olympic road champion, once described it as trying to breathe through a straw while riding. Grewal is among the 10 to 15 percent of the population who suffers from asthma, 60 to 90 percent of whom are susceptible to exercise-induced asthma (EIA) attacks.

Exactly how exercise leads to an asthma attack is not firmly established, but breathing a lot of cool, dry air seems to be the most common trigger. Incoming air must be warmed and moistened before it reaches the alveoli, the minute air sacs deep in the lungs where oxygen and carbon dioxide are exchanged. Cool, dry air saps the bronchi of heat and moisture, triggering broncospasms (narrowing of the breathing passages), which restrict air flow to the alveoli.

One of the best courses of action for cyclists who experience EIA is to warm up properly and gradually increase riding effort or speed. Asthmatic athletes who use a good warm-up or increase the workload gradually are less likely to induce EIA than those who rapidly increase their level of work. Often cyclists who experience EIA will ride with a balaclava or a mask to moisten the air when the temperature is below 50 degrees Fahrenheit.

There are some medications that athletes can use for asthma. One of the more popular asthma medications is albuterol. Effective in relieving the symptoms after they begin, albuterol provides protection from EIA in 80 to 95 percent of the athletes who use it before exercise. When it is administered with a special inhaler 10 to 20 minutes before a ride, albuterol helps prevent broncospasms from occurring. Another medication, cromolyn sodium, is slightly less effective but has the fewest complaints of side effects.

Some foods, air pollutants, pollens, and other allergens can trigger asthma. Because asthma is a chronic disease, there's no instant remedy. By continually managing their illness through medication, proper warm-up, and relaxation techniques, asthmatic cyclists can keep their competitive edge.

Diabetes

Recent findings in diabetic care have solved the problems that used to keep people who have diabetes from becoming active in cycling. But there are still too many people with diabetes who are a lot less active than they would like to be only because they do not understand how to cope with the disease. If you have diabetes, not only can you become an active and successful athlete, but cycling can even help you control the condition. To perform at your best safely, however, you need to understand how exercise and diabetes interact and how to adjust your exercise program to allow for the physiological changes that training and competition will cause.

Basically, there are two types of diabetics. Type 2, or late-onset, diabetes means that there is enough insulin in the blood to pass sugar into the muscle cells where it is converted to energy. Insulin is a hormone used to help transport glucose from the blood into the cells. In type 2 diabetes, however, the cells do not respond adequately to the hormone, and blood sugar levels remain high. This form of diabetes usually occurs in middle-aged people who are overweight and inactive, and it can be dramatically improved through diet and exercise.

In type 1 diabetes, the pancreas doesn't produce enough insulin to help transport the glucose into the muscle cells. This form of diabetes usually occurs in younger people, before the late 20s, and injections of insulin and a controlled diet must be followed to compensate for the body's lack of insulin. In either type, if diabetes is left untreated, the results are high levels of blood glucose, which can cause heart, kidney, and vision problems.

The three major influences on blood glucose levels are insulin, diet, and exercise. In nondiabetic people, the pancreas automatically releases the proper amount of insulin needed to regulate blood glucose. The person with diabetes, on the other hand, lacks this built-in mechanism and must control his body's delicate balance. Because insulin, diet, and exercise affect one another, exercise cannot be changed without a corresponding change in insulin or diet, and diet cannot be altered unless insulin therapy is changed. Further adjustments must be made to account for illness, emotional stress, menstruation, and infection, all of which affect insulin levels.

What happens when a person with diabetes becomes a cyclist? Although exercise cannot cure diabetes or end insulin injections, it does help lower blood glucose and can reduce the amount of insulin needed daily. Exercise has an insulin-like effect on the muscles in that it increases the permeability of the muscle membranes. By doing this, it also reduces the amount of insulin required. Over the long run, being active lowers the amount of glucose in the blood, which is the main objective of controlling diabetes.

Increasing the level of activity and exercise for a person with diabetes requires careful planning and scheduling. To compensate for the glucose-lowering effects of exercise, a diabetic athlete must go into a ride with a normal or slightly elevated blood glucose level. This is easily achieved by eating a carbohydrate snack about 30 minutes before exercising.

Remember, the key to controlling diabetes is maintaining a consistent balance between exercise and energy output, food intake and insulin. A spur-of-the-moment ride or run may sound like fun, but if you have diabetes, you cannot modify your exercise routine without also modifying your medications or diet. This kind of planning takes practice. Keep an accurate training diary in order to plan meals and the amount of insulin needed for a training session or race.

People with diabetes who require insulin injections must plan carefully so that they are not cycling miles away from their homes when insulin levels are peaking in the blood. The combined effect of insulin and exercise may allow too much glucose to enter the cells and result in low levels of blood glucose (hypoglycemia). If you have diabetes, carry carbohydrates in the form of candy or a sports drink with you on the bike in case of an emergency (weakness, headache, dizziness, confusion). To prevent hypoglycemia you will need to either decrease your insulin dosage or eat more food before your workout.

One technique that many diabetic athletes use is to eat immediately before and after exercise. The food you eat before the workout provides the glucose during the session. Eat immediately after the workout and again a few hours later. Hypoglycemia episodes are not uncommon three to four hours after a hard workout or race, probably because of the muscles' need to replenish glycogen stores and their increased demand for glucose. Remember, exercise also increases insulin sensitivity, making the diabetic athlete even more susceptible to postexercise hypoglycemia.

Make sure you inform your training partners and coach of your condition. Your companions also should be informed of what to do in an emergency. If you are out on the road, your coach or partners should know the symptoms of hypoglycemia and hyperglycemia. Hyperglycemia (high blood glucose) may occur if you have not taken enough insulin or have consumed too much carbohydrate. Above all else, train with another person, carry carbohydrates with you at all times, and wear a medical-alert tag identifying your condition.

Women's Health Issues

Before 1984, female cyclists were not participants in the Olympic Games. The limitation on women's road racing was defended on the grounds that long-distance sports (such as cycling and running) might be harmful to women's health. But research and position statements by the American College of Sports Medicine have done much to dispel the idea that endurance exercise is harmful for the healthy, trained female athlete. Since 1984 other endurance events for women, such as the 40-km individual time trial, the 3,000-meter individual pursuit, and the 30-km points race, have been added to the World Championships and/or Olympic Games.

Scientific studies show that men and women adapt to exercise training in a similar manner. Female road cyclists have high maximal oxygen consumptions and low relative fat content. The challenge of heat stress in long-distance cycling and the changes in oxygen pressure at altitude seem to be well tolerated by women. The limited amount of studies available suggests that women have the same rate of orthopedic injuries. Still, women have to contend with some health issues that men never have to face.

Menstrual Patterns

Strenuous cycling can have an impact on just about every part of the body, including a woman's reproductive system. When women suddenly increase their levels of cycling activity, they often detect changes in the heaviness of their menstrual flows and in the amount of menstrual discomfort. Some women stop menstruating altogether (amenorrhea) or may have irregular menstrual cycles (oligomenorrhea).

According to Charlotte Sanborn and Wiltz Wangner, Jr., athletic amenorrhea is most common in girls and young women who engage in heavy physical training. Among cyclists, amenorrhea is most common among women who put in long miles and are dieting to lose weight or maintain very lean physiques. There is also some evidence that being driven toward stressful patterns of achievement may lead to irregular menstrual patterns ("The Female Athlete and the Menstrual Cycle," pp. 111–30 in *Sport Science Perspectives for Women*, J. Puhl, C.H. Brown, and R.O. Voy, eds.).

If you experience menstrual irregularity, it is important to rule out possible medical disorders and pregnancy. Many female cyclists assume that irregular menses are a normal result of hard training and are no cause for concern. Indeed, in most cases a short period without menstruation will cause no lasting negative health risks, but you want to make sure that you do not have a more serious problem. Never assume that amenorrhea is either due to or related to cycling.

After a physician has ruled out a medical disorder, she may simply want to monitor you periodically during training. Many times, the menstrual cycle will return to normal when training is decreased (as in the off-season). However, recent research indicates that women who go for long periods without normal menstruation have some cause for concern. Amenorrhea and oligomenorrhea often indicate that levels of the hormone estrogen are low. Estrogen is important not only for normal reproductive function but also for controlling bone density. Research has shown that amenorrheic athletes have a much higher incidence of stress fractures, tendinitis, and muscle strains.

Studies of female athletes have shown that some have the bone densities of women in their 50s and 60s: They are exhibiting the symptoms of osteoporosis. Women who are training and dieting to be healthy and fit are in fact aging rapidly. When bone density decreases in the spinal column, these cyclists may be more susceptible to chronic back problems.

Bone loss may be slowed or prevented by calcium supplementation and/ or estrogen or progesterone replacement. The American Academy of Pediatrics recommends low-dose oral contraceptives (less than 50 micrograms of estrogen per day) to protect against skeletal demineralization in amenorrheic females over age 16. As with any medication, however, the harmful side effects must be weighed against the benefits of another treatment with less severe side effects. The key is to seek out medical care at the first signs of menstrual irregularity.

Cycling During Pregnancy

Not many years ago, pregnant women were told to take it easy. Today, women are hearing that regular exercise during pregnancy is healthy for both the mother and the child. As we know, everyone responds differently to exercise, and this includes pregnant women. Factors that influence individual response to exercise are body composition, age, body weight, environmental conditions, and physical conditioning.

As the pregnancy progresses, changes in endocrine, cardiovascular, and respiratory functioning will affect a woman's response to exercise. Cardiac output (blood pumped by the heart per minute) and blood volume will increase by 30 to 45 percent during pregnancy. Resting heart rate also will be higher, though arterial blood pressure tends to remain stable.

Many women are concerned about fetal responses to activity. They wonder if there will be a reduction in blood flow to the uterus during cycling. Research has shown that during moderate exercise there may be a slight decrease in overall uterine blood flow, but blood flow appears to be redistributed favoring the placental flow.

Many female cyclists choose to continue training during pregnancy but have to modify the duration and intensity of exercise. Some programs may need to be modified as pregnancy progresses. Mountain biking will have to be eliminated, road training will have to be cut to shorter distances, and eventually a pregnant woman may have to switch to stationary cycling.

Cycling is a good non-weight-bearing activity. Many women find riding stationary bikes safer than riding on the road, especially when changes in their center of gravity affect their balance. Swimming is also an excellent non-weight-bearing activity.

Weight training may be continued during pregnancy, provided that the goal is strength maintenance and that proper breathing technique is practiced. Avoid waterskiing, horseback riding, scuba diving, and the like; stick to low-impact activities such as cycling. If it hurts while you're doing it or later in the evening or the next day, don't do it.

Follow these exercise precautions during pregnancy:

- Your core temperature should not exceed 101 degrees Fahrenheit. Check your temperature rectally early in your pregnancy after a standard workout and use this measure to help you guide workout intensity.

- Avoid saunas and hot tubs.

- Follow the American College of Obstetricians and Gynecologists' recommendation to keep your heart rate below 140 beats per minute during exercise.

- Proper hydration and good nutrition are essential. Drink plenty of water during exercise and establish sound eating habits.

- Discontinue exercise if any unusual symptoms occur, and consult your physician.

Cycling After Pregnancy

Listen to your body, which will tell you when to resume exercise after delivery. If you had a normal delivery, you probably can resume exercising as soon as you are able to do so without pain. A return to high-intensity cycling should be avoided prior to the postpartum examination because your muscles have not yet returned to your prepregnancy state and your chances of injury are greater. If you are breast-feeding, you can exercise provided you have adequate breast support and you maintain hydration. Include activities such as cycling and walking in your program.

Many female athletes feel that they are stronger and actually improve their performance after pregnancy. It has even been postulated that the stresses of labor and delivery somehow make a woman tougher and better able to compete.

WOMEN AND ENDURANCE CYCLING

For many years, those studying women's sports such as running and cycling have tried to understand the demands and limitations of endurance training on female endurance athletes. Current available research and evidence provide no support for treating men's and women's training programs differently. Although men and women do differ in their responses to vigorous exercise, there are probably more differences within each sex than between them. Studies have found that the level of physical fitness makes more difference than gender does. Further, when differences are observed in trained male and female athletes, in most cases the response is one of adapting and conditioning to chronic exercise.

(continued)

Research shows that women respond to endurance training in the same manner as men; therefore, restrictions should not be placed on women in endurance events. Although it is generally true that a woman has a smaller heart mass, less cardiac output (amount of blood pumped by the heart per minute), and less blood volume and hemoglobin, training can increase the efficiency of her oxygen transport system. When maximal oxygen consumption is expressed in terms of lean body mass (total weight minus fat weight), the highly trained woman is nearly identical to the man. However, generally speaking, women will have a higher percentage of body fat than men will.

For many years, women were kept from endurance events on the grounds that they could not tolerate heat or the race distance for extended periods of time. It was not until the 1984 Olympic Games that the women's road race was added to the event schedule. Many of these misconceptions were fostered by poorly designed studies. Researchers compared trained men and sedentary women and used standardized work tasks that might be considered moderate for men but significantly harder for women.

The biggest problem for a female cyclist is that she cannot leave her higher percentage of fat on the starting line. She must carry it on the bike along with her muscle mass, and it will cost her more oxygen to cycle at the same speed as someone with a lower fat percentage. Again, training can help. Several years ago, a study of lean female distance runners found that their maximal oxygen consumption was only 4.1 percent lower than that of a comparative group of male marathoners when compared by lean body mass.

One of the great debates about women's performance in athletics concerns menstruation. There seem to be differences among women regarding exercise and competition during menstruation. Many have few or no menstrual difficulties under any conditions, active or sedentary. On the other hand, a significant number of women have oligomenorrhea (infrequent menstrual flow) or other menstrual difficulties that apparently are neither helped nor aggravated by vigorous activity. Several cyclists have reported a total absence of menstruation when training for long distances. This phenomenon may be related to low body weight and reduced levels of body fat: Several studies have reported no menstruation (secondary amenorrhea) in chronically underweight women.

For a survey conducted at a major women's stage race, 33 women were questioned on the mileage ridden each week and the incidence of secondary amenorrhea. Approximately 12 percent of the women experienced this condition. These women were training 200 to 300 miles per week.

Many factors may contribute to amenorrhea in cyclists, but it is primarily characterized by loss of body weight and many miles of training on the bicycle each week. Besides loss of body fat, cycling long distances may lead to decreased levels of certain hormones that control various phases of the menstrual cycle, which may lead directly or indirectly to amenorrhea. The role of cycling and the causes of these menstrual irregularities remain unknown.

It is well recognized that the average man is considerably stronger than the average woman. Several different studies suggest that men are approximately 30 to 40 percent stronger than women. However, for men and women of comparable body weight and lean body weight, lower body strength is similar, although men maintain a clear superiority in upper-body strength. Strength training, formerly condemned as a form of training for women because of its supposed masculinizing effects, is now recognized as valuable in building up the physiological profile of the female cyclist.

Stretching

If you are a serious cyclist, stretching regularly will help you avoid tight muscles and injuries. Hard riding is great exercise, but it does lead to a gradual loss of muscle elasticity and an overall decrease in joint flexibility. Fortunately, stretching enables your muscles and joints to adapt to the rigors of cycling.

Stretching improves flexibility and increases range of motion, so well-exercised muscles and joints will undergo less severe stress in competitive conditions. Proper stretching after a workout also can reduce or even eliminate muscle stiffness after a ride. Stretching keeps the body fine-tuned and hastens recovery.

In his book *Road Racing*, Bernard Hinault, five-time winner of the Tour de France, speaks of the benefits of regular stretching in a cycling program: "Stretching just before competition, like a time trial, prepares the muscles for the effort by making them more supple and increasing their tone. The alternating pattern of contraction-relaxation is more completely guaranteed, enhancing your effectiveness if you must ride fast and gives you a more efficient style if you must ride for a long time" (p. 182).

Hinault further explains, "You will be able to raise your saddle and still be able to pedal with suppleness and retain good speed. You'll be able to do this because of an improved decontraction of the opposing muscles with each pedal revolution. The hamstrings, which instinctively attempt to hold back the descending leg, reap a great benefit from stretching. It is their imperfect decontraction that prevents you from raising your saddle enough." Raising your saddle will allow your leg muscles a greater range and will put less strain on your spinal column and lower back.

Bob Anderson, author of *Stretching* and an avid cyclist, says, "One of the best ways to stretch is with static stretching, in which you stretch each muscle group slowly and gently, until a mild amount of tightness (not pain) is felt in the muscle. Then maintain this position for about 30 seconds or until the muscle begins to relax. As you hold the stretch, the feeling of tension should diminish. If it doesn't, just ease off slightly into a more comfortable stretch."

After holding the easy stretch, move a bit farther into the stretch until you feel mild tension again. This, the developmental stretch, should be held for another 10 to 30 seconds. The tension should again slightly diminish or stay the same. If tension increases or becomes painful, you are overstretching and should ease off to a more comfortable stretch. The developmental stretch reduces tension and will safely increase flexibility. Repeating this process a few times for each muscle group will yield the best results.

The rapid, jerky movements involved in ballistic (bouncing) stretches are ineffective and can lead to injury. If you bounce, the muscle responds by contracting to protect itself from overstretching. Thus, an internal tension develops in the muscle and prevents it from being fully stretched. Bouncing also may cause tiny tears in the muscle, leaving scar tissue behind, which can make the muscle less flexible than it was before.

I suggest you experiment with stretching for 5 to 10 minutes before and after you ride. The areas of your body that tend to tire first are the ones that you should pay particular attention to when you are preparing for a ride. Hold the degree of tension in the muscle that feels good to you. The key to stretching is to be relaxed while you concentrate on the muscles being stretched. Your breathing should be slow, deep, and rhythmical. Don't worry about how far you stretch. Relax into it and limberness will become just one of many by-products you receive from regular stretching.

Stretching will get your blood circulating through your muscles and warm them up for the tasks ahead. Once you start riding, don't forget to pedal easily for a few minutes until your heart rate gets up to 120 before beginning any hard efforts.

Michael Alter's book, *Sport Stretch*, contains an excellent stretching routine for cycling. It will take you about 10 minutes to do the following stretching exercises before and after your ride, just 10 minutes to keep injuries and tightness to a minimum. As you stretch, you will learn about how your body moves and feels. Stretching is a great form of physical education.

Achilles Tendon Stretch

Stand upright four to five steps from a wall. Lean against the wall without losing the straight line of your head, neck, spine, pelvis, legs, and ankles. Keeping both heels down, flat, together, and parallel to your hips, exhale as you bend your arms and move your chest toward the wall, shifting your weight forward (photo). Hold the stretch and relax.

Hip Flexors Stretch

Lie on a table near the edge, flat on your back. Allow one leg to hang over the side. Inhale, flex the opposite knee, grasp it with your hands, and bring it to your chest (photo). Inhale and compress your thigh to your chest. Hold the stretch and relax. Repeat with the other leg.

Adductors Stretch

Sit upright on the floor with legs flexed and heels touching each other. Grasp your feet or ankles and pull them as close to your buttocks as possible (photo A). While leaning forward from the hips without bending your back, exhale and attempt to lower your chest to the floor. Hold the stretch and relax.

For those who are less flexible, assume a squat position with your feet about 12 inches apart and your toes turned slightly out. Place your elbows on the inside portions of your upper legs (photo B). Exhale and slowly push your legs outward with your elbows. Remember to keep your feet flat on the floor to reduce strain on the knees. Hold the stretch and relax.

a

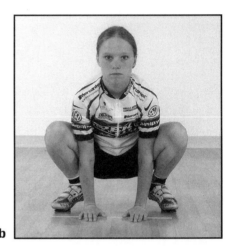
b

Abdomen and Hips Stretch

Kneel upright on the floor with legs slightly apart and parallel and with toes pointing back. Reach around your back and place your palms on your upper hips and buttocks. Inhale, slowly arch your back, contract your buttocks, and push your hips forward. Exhale. While continuing to arch your back, drop your head backward, open your mouth, and gradually slide your hands onto your heels (photo). Hold the stretch and relax.

Quadriceps Stretch

Lie on your back at the edge of a table with your left side toward the edge. Flex your left leg and slide it toward your buttocks to help anchor and stabilize your hips. Grasp your leg under the left thigh with your left hand. Exhale, slowly lower your right leg off the table, and grasp the ankle or foot with your right hand (photo A). Inhale, and slowly pull your right heel toward your buttocks. Hold the stretch and relax, then repeat with the other leg.

As an alternative stretch, kneel upright with knees together, buttocks on the floor, heels by the sides of your thighs, and toes pointing back. Exhale as you lean back until you are flat on your back (photo B). Do not let your feet flare out to the sides. Hold the stretch and relax.

a

b

Buttocks and Hips Stretch

Sit upright on the floor, resting your left leg in front of you with your knee flexed and your foot pointing to the right. Cross your right leg over your left leg and place the foot flat on the floor. Exhale, round your upper torso, and bend forward (photo). Hold the stretch and relax, then repeat with the other leg.

Lateral Neck Stretch

Sit or stand upright with your left arm flexed behind your back. Grasp the elbow from behind with the opposite hand. Exhale, pull your elbow across the midline of your back, and lower your ear to the right shoulder (photo). It is essential to keep your left shoulder stabilized. Hold the stretch and relax, then repeat on the other side.

Lower Back Stretch

Lie flat on your back with your arms by your hips, palms down. Inhale, push down on the floor with your palms, raise your legs up in a squat position so that the knees almost rest on your forehead, and bring your hands up to support your back (photo). Hold the stretch and relax. Perform this stretch with care.

Posterior Neck Stretch

Lie flat on the floor with both knees flexed while interlocking your hands on the back of your head near the crown. Exhale and pull your head off the floor and onto your chest (photo). Keep your shoulder blades flat on the floor. Hold the stretch and relax.

Hamstrings Stretch

Sit upright on the floor with both legs straight. Flex your right knee and slide your heel toward your buttocks. Lower the outer side of your right thigh and calf onto the floor. Place your right heel against the inner side of your left thigh so that a 90-degree angle is formed between your extended left leg and flexed right leg. Exhale, keeping your left leg straight, bend at the waist, and lower your extended upper torso onto your thigh (photo). Hold the stretch and relax, then repeat with the other leg.

From *Sport Stretch* (2nd ed.) by M.J. Alter (pp. 92, 102, 115, 118, 132, 136, 138, 147, 157, 165, 182, 187), 1998, Champaign, IL: Human Kinetics. Copyright 1998 by Michael J. Alter. Adapted by permission.

 *The Final Spin*

It's safe to say that every year the competitive cyclist will become injured or ill at least a few times. Your best bet for treating the injury or illness is to be conservative and return to training cautiously. The competitive cyclist will find the line between overtraining and undertraining a fine one. Too much mileage and intensity may lead to injury and illness, too little to underachieving. Often this is what makes the difference between winning and losing at all levels of competition.

The cyclist who repeatedly loses training time will be in worse condition than the conservative and healthy cyclist. An important part of training is learning to prevent injuries and illnesses and knowing how and when to return to training.

Preventing injury and illness means eliminating their causes and reacting to the early warning signs. Most problems can be prevented, but once one occurs you must treat the cause, treat the injury, and rehabilitate your body in order to return to competitive fitness.

PART II

The Nutritional Edge

We all want to get the most out of our training programs. Some exercise for fitness, others train for competition, but all of us push our bodies to the limit, sometimes daily, to maximize our workouts. As dedicated cyclists, we may put in several hours of strenuous exercise to improve beyond base conditioning and to develop strength and endurance. Intense, exhaustive exercise is only one aspect of an effective training program.

Successful cyclists and their coaches know that it's impossible to train extremely hard on consecutive days for any extended period of time. This is especially true for endurance cyclists. To adequately rebuild muscle glycogen stores, the body needs 24 to 36 hours to recover from strenuous training. These days, a "hard-easy" schedule, which incorporates easy days of less-intense training, is an accepted part of every smart endurance athlete's routine. It's as simple as listening to your body. You know when you have maximized your workout or raced to your limit because your body will not allow you to continue, and you won't be able to go at the same level the next day—no matter how hard you try.

This part of the book explores many facets of sound nutrition for cyclists. This section will be helpful if you've become confused by conflicting information. In fact, if you're not uncertain about what to eat and drink for peak performance, it's probably because you haven't been trying to figure it out. After all, cyclists are regularly bombarded with claims (sometimes contradictory) that certain foods or diets will help them live longer, lose weight, improve strength, and, of course, ride better.

If you're tired of feeling perplexed—and perhaps bouncing from one food fad to another—this section is for you. It lays the foundation for what you need to know about good eating, supplementation, and recovery for better cycling.

6

FUELING FOR TRAINING AND COMPETITION

As a cyclist, you may be tempted to purchase a high-tech bicycle to improve performance, but you may only need to look at your diet. No amount of money spent on equipment, training, and coaching will ensure a winning performance if you do not have the proper fuel in your tank.

Nutrition and fluid replacement play a significant role in successful training and competition. You have trained hard, purchased the proper equipment, and honed your cycling skills. Proper nutrition may be all you need to perform at your maximum in training and competition. This chapter will provide you with information on optimal nutrition, which is an essential component in achieving top physical performance in cycling.

Total Nutrition for Improved Performance

The main nutritional need of cyclists is increased energy. The more intensive your cycling, and the longer it lasts, the larger your total energy expenditure. From published reports on cyclists in the Tour de France and from personal observations, it can be estimated that racing cyclists require 3,000 to 7,000 calories daily. Sedentary, normal-weight women typically consume 1,400 to 2,000 calories per day, their male counterparts 2,500 to 2,800. This wide range highlights the need for individual assessment. In daily practice, estimate your energy needs by monitoring your weight and satisfying your appetite. Inadequate energy intake will lead to decreased physical performance, weight loss, and chronic fatigue.

Fluid Facts

You may not think of water as a nutrient, but it is the most critical one in your diet. You can live only three to four days without water. About 60 to 70 percent of an adult's body weight is water.

You lose water from the body in many ways. Through breathing, urinating, and sweating, you lose up to 12 cups of water each day. If you exercise in hot weather, you could easily double or triple that amount.

Without sufficient water intake, fatigue will set in, and performance will be affected. Even small variations in fluid levels will begin to affect performance. Losing only 2 to 3 percent of the body's fluid through sweat (about 3 to 4 pounds in a 150-pound individual) decreases cycling performance 3 to 7 percent. Figure 6.1 shows the effects of dehydration on cycling performance.

It is best to drink one to two cups of fluid before exercise and then drink often during exercise. It is also important to include some form of carbohydrate with the fluid to help supply energy to your muscles.

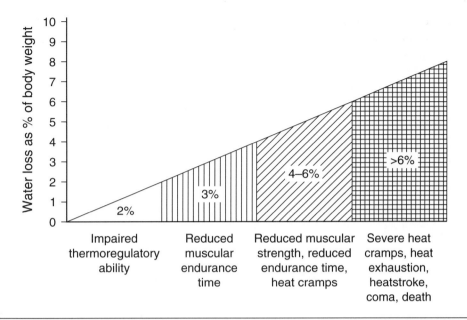

Figure 6.1 The effects of various levels of dehydration on endurance performance.

From *Serious Training for Serious Athletes* (p. 135) by R. Sleamaker, 1989, Champaign, IL: Human Kinetics. Copyright 1989 by Robert Hayes Sleamaker. Reprinted by permission.

Carbohydrate: Main Source of Energy

Carbohydrate, the primary fuel for muscle contraction, is the nutrient most important for cycling. Energy from carbohydrate can be released within exercising muscles up to three times faster than energy from fat. There are two major types of carbohydrates: complex (found in spaghetti, potatoes, breads, and rice) and simple (naturally occurring simple sugars). Carbohydrate stores in the body (glycogen) are limited. When depleted, cyclists can't train or race hard and may experience fatigue.

To accomplish glycogen repletion on a daily basis, consume a significant amount of carbohydrate, about 60 percent of your total caloric intake. This amounts to 500 to 600 grams of carbohydrate (2,000 to 2,400 calories per day). Such a diet means eating large quantities of carbohydrate foods (see table 6.1). Eat carbohydrate-rich breakfasts, such as cereals and pancakes, instead of eggs. For lunch and dinner, have large portions of rice, pasta, potatoes, vegetables, and fruits. Your plate should be two-thirds covered by carbohydrates. The remaining calories in the diet should be obtained from fat (20 to 25 percent) and protein (15 to 20 percent).

TABLE 6.1 Foods Containing High Sources of Carbohydrate

Food	Energy (calories)	Carbohydrate (g)*
Baked potato, large	240	55
Pancakes, 3, 4-in.	260	51
Rice, 1 cup	205	45
Whole-wheat bread, 4 slices	224	44
Pizza, cheese, 2 slices	340	42
Stuffing, 1 cup	220	40
Spaghetti, 1 cup	200	40
Sports bar, 1 bar	225	40
Instant oatmeal, maple, 1 serving	160	30
Bagel, 1	160	30
Raisins, 1/4 cup	120	30
Banana, medium	105	27
English muffin, 1	130	25
Cream of wheat, 1 serving	100	22
Apple, medium	81	21
Honey, 1 tbsp.	60	15
Fig cookie, 1	50	11
Peas, 1/2 cup	50	10
Carrot, medium	40	10
Greenbeans, 1/2 cup	30	7

* 1 gram of carbohydrate = 4 calories. Some of these foods contain fats and proteins.

Not only does the amount of carbohydrate in the diet affect performance, but daily carbohydrate stores dictate day-to-day energy levels. Figure 6.2 shows what can happen to glycogen stores if you do not eat a daily diet high in carbohydrate. A high-carbohydrate (high-CHO) diet allows you to recover faster from your workouts. Getting inadequate carbohydrate can lead to chronic fatigue. Without adequate carbohydrate stores, you'll feel like you are always riding in low gear.

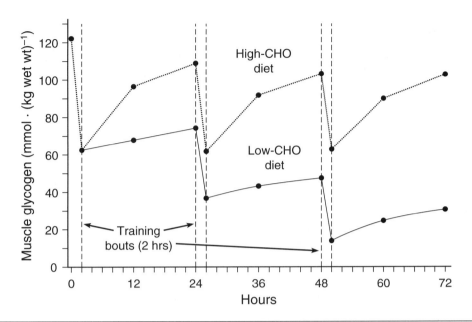

Figure 6.2   A high-carbohydrate diet speeds recovery from training.

From "Nutrition for Endurance Sport: Carbohydrate and Fluid Balance" by D.L. Costill and J.M. Miller, 1980, International Journal of Sports Medicine, 1, p.2. Reprinted by permission of Georg Thieme Verlag.

Protein Needs

High protein intake usually is associated with weightlifting and bodybuilding, but recent evidence suggests that endurance athletes also may need additional protein. The extra protein is probably necessary to repair damaged muscle tissue and be used as an auxiliary fuel source during long-term exercise. Such exercise increases protein demands from the .8 gram per kilogram of body weight suggested by the recommended dietary allowance (RDA) for protein to between 1 and 1.5 grams per kilogram (2.2 pounds). For a 120-pound cyclist, this would be 60 to 85 grams of protein per day.

Most cyclists will not have to make major changes in their diets to meet this requirement. For example, a cyclist who consumes 3,500 calories a day in a diet that is about 12 percent protein will easily meet this requirement. Aim for 1.5 grams per kilogram of body weight. If you eat 10 to 20 percent of your diet in protein, your protein intake will be adequate to meet the increased needs of hard training and racing.

A rule of thumb to get adequate protein in your diet is to include two cups of low-fat milk or yogurt plus four to six ounces of protein-rich foods per day.

Foods high in protein are meat, poultry, fish, eggs, dried peas, beans, and lentils.

Some individuals may need to modify this diet. A female cyclist eating a low-calorie diet of mostly vegetables and salads may be at risk for protein deficiency, which would manifest itself in anemia, fatigue, and possibly amenorrhea. She should consume more protein-rich foods such as dairy products, fish, poultry, and lean meats. Be sure to include products such as yogurt, lean meats, and low-fat milk, which are considered complete proteins when you are on a high-carbohydrate diet.

Fat Facts

The recommended diet for healthy and active individuals has 20 to 25 percent fat. There is no need to supplement your diet with fat. Research on Tour de France cyclists confirms this. On average, the diets of these cyclists contained 23 percent fat, 62 percent carbohydrate, and 15 percent protein. Although cycling stimulates adaptive changes that increase the body's ability to mobilize and utilize fat as an energy source, you do not need to increase fat intake above the prescribed percentages. Adequate carbohydrate and fat intake can be obtained from a diet containing grains, vegetables, fruit, dairy products, and lean meats.

All fat—saturated (found in butter, beef fat, coconut and palm oil, and hydrogenated vegetable oil), monounsaturated (found in olive and canola oil), and polyunsaturated (found in most vegetable oils such as corn and safflower oil)—has 9 calories per gram, compared to the 4 calories per gram of carbohydrate and protein. By having fat in the diet, cyclists who expend a lot of calories each day can get the calories they need with less food. It can be difficult for a cyclist who needs 4,000 to 6,000 calories a day to eat this large amount of calories on a diet of less than 20 to 25 percent fat.

In getting your 20 to 25 percent fat allotment, try to consume similar amounts of saturated, monounsaturated, and polyunsaturated fat. Fat helps provide energy, helps store and use fat-soluble vitamins (A, D, E, and K), and is vital to moving nutrients into and out of cells. Fat is needed in your diet, but it needs to be kept in the recommended range of total calories.

Vitamins and Minerals

Although a lot of research on vitamins and minerals has focused on their use as enzymes to speed up metabolic reactions in the body, there is now evidence that they protect your body from the damage of hard cycling. Little did you know that increased exercise may have a negative effect on your body. Yes, after all these years of telling about the benefits of exercise—reduced body fat, increased cardiorespiratory fitness, increased strength,

INVESTIGATING THE 40-30-30 DIET

The 40-30-30 diet recently has become a popular nutritional regimen in the sport and fitness world. Athletes on this diet plan obtain 40 percent of their calories from carbohydrate, 30 percent from fat, and 30 percent from protein, in contrast to the 60-25-15 ratio that traditionally has been recommended by nutritionists. Supporters of the 40-30-30 plan say that decreasing carbohydrate intake and boosting protein consumption enables dieters to burn more fat. For athletes, this translates into a glycogen-sparing effect, which can extend endurance.

The theory behind the 40-30-30 diet is that a lower carbohydrate intake, coupled with an increased percentage of protein, helps keep blood insulin levels low. From our discussion about insulin's importance in glycogen manufacture and storage (chapter 5), you might be wondering what benefits low insulin levels would offer. While insulin is essential for processing carbohydrate, it also has been shown to inhibit fat metabolism. According to 40-30-30 proponents, lowering blood insulin levels allows the body to burn fat more efficiently.

Furthermore, whereas a high-carbohydrate, low-fat meal triggers the release of insulin, a higher percentage of protein triggers the release of glucagon. This hormone has the opposite effect of insulin: it enables the body to burn fat. Therefore, in theory, an athlete who is looking to use more fat for energy during exercise wants to eat less carbohydrate and more protein and fat.

Many researchers in sports nutrition, however, have stated otherwise. The fact remains that the consumption of any moderate meal consisting of 60 percent carbohydrate, 25 percent fat, and 15 percent protein will produce a moderate amount of insulin. The primary role of insulin is to metabolize carbohydrate, not to store fat. Since insulin is busy doing its job on a carbohydrate-rich meal, the concentration of insulin soon falls.

The claim that the 40-30-30 diet helps athletes lose body fat also remains unproved. Athletes would not lose body fat because 40-30-30 keeps insulin low in the blood. Instead, those who lose body fat are more likely to have done so because they've benefited from calorie counting to stay within the recommended 2,000-calorie limit. An athlete following the 40-30-30 plan ends up eating less simply because he is taking greater care to count calories and regulate food consumption.

In the end, most nutrition researchers, sport dietitians, and exercise physiologists remain firm in their conviction that the optimal athletic diet consists of 60 percent carbohydrate, 20 to 25 percent fat, and 15 to 20 percent protein. This recommendation is based on a veritable mountain of validated and convincing research. The experts also advocate supplementing with carbohydrate before and during exercise to improve endurance performance and consuming carbohydrate after exercise to replenish glycogen stores.

and less stress—scientists are now discovering a link between exercise and the formation of free radicals. They sound like a group of terrorists loose in your body, and they are.

We inhale a lot of free radicals in the air we breathe. Yes, oxygen is critical for life and for the production of energy for strength training, running, cycling, or swimming. Ironically, however, some of the chemical reactions oxygen triggers within your body create toxic compounds called free radicals, highly reactive, unstable entities that have the potential to cause severe damage to a cell's structure. They attack the cell walls of muscles, mitochondria, the heart, and blood vessels. They damage cell structure and reduce the cell's ability to function and regulate itself.

Free-radical damage has been linked not only to reduced exercise ability but also to problems specifically associated with aging, such as a declining immune system, atherosclerosis, and Parkinson's disease. Free radicals also may be directly linked to cancer and heart disease, which together account for 80 percent of all deaths in the United States.

Fortunately, our bodies are equipped to fight the ravages of free radicals with substances called antioxidants, which halt or inactivate these dangerous molecular by-products and help repair the cellular damage. Antioxidants keep the damage from getting out of control. Antioxidants are to cells what traffic lights are to cars: they both prevent destruction and mayhem, but the more activity there is between oxygen and the cells of your body (traffic), the more antioxidants (traffic lights) you need.

The body creates antioxidants in the form of enzymes such as superoxide dismutase. But antioxidants also are found in vitamins C and E and in beta carotene, a precursor of vitamin A. Selenium, zinc, the peptide glutathione, and bioflavonoids are other minerals and nutrients that have been found to be synergistic in the fight against free radicals. Also, scientific research has shown that some herbs may be linked to combating free radicals. Siberian ginseng, turmeric, rosemary, ginkgo, and milk thistle are some of the more popular antioxidant herbs.

Exercise and Free Radicals

As a cyclist, you may be at a greater risk than more sedentary individuals for higher levels of free-radical production in your body. While you exercise you take in many more times the oxygen than you would at rest, which leads to an increased number of mitochondria in the muscle cells. Mitochondria are the structures involved in your muscles' aerobic metabolism. The resulting mitochondrial activity is thought to increase oxidation and free-radical production.

Exercise increases the release of the hormones epinephrine and norepinephrine, which helps charge up your nervous system, release fats from your body's stores, and supply glycogen to the muscles. The oxidation of these hormones has been shown to be related to free-radical formation.

Just as exercising leads to greater oxygen intake, exercising in smoggy conditions can lead to the increased intake of ozone and nitrogen oxide. When the oxygen combines with the ozone or nitrogen oxide, even more free radicals are produced.

Combating Free Radicals With Vitamins

Free radicals are at least partially to blame for muscle damage, soreness, and reduced endurance. Free radicals damage muscle cells during hard exercise, leading to inflammation and acute muscle soreness. Several studies have shown that optimal levels of antioxidants may reduce muscle injury and improve endurance.

Research at the University of California, Davis, showed that when athletes ran to exhaustion on a treadmill, two important enzymes normally found in the muscle cells appeared in high concentrations in the athletes' blood. In a second trial the runners received supplements of 1,000 milligrams (mg) of vitamin C, 10 mg of beta carotene, and 800 international units (IU) of vitamin E for eight weeks. When the tests were repeated, the athletes had much lower concentrations of the enzymes in their blood. This suggests that the athletes had less muscle-cell damage when they took the antioxidants. They also had significantly higher levels of glutathione preoxidase in their blood, an antioxidant that helps prevent damage to muscle-cell membranes.

Vitamin C has many important functions, including enhancing iron absorption, producing collagen, assisting in wound healing, and stimulating the immune system. As an important water-soluble antioxidant, vitamin C specializes in scavenging oxidants and free radicals in the watery fluids of cells and blood. The U.S. RDA for vitamin C is 60 mg a day, but many researchers recommend 250 to 1,000 mg per day to prevent cell damage, serve as an antioxidant, prevent heart disease, and help prevent cancer.

Beta carotene and vitamin A are related. Beta carotene is a precursor to vitamin A and also serves as an antioxidant itself. Although vitamin A is not a very active antioxidant, it helps your body resist infection, neutralizes the effect of free radicals, and has been shown to reduce the incidence of cancer. The U.S. RDA for vitamin A is 5,000 IU per day. Many people believe you need 10,000 to 20,000 IU of vitamin A to help fight infections and battle free radicals.

Beta carotene is a plant pigment that the body converts to vitamin A if the need exists. When you eat a carrot or an orange, part of the beta carotene is converted to vitamin A. The remaining beta carotene acts as an antioxidant, dousing free radicals and preventing oxidative damage. There is no RDA for beta carotene, but most scientists recommend a minimum intake of 5 to 10 mg daily.

Many in the medical community claim that vitamin E is the master antioxidant. Vitamin E has been shown to mend some of the signs of aging and other changes that occur as the result of oxidative damage. Older individuals have greater levels of markers called lipid peroxides, which are signs of oxidative damage. Yet when elderly people in one research study took vitamin E supplements in amounts 20 to 40 times the U.S. RDA, the levels of these markers went down, which suggests the slowing down of cell aging.

What about the effects of vitamin E on athletes, who experience oxidative damage to muscle cells during exercise? In one study, athletes who received vitamin E supplements of as little as 400 IU per day showed decreased levels of malondialdehyde (MDA, a marker for muscle-cell oxidation) after running. A group of 25 female runners were measured for MDA before and after a 30-minute treadmill run. The post-run levels of MDA increased over 30 percent in the group that did not take vitamin E supplements.

The U.S. RDA for vitamin E is 30 IU, but studies have used much higher levels, up to 800 IU for three years, without finding toxic effects. A minimum intake of 200 to 800 IU is recommended for people who exercise intensely or are routinely exposed to air pollutants during exercise.

Exercise also may have an effect on your immune system. There is probably a link among hard exercise, immunity, and antioxidants. When you exercise vigorously and often, fighting free radicals may strain your immune system, leaving you susceptible to colds, flu, and infection. After hard exercise your immune system needs a boost, and antioxidants are essential for optimal functioning of your immune system.

Additional Free-Radical Fighters

When you exercise hard, when you are exposed to stress or poor air quality, or when you ingest certain medications or processed foods, you may not be obtaining enough key antioxidant nutrients. Recently, numerous studies have reported that the RDA of antioxidants may not be sufficient to provide a strong defense against free radicals and infections. You might want to use glutathione and N-acetyl cysteine, selenium, zinc, or bioflavonoids for supplemental protection against free radicals.

Glutathione and N-Acetyl Cysteine

The peptide glutathione converts oxidized vitamin C back into a form that can once again serve as an antioxidant. Research on animals has shown that intense exercise can reduce muscle glutathione by 40 percent and liver glutathione (from which muscles increase their supply) by 80 percent. After exercise, liver and muscle glutathione levels continue to fall, indicating continued use of this antioxidant in fighting free radicals. If glutathione levels drop too low, severe muscle damage may take place.

Glutathione can be taken preformed, but some of it will be destroyed in the digestive tract. The body produces glutathione from L-cysteine and other amino acids. Research has shown that increasing intake of N-acetyl cysteine helps the body supercompensate its levels of glutathione. N-acetyl cysteine is preferred over L-cysteine because it is more stable and less toxic.

To ensure that your intake of cysteine is adequate to produce glutathione, eat quality protein or take a supplement containing N-acetyl cysteine. Currently there are no RDAs for glutathione or N-acetyl cysteine, but intakes of 50 mg or more of each antioxidant should be ingested. Read the label on any antioxidant supplement to ensure that these forms of peptide and amino acids are listed. Be sure to take three times the amount of vitamin C as N-acetyl cysteine to avoid the possibility of it precipitating in the kidneys as cysteine and possibly causing kidney stones.

Selenium

Selenium is a potent antioxidant that works synergistically with antioxidant nutrients such as glutathione preoxidase, vitamin E, zinc, and vitamin C to combat cellular damage caused by free radicals. We receive selenium from plants, which receive it from soil, but many areas have too little selenium in the soil. If the soil that produces your food is too low in selenium, chances are you will not receive enough from your diet alone.

The RDA for selenium is 50 mg, but Colgan Institute, a leading center dedicated to sport nutrition research, and other exercise-research institutes have shown that 200 to 400 mg per day may help fight against free-radical damage of heart tissue and decrease the incidence of cancer.

Dr. Michael Colgan also recommends the Seleno-L-Methionine form of selenium for better absorption into your body. Seleno-L-Methionine is one of the most potent and nutritionally safe forms of selenium. Be sure to keep your intake of selenium under 800 mg per day; selenium can become toxic above this dosage.

Zinc

Zinc stimulates superoxide dismutase (SOD), the main antioxidant enzyme manufactured by the body. This enzyme is crucial to cell life. Most of the clinical research on SOD has centered on the inflammation resulting from excessive free radicals, such as in arthritis, bursitis, and gout. SOD supplements do not work; they often are missing cofactors or are mostly destroyed in the digestive tract. Eating a balanced diet and taking zinc and other supplements will ensure production of SOD. You should be taking a minimum of 15 mg of zinc per day.

Bioflavonoids

The bioflavonoids are a family of related compounds that includes rutin, flavones, flavonols, and the flavonones. The bioflavonoids are not vitamins or minerals, although at one time they were called vitamin P or substance P. They are found in the inner peel of citrus fruits, the white core of peppers, buckwheat, and leafy vegetables.

Bioflavonoids are essential for the proper absorption and use of vitamin C. They help vitamin C keep collagen, the intercellular cement, in healthy condition. Bioflavonoids also act as antioxidants to keep vitamin C and adrenaline from being oxidized by copper-containing enzymes. Limited evidence shows bioflavonoids might prevent bruising and damage to artery walls caused by free radicals.

There is no RDA for bioflavonoids. Ensure a daily intake of good food sources of bioflavonoids and take a supplement that contains bioflavonoids to aid in vitamin C uptake.

Your Personal Antioxidant Program

So what should a smart athlete do? First, eat lots of fresh fruits, vegetables, and whole grains. Citrus fruits provide vitamin C. Two to three servings per day of dark green and orange vegetables, such as spinach and carrots, will increase beta carotene intake. Whole grains are good sources of selenium and zinc. Vitamin E can be found in wheat germ, nuts, and sweet potatoes.

A balanced diet is important to the complete profile of antioxidant support to fight free radicals and infection. But getting a balanced diet in today's society may be as difficult as riding a 40-km time trial in less than an hour. We often do not like the foods that are high in antioxidants, often eat processed or overcooked foods, and often cannot eat enough food to reach the necessary antioxidant levels. According to the National Cancer Institute, less than a tenth of the population of the United States eats five or more daily servings of food sources of antioxidants, the minimum recommended by most health and nutritional organizations. And the RDA for antioxidants may not be adequate for people who exercise regularly.

Many experts now recommend enhancing antioxidant intake with supplements of vitamins, minerals, and herbs. Your best bet is a multivitamin and mineral supplement that includes antioxidant-helping herbs. The decision to supplement is one only you can make. However, given the harmful effects of free radicals and the lowering of immunity during hard training and competition, the best offense may be an adequate diet and a solid multivitamin-and-mineral defense. There is now enough research available to make it clear that antioxidant vitamins and minerals are important nutrients for health and that many athletes probably do not get enough.

Iron-Poor Blood

It had been a long, hard road back in the first half of the 1989 season for Greg LeMond, and the results had not been promising. To not do well after putting in many miles of hard work and training was frustrating. As late in the season as the Tour of Italy, he still felt he was running on empty and decided it was time to have a physical examination and blood test. He was diagnosed as having a low iron count and anemia. Once this physical problem was resolved, the season turned around, and he went on to win the Tour de France and the World Championships.

Hard-training athletes must maintain a proper level of iron in order to compete in top form. Iron helps hemoglobin carry oxygen to exercising muscles and also plays a key role in energy production in working muscles. If iron stores are not adequate, an individual can develop anemia, a condition identified by low hemoglobin and/or serum (blood) ferritin. The normal value for males is 14 to 18 grams per 100 ml of blood; for women, 12 to 16 grams.

Iron stores can be reduced in several ways. Periods of heavy sweating, for example, can decrease iron stores. Cyclists who sweat two to three liters per day may double their loss of iron. This increased drain of iron, if continued for months, could lead to exhaustion. Cyclists who are vegetarian can have reduced iron stores because their diet is poor in iron. Hemeiron, the iron-rich red pigment in the blood hemoglobin, is found only in meat, not in vegetables. Cyclists who are vegetarians should be conscious of their iron consumption and make an extra effort to eat plenty of whole grains, nuts, dried fruits, and other iron-rich foods.

Female cyclists also need to be concerned with iron loss. The average cyclist, male or female, normally loses .9 mg of iron every day in sweat, urine, and stool. Women lose an additional 15 to 45 mg each time they menstruate and may not eat enough iron-rich foods to compensate for that loss. For this group, RDA is 18 mg. Nonmenstruating female cyclists have reduced blood losses and reduced iron needs, and their requirements are similar to those for men—10 mg.

To reduce your risk of becoming iron-deficient or anemic, incorporate the following practices into your diet:

- Eat foods rich in vitamin C at every meal. Vitamin C helps the body absorb iron. For example, a glass of orange juice with an iron-enriched breakfast cereal enhances vitamin C absorption by 250 percent. The enhancing effect is proportional to the amount of vitamin C ingested. You also may consider taking a vitamin supplement.

- Make lean meat a part of your diet three times a week. Other good sources of iron are beans, spinach, broccoli, prunes, and dried apricots. But remember, fruits and vegetables do not contain the essential hemeiron your body needs.

- Eat enriched or fortified breads, cereals, and pasta whenever you can.

- When it's feasible, cook your meals in a cast-iron pan or skillet; this will help increase the iron content of the food.

- Eat fish or chicken with vegetable proteins such as lentils, chili beans, or split peas. The hemeiron from animal protein enhances the absorption of vegetable protein.

- Avoid drinking tea and coffee at meals. They reduce iron absorption by as much as 40 percent.

EXERCISING ON VEGGIES: BENEFITS AND RISKS

There are basically two types of vegetarians: lacto-ovo vegetarians and vegans. Lacto-ovo vegetarians consume dairy products and eggs as well as all foods of plant origin, such as vegetables, fruits, breads and cereals, dried beans and peas, nuts and nut butters, and seeds. They refrain from eating red meat, chicken, and fish. A variation is the lacto vegetarian, who also avoids eggs. Vegans consume only foods of plant origin and avoid all foods of animal origin, including dairy products, eggs, meat, fish, and poultry. People who avoid only red meat but consume chicken or fish are not true vegetarians.

The misconception that athletes and people who exercise need to eat large amounts of meat for protein is one of the most persistent of the diet-exercise myths. In reality, vegetarian athletes can easily consume high-quality protein in ample amounts to meet the extra demands of exercise without jeopardizing their performance or health.

Everyone needs protein. A proper supply and balance of amino acids, the building blocks of protein, are necessary for cells to make antibodies, the hemoglobin in red blood cells, the specialized proteins in muscle cells, enzymes, hormones, and other essential protein-containing compounds. Most amino acids can be made by the body, but 8 to 10 of them must be supplied by the diet and are called essential amino acids. Red meat, chicken, fish, dairy products, and eggs contain all of the essential amino acids and are called high-quality proteins. Grains, dried beans and peas, nuts, seeds, and vegetables contain some of the essential amino acids but not all of them. Therefore, these foods are called incomplete proteins.

However, nature, in her infinite wisdom, has balanced the amino acids in grains and legumes so when these two foods are combined, the end product is a high-quality protein. For example, grains are low in the amino acid lysine and high in methionine, whereas cooked dried beans and peas are high in lysine and low in methionine. A meal that combines grains and legumes, such as chili beans and cornbread, supplies all of the essential amino acids. Combining two foods with incomplete proteins to create a high-quality protein or combining a high-quality-protein food (such as milk or eggs) with an incomplete-protein food (such as oatmeal or cooked dried beans) is called complementing proteins.

In the past, it was believed that complementary proteins had to be consumed at the same meal for optimum protein production. This belief has been proven false. The body maintains a fluctuating, temporary source of amino acids called the amino-acid pool, and as long as complementary proteins are consumed sometime during the day or even every few days, normal protein synthesis and tissue functioning are maintained.

For lacto-ovo vegetarians, complementing proteins is a minor issue because their diets contain the high-quality-protein foods milk and eggs. But, lacto-ovo vegetarians still need to watch their nutrition because they often rely solely on milk products for protein, thus increasing their risk of developing deficiencies of iron and other trace minerals not supplied by dairy foods. It is important to include at least two servings of cooked dried beans or peas, nuts, or seeds in the daily diet to avoid these deficiencies.

While there is a substantial amount of information on the nutritional adequacy of vegetarian diets, little is known about the effects of vegetarianism on athletic performance. Athletes should not attempt a vegan diet without previous experience with this type of diet or without consultation with a dietitian or physician. The athlete should consider such a diet only if she is willing to devote time and effort to learning the proper combinations and amounts of foods necessary to achieve a balanced diet.

For cyclists who wish to consume a vegetarian diet, a sound recommendation would be to include dairy products and eggs and occasionally (weekly) a small portion of fish or chicken. Such a diet requires bulkier or more frequent meals and careful attention to variety and food combinations. You also should consider supplementing with a protein powder or metabolic-optimizer powder drink to ensure that you get enough quality protein and amino acids.

The vegan is more susceptible to vitamin and mineral deficiencies, particularly vitamins B_2, B_{12}, and D, and to deficiencies of calcium, iron, and zinc, which must be eaten each day. She can consume fortified foods, such as soy milk fortified with vitamin B_{12}, and she can add a multivitamin-and-mineral supplement to the diet.

Nutrients to which vegans must pay particular attention include vitamins B_2, B_{12}, and D; and calcium and iron. Vitamin B_2 is commonly obtained from dairy products, which vegans avoid. However, it is also found in dark-green vegetables, which usually are abundant in the vegan diet. Vitamin B_{12} is found only in animal products. Because of this, vegans must get B_{12} from a supplement, such as B_{12}-fortified soy milk. Of particular concern is deficiency of vitamin B_{12} in growing children, pregnant or lactating women, and people who have followed a strict vegan diet for several years. The body stores only up to four years' worth of B_{12}. Vitamin D is found in fortified milk and is made by the body when the skin is exposed to the sun. A deficiency of vitamin D would be of concern to vegans who don't get much sun.

Although a diet low in fat and high in carbohydrates can lower the risk of certain diseases in sedentary individuals, a poorly planned vegetarian diet in an active person can lead to metabolic, endocrine, and nutritional changes that impair health and performance. Therefore, gathering as much information as possible on vegetarianism and meal planning is a must.

You may wonder how vitamin B_{12} affects iron absorption and prevents anemia. Actually, vitamin B_{12} is known to cure only one form of anemia: pernicious anemia, which occurs when you cannot adequately absorb vitamin B_{12} in the intestine. Vitamin B_{12} is important for the proper development of red blood cells, and deficiency of this vitamin can lead to improper oxygen transport in the circulatory system. People who eat meat are assured an adequate intake of vitamin B_{12}. Strict vegetarians will have to supplement their diets with vitamin B_{12} because they will not receive any in their meals.

With an iron-rich diet, iron supplementation may not be needed. But if your diet is deficient in iron, consider taking a multivitamin. A multivitamin supplement will provide not only iron but also vitamin C to advance iron absorption. If you experience recurrent iron deficiency, your physician can prescribe an iron supplement. A common supplement is 325 mg of ferrous sulfate two or three times a week. Be careful not to take megadoses of iron because that can cause intestinal distress and may result in conditions such as cirrhosis of the liver, diabetes, and possible damage to the heart.

If you suffer the symptoms of chronic fatigue that Greg LeMond had, don't waste time. Review your entries in your training diary because lack of sleep, lots of travel, or overtraining also may produce the same symptoms. Then call your physician and have a blood test. Early diagnosis, proper diet, and supplementation can be the keys to restoring peak performance.

Carbo Loading

Glucose is a simple form of sugar and is the basic form of carbohydrate used in your body. Almost all ingested carbohydrate is converted to glucose before it is used in your body. Blood glucose serves as the metabolic fuel for your skeletal muscle. Some glucose supplied to your muscles is converted to glycogen and is stored intramuscularly. Glycogen is a polymer of glucose, that is, a number of glucose molecules chemically linked together. Glycogen is the stored form of glucose and serves as a metabolic fuel for cycling.

The amount of glycogen stored in muscle determines how long and at what level you will perform in training and racing. As you can see in figure 6.3, the glycogen level is low on a high-fat, low-carbohydrate diet. Cycling on low levels of glycogen will lead to early fatigue. If you eat a low-carbohydrate diet (40 percent or less), your cycling abilities will be greatly reduced and you will fatigue more quickly than if you ate a high-carbohydrate diet (60 to 70 percent).

Glycogen supercompensation, or carbohydrate loading, is the term used to describe the technique whereby muscle-glycogen levels are overloaded to enhance cycling performance. You may want to practice this technique several times during the season to ensure that your muscles are filled with carbohydrate. The classic approach to carbohydrate loading has been to exercise hard

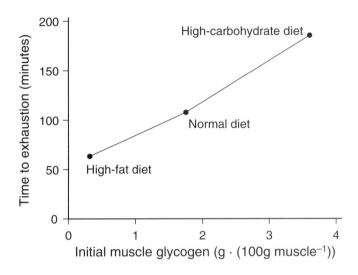

Figure 6.3 The effects of various diets on time-to-exhaustion in endurance athletes. Time-to-exhaustion is related to the amount of glycogen stores the athlete has. A high-carbohydrate diet is the most effective means of building glycogen stores.

From "Diet, Muscle Glycogen and Physical Performance" by J. Bergstrom, L. Hermansen, E. Hultman, et al., 1967, *Acta Physiologica Scandinavica*, 71, p. 140. Reprinted by permission of Acta Physiologica Scandinavica.

and eat a low-carbohydrate diet for three or four days. This depletion phase is followed by three or four days of high-carbohydrate meals while tapering training intensity for an upcoming event. Several studies showed that a cyclist could enter the event with increased carbohydrate stores.

However, this regimen has its problems. It increases your chance of injury, and your workout quality suffers during the depletion phase. Many athletes have complained of not peaking physiologically and psychologically for competition after following this program.

A modified regimen has become popular with athletes who want to supercompensate before major competitions. Athletes follow a diet of 50 percent carbohydrate for three days followed by a diet of at least 70 percent carbohydrate for another three days before competition (see table 6.2). During this six-day period, cycling exercise is decreased from 90 minutes on day 1, to 40–60 minutes on days 2 and 3, to 20–30 minutes on days 4 and 5, with complete rest or a short ride the day before competition. This method has been shown to be just as successful in loading the muscles with glycogen but with fewer side effects than the classic method.

Glycogen supercompensation results in a 1- to 4-kg weight gain because each gram of glycogen is stored with 3 to 5 grams of water, and some athletes complain of feeling heavy or bloated during this loading program. For this reason, you may want to practice this regimen in training or before a minor competition before trying it prior to a major competition.

TABLE 6.2	Modified Carbohydrate (CHO) Loading Regimen	
Day	**Exercise time**	**Dietary CHO (%)**
1	90 min.	50
2	40 to 60 min.	50
3	40 to 60 min.	50
4	20 to 45 min.	70
5	20 to 45 min.	70
6	Rest to 30 min.	70
7	Race	70

Such overcompensation does lead to increased performance in events more than 60 to 90 minutes but is of no value in shorter races, such as track events or short criteriums. Glycogen loading should not be used on a routine or weekly basis but reserved for a few major competitions each year.

It is not easy to eat a diet of over 70 percent carbohydrate. The volume of food eaten in a high-carbohydrate diet is enormous, and several companies have come up with liquid products to help athletes increase carbohydrate intake. High-carbohydrate drinks such as Gatorade Gatorlode and TwinLab Ultra Fuel can supplement your meals. One advantage to liquid carbohydrates is that they do not provide the bulk of solid carbohydrates.

Competition and Nutrition

A pre-event meal prevents hunger during cycling. Food eaten at least three hours before an event can raise blood glucose and liver glycogen, particularly after an overnight fast. This may supply a small competitive edge for an upcoming road race. The liver, which helps maintain blood glucose during exercise, relies on frequently scheduled meals to fill its stores of glycogen.

A pre-event meal should be low in fat and fiber and contain 70 to 150 grams (280 to 600 calories) of carbohydrate. Choose high-starch foods such as English muffins, pancakes, waffles, bagels, and pasta because these foods are easily digested and will help maintain your blood glucose levels. Drink low-fat milk, juice, or an energy drink with your meal.

The closer to competition the meal is consumed, the smaller it should be. For example, a meal containing two or three calories per pound of body weight is suggested during the last one or two hours before competition, whereas a meal of seven to eight calories per pound is all right three or four hours before the event. This should help prevent an upset stomach before a race.

Balanced liquid meals may be an excellent alternative for cyclists who have difficulty eating solid food before events. These products leave the stomach quickly and provide quality nutrients.

Eating on the Line

Cyclists often consume simple carbohydrates such as energy drinks, carbohydrate gels, and sports bars on the line before the start of their event. Does this late intake of carbohydrates have an effect on race performance? It seems that athletes differ in their responses to eating 30 to 45 minutes before exercise. Some athletes experience hypoglycemia (low blood glucose) because of high insulin levels induced by the pre-exercise sugar. Other athletes are not as sensitive to these pre-exercise snacks and do not experience fatigue during cycling. The best time to experiment with pre-exercise eating is in training.

"Dairy Queen. God, I dream about Dairy Queens during long races."

Greg LeMond, three-time Tour de France winner

Consuming sugar before short events such as the kilometer, match sprints, or a pursuit will not improve performance because the body already has enough energy stored in the muscles in the form of glycogen and adenosine triphosphate. However, you may benefit from such snacks before a long road race because they will provide you with additional glucose during the first hour of the race. If you are concerned about a possible insulin reaction and hypoglycemia, you should not eat sugar until a few minutes before the event. The rise of specific hormones before racing, such as epinephrine and growth hormone, will inhibit insulin responses.

Carbohydrate and Fluid Intake During Training and Racing

Consuming fluids during cycling is vital to your optimal performance. Dehydration of as little as 2 percent of your body weight can impair endurance. Prepare for cycling in warm weather by drinking 15 to 20 ounces during the last 15 minutes before training or racing. If you are participating in events lasting more than 60 minutes, continued fluids and carbohydrates are essential to improved performance.

Consuming carbohydrates during prolonged cycling enhances performance by providing glucose for the muscles to use when glycogen stores begin to drop. Carbohydrate consumed during the ride maintains blood glucose levels and supplies energy to the working muscles. Your body will utilize carbohydrates at a higher rate and endurance will improve.

When I first started racing, a bottle would last me 150 km. But now, for a 300-km race in moderate weather, I need 10 to 12 bottles including nutritional drinks. Normally, a rider should lose hardly any weight during a stage, and that means drinking a lot.

Bernard Hinault, five-time Tour de France winner

Research has shown that trained cyclists need to ingest carbohydrate at the rate of 1 gram per minute (60 grams per hour, or about 240 calories) to maintain normal blood glucose levels during prolonged rides. As shown in table 6.3, you can accomplish this by drinking beverages containing various combinations of fluid and carbohydrate. Use this table to formulate your own ideas for mixing weaker or stronger concentrations. The amount of carbohydrate that athletes feel they can tolerate in their drinks varies. The best time to discover your preference is in training, when you can experiment with different concentrations of carbohydrate.

As indicated in table 6.3, beverages containing 6 percent or less carbohydrate probably cannot be ingested in large enough volumes to provide adequate carbohydrate and should be viewed only as fluid-replacement drinks. Drinks of greater than 10 percent carbohydrate can easily provide one gram of carbohydrate per minute, but they supply very little fluid. They are best used only as carbohydrate-supplement drinks. Drinks of 6 to 10 percent carbohydrate in volumes of 600 to 1,000 ml per hour provide both adequate carbohydrate and fluid.

TABLE 6.3 **Volume of Carbohydrate (CHO) Drink to Provide the Indicated Amount of Carbohydrate**

Concentration of CHO in drink (%)	Rate of CHO supplementation g/hr (ml/hr)			Comment
	40 g/hr	60 g/hr	80 g/hr	
2	2,000	3,000	4.000	Volume too large
4	1,000	1,500	2,000	Volume too large
6	667	1,000	1,333	Volume too large
8	500	750	1,000	Fluid and CHO supplement
10	400	600	800	Fluid and CHO supplement
15	267	400	533	CHO supplement
20	200	300	400	CHO supplement
25	160	240	320	CHO supplement

From "Carbohydrate Feeding During Prolonged Cycling to Improve Performance" by Andrew Coggan, 1990, *Cycling Science,* 2(1), p. 10. Copyright 1990 by Cycling Science Publications. Adapted by permission.

I would suggest the following regimen to help maintain an optimum flow of fluid and carbohydrate from the stomach and intestine into the bloodstream. Drink about 400 ml (about 14 ounces) of an energy drink of 10 percent or less carbohydrate just before a long race or training ride, then ingest about 100 ml (3 to 4 ounces) every 10 minutes during the race.

This pattern of filling your stomach before a race and then taking in more fluid at regular intervals will keep your stomach full enough to maximize gastric emptying. As a result, you'll optimize water absorption during hot weather, and the carbohydrate in the drink will be carried into the intestine along with the fluid. Remember, drink only a few minutes before the start of the race to ensure that the fluid will end up in the bloodstream, not in the bladder.

This volume of fluid in the stomach during cycling may take some getting used to. You should practice this regimen in training. If you "train" the stomach and intestine to tolerate a particular energy drink by using the drink during your practice rides, you will be less likely to have stomach problems during a race.

Some athletes do not have as many stomach problems when they consume drinks that use maltodextrins or glucose polymers as their primary carbohydrates. Glucose, maltodextrin, and sucrose all stimulate fluid absorption in the small intestine. It may be best to avoid a fructose-based drink. Fructose, which is absorbed more slowly in the intestine than other carbohydrates, does not stimulate as much fluid absorption. In fact, diarrhea and gastrointestinal distress are common side effects in athletes who consume large volumes of fructose drinks during exercise. Table 6.4 compares the sources of carbohydrates, percentages of carbohydrates, numbers of calories, and amounts of sodium in commercially available energy drinks.

TABLE 6.4 Commercial Sport and Energy Drinks

Product	Carbohydrate source	Carbohydrate (%)	Calories per 8 oz.	Sodium (mg)
Gatorade	Sucrose, glucose	6	50	110
Exceed	Glucose polymer, fructose	7.2	70	50
Cytomax	Polylactate, maltodextrin	8	83	100
Powerade	High-fructose corn syrup, glucose polymers	8	70	70
Sobe Sport System	Fructose, dextrose, maltodextrin	8	70	70
All Sport	High-fructose corn syrup	8.5	80	55
HydraFuel	Glucose, glucose polymer	7	66	25
Accelerade	Glucose, fructose, maltodextrin	8	93	127

MONITORING HEAT STRESS AND DEHYDRATION WITH THE HELP OF HEART RATE

In the summer season, you will experience more days of hot and humid weather. Heat stress occurs when elevated air temperature, humidity, and radiant heat from the sun combine to impede your body's ability to dissipate heat. This places considerable demands on your body's ability to not become overheated. Heart rate can be used as a tool to help you monitor yourself so you won't become overheated, and monitor your fluid (sweat) losses so you can train more effectively and safely in the heat.

Training in hot weather causes your heart rate to rise significantly, as your body sends more blood to the skin in an attempt to cool the body. This is particularly true after the first 30 minutes of exercise, when core temperature starts to climb rapidly. What this simply means is that you have to slow down—sometimes drastically—in hot weather to stay within a comfortable exercise zone and not cause your body temperature to rise out of control.

An increase in temperature of about 20 degrees Fahrenheit may cause your heart rate to increase by 10 beats for the same workout done on a cooler day. Higher ambient temperatures cause more blood to be sent to the skin to help with cooling, increasing heart rate. A heart rate monitor will help you hold back your speed or exercise intensity so you do not overstress your body, overheat, or get too dehydrated, which will cause you to "hit the wall" at the end of a hard training session or competition.

Exercise physiologist John Booth of Australia conducted an experiment in which runners ran on a treadmill at about 9 mph in a warm laboratory (90 degrees Fahrenheit and 60 percent relative humidity). The heart rates of the runners increased from 168 beats per minute to 188 beats per minute after 30 minutes. The body mass of the runners in the study also decreased 2.2 to 4.4 pounds. The 20-beats-per-minute increase in heart rate of these runners, which may have been related to fluid loss, can perhaps be explained by Scott Montain and Ed Coyle from the University of Texas. These scientists showed that for every 1 percent loss in body weight due to dehydration, heart rate increases by about 7 beats per minute. Their results also showed that adequate fluid replacement during exercise considerably reduced the rise in heart rate.

Table 6.5 shows the magnitude of heart rate increase after fluid loss and can be used as a guide for adjusting heart rate during exercise. Use a heart rate monitor to accurately monitor your heart rate during exercise. You will not only know how your cardiovascular system is affected by heat stress and dehydration, but you will have a tool to help you rehydrate more effectively during exercise and keep dehydration at bay.

To help combat dehydration, begin drinking even before you start your exercise session. Drink 6 to 8 ounces of water or a sports drink as you are going out the door and getting on your bike. During the exercise session, slow down your intensity by monitoring your heart rate and try to drink at least 8 ounces of

TABLE 6.5 Heart Rate Heat Stress Index: Heart Rate Increases After Fluid Loss for Individuals of Various Body Weights

Change in body weight	Change in heart rate (bpm) according to starting body weight				
	110 lbs	130 lbs	155 lbs	175 lbs	200 lbs
1 lb	7 bpm	6 bpm	5 bpm	4 bpm	4 bpm
2 lbs	14 bpm	12 bpm	10 bpm	9 bpm	8 bpm
3 lbs	21 bpm	18 bpm	15 bpm	13 bpm	12 bpm
4.5 lbs	38 bpm	43 bpm	20 bpm	18 bpm	16 bpm

fluid every 20 minutes (sip fluids to avoid stomach discomfort). If you cannot carry enough fluid in your water bottles on a long ride, wear a back- or hip-mounted hydration system to ensure you drink enough. Such systems also keep fluids colder, and cool drinks tend to taste better, so you are apt to drink more.

Training, acclimatization, proper fluid replacement, pacing, and using a heart rate monitor will help you perform your best in summer heat. The bottom line is to know your body. By planning ahead, you can minimize the effects of heat stress. Remember you can't change the weather, but with a little planning, you can beat the heat.

Don't underestimate the importance of taste. If a drink tastes good, you will drink more of it. Research by Gatorade has shown that the optimal beverage or bar must strike a balance between physiological effectiveness and palatability. What seems pleasant tasting when you are at rest may not be right several hours into the race on a hot day. So try out various nutritional products and volumes during training.

When possible, drink cool fluids. A cool fluid tastes better and is more refreshing. It helps lower body temperature and may empty from the stomach quicker.

Electrolytes

Athletes often wonder how important electrolytes are in energy drinks. Electrolytes such as sodium, chloride, potassium, and magnesium are necessary elements for muscle contraction and relaxation. In addition, electrolytes help maintain your body's fluid balance. During cycling, your body loses some amount of these minerals with water through sweating. Because electrolytes are found in blood plasma and muscle tissues in varying concentrations, measured in milliequivalents per liter (mEq/L), the concentrations lost through sweat vary, as well (see table 6.6).

TABLE 6.6 Electrolyte Concentrations in Blood Plasma, Muscle Tissue, and Sweat				
	Sodium (mEq/L)	Chloride (mEq/L)	Potassium (mEq/L)	Magnesium (mEq/L)
Blood plasma	140	100	4	1.5
Muscle tissue	9	5	160	30
Sweat	40 to 60	30 to 50	4 to 5	1.5 to 5

Fred Brouns, PhD, from the Department of Human Biology at the University of Limburg, the Netherlands, who has worked with many professional cycling teams, recommends that you look for the following on the label of a sports drink: sodium, 400 to 1,100 mg per liter (mg/L); chloride, 500 to 1,500 mg/L; magnesium, 10 to 100 mg/L; and potassium, 120 to 225 mg/L. Many sports drinks report electrolytes in milligrams per 8-ounce serving. To convert that amount to milligrams per liter, simply multiply that amount by 4.

Sodium and Chloride

An electrolyte imbalance called hyponatremia—low blood sodium, also called "water intoxication"—has been reported in endurance athletes. Hyponatremia may occur during endurance events for a couple of reasons. First, sodium is lost in sweat, and after several hours this amount may be significant. Second, consuming only water and/or carbohydrate drinks dilutes the amount of sodium in the bloodstream. Although water intoxication is rare, the potential still exists. Water intoxication causes headaches, cramping, loss of strength, and nausea. Drinking sports drinks that contain sodium can help reduce the risk of hyponatremia.

The electrolytes sodium and chloride help maintain the volume and balance of all the fluid outside body cells, such as blood. Sodium plays a particularly important role because it helps transport nutrients into cells so they can be used for energy production, tissue growth, and repair. In addition, sodium functions in muscle contraction and nerve impulse transmission.

The concentration of sodium and chloride lost in sweat is about one-third the concentration found in blood plasma. Therefore, if you lose 9 pounds of sweat during a long race or training session, the electrolyte loss would be roughly 5 to 6 percent of your body's total sodium-chloride content.

Sodium and chloride are found in most foods and can be obtained easily through a balanced diet. Therefore, sodium or chloride deficiency generally occurs because of severe dehydration, during long periods of exercise without proper fluid or electrolyte replenishment. The side effects include reduced performance, dizziness, and fainting. Ingesting sodium during exercise can help maintain blood plasma volume, the fluid portion of the blood volume. Beverages containing sodium help maintain water in the bloodstream and plasma volume.

Potassium

Potassium is needed for nerve transmission, muscle contraction, and glycogen formation. It also aids in maintaining cardiovascular system function. Whereas sodium and chloride are highly concentrated in the fluids outside cells, the concentration of potassium in the fluid within cells is almost 40 times greater than the concentration in blood. Therefore, potassium losses, which result in a decrease of less than 1 percent through sweat, are not as great as sodium and chloride losses. It has been suggested, however, that this small percentage is enough to cause muscles to contract involuntarily, resulting in painful cramps that can stop you in your tracks. In addition, potassium loss can lead to heat intolerance.

Potassium is lost in a number of ways during and after hard training. Because potassium is stored with glycogen in the muscle fibers, the breakdown of glycogen to supply energy to your muscles leads to an increased loss of potassium from the muscle cells. This results in a corresponding increase in the potassium concentration of your blood. After exercise, potassium is excreted in greater quantities in the urine.

To replenish potassium loss resulting from exercise, try drinking a sport recovery drink that contains potassium. It's also wise to eat a balanced diet that includes foods high in potassium such as dairy foods, bananas, oranges, kiwi fruit, potatoes, and tomato juice.

Magnesium

Magnesium is found in all body cells, although it is primarily located in the bones, muscles, and soft tissues. It's a necessary element in more than 300 enzyme reactions involving nerve transmission, muscle contraction, and, especially, adenosine triphosphate production.

Research has shown that increased physical activity can deplete magnesium stores. In one study, 26 runners were found to have significantly lower levels of magnesium in their blood and urine after they completed a marathon. This could be because the body uses more magnesium during prolonged intense exercise. When magnesium levels fall below a critical point, performance suffers, and athletes run a greater risk of developing muscle cramps.

Low blood magnesium levels during exercise also have been cited as causes of muscle fatigue and irregular heartbeat. Magnesium deficiency can lead to dizziness, muscle weakness, irritability, and depression. It's important to consume a sports drink that contains magnesium in order to replenish what is lost during exercise. Sufficient magnesium also can be obtained by eating a balanced diet including magnesium-rich foods such as apples, avocados, bananas, brown rice, dairy foods, garlic, green leafy vegetables, soybeans, and whole grains.

Several studies have shown that supplementing the diet with moderate amounts of magnesium is not only beneficial in avoiding depletion, but it also may improve endurance and strength. In a study of untrained subjects, ranging from 18 to 20 years of age, who underwent a seven-week training schedule, greater improvements in muscle strength were found among those who took 560 mg of magnesium daily compared with those who received a placebo.

Meals on Wheels

As you have seen, drinking small amounts of carbohydrate and fluid throughout the ride can ward off hunger, provide needed calories, help maintain blood glucose, and meet your fluid needs. If you prefer something to eat during the ride, a nutritious, convenient energy bar may be the answer.

Most sports bars are high in carbohydrate with moderate amounts of fat and protein. They also supply vitamins, minerals, and fiber. Along with energy drinks, these bars should have a definite place in your pantry.

Top road cyclists often consume large quantities of energy bars during road races. Some cyclists have suggested that on cooler days or when they cannot tolerate a lot of fluid in their stomachs, energy bars supply their carbohydrate. Be careful, though, in selecting energy bars. Check the bar's label to ensure that it is high in carbohydrate, low in fat, and low in protein. Select bars that are over 80 percent carbohydrate, less than 10 percent fat, and not much more than 10 percent protein. Remember, there are 4 calories per gram of carbohydrate and protein and 9 calories per gram of fat. A 225-calorie bar with 11 grams of fat and 5 grams of protein is 44 percent fat calories, 9 percent protein calories, and only 47 percent carbohydrate calories. PowerBars, Cliff Bars, and other sports bars are excellent products for active cyclists.

While riding—or even cross-country skiing in the off-season—over long distances, it may be wise to consume some solid food. Energy bars not only supply carbohydrate but also give you a sense of having something solid in your stomach.

Some athletes do not like drinking excessive fluid during exercise. Nutritionists have suggested that exercise-induced nausea can be accentuated by having liquids sloshing around in the stomach for a long time. Eating solid food will help settle the stomach when large volumes of fluid are being digested.

Remember these points about eating energy bars before, during, or after training or competition:

- Drink several ounces of fluid with the energy bar, especially during exercise when you need the fluid in addition to the energy from the bar.

- Stay away from high-fat, high-protein bars. Your primary fuel during exercise is carbohydrate, and that should be first on the label.

- Eat before you are hungry. If you wait until you are hungry, your blood glucose and muscle glycogen stores may be too low for peak performance.

- During cold weather, you may need to keep your energy bars close to your body to prevent their freezing.

- Just as you do with energy drinks, you need to experiment with energy bars in training before using them in competition. Trying something new on race day can increase your risk of abdominal distress.

Energy bars—along with sports drinks, bananas, and other fruits—are important tools in the nutritional arsenal of any cyclist. Try several of the brands and flavors available at your local sports or nutrition outlet. Whichever one works best for you is the one to use in training and competition. Taste and palatability are your biggest concerns. Keep the carbohydrate content high, the fat content low, and, most importantly, your energy level high.

 ## The Final Spin

Everything you do influences performance, but your food choices can have the most effect because of their long-term and short-term benefits. A proper diet will help training and performance. The ideal training and competition diet should contain 60 percent calories from carbohydrate, 20 to 25 percent from fat, and 15 to 20 percent from protein.

There are three stages in cycling in which nutrition can affect performance:

1. **Nutrition during training.** You will spend most of your time training; therefore, training is the most critical stage. A diet high in carbohydrate is important because it is not uncommon to train four to six hours a day and burn 2,500 to 5,000 calories. The best way to replenish these calories is with a high-carbohydrate diet.

2. **Pre-event nutrition.** Your main dietary concern before an event is to ensure sufficient energy and fluid. Emphasize a high-carbohydrate diet with plenty of fluids two to three days before competition.

3. **Nutrition during competition.** You will need to ingest adequate amounts of fluid and carbohydrate during rides lasting 60 minutes or longer. Proper nutrition during exercise helps maintain glucose in the bloodstream, which supplies the muscles with glucose for energy.

Optimal nutrition is essential to achieving top physical performance in cycling.

REFUELING FOR RECOVERY

7

The race is over. You pack up your bike and drink 10 to 12 ounces of water. After collecting your prize, you jump into your car and drive the three hours home before you sit down to dinner. This is your first food after a hard road race.

Then you're tired the whole next day, and even after a good warm-up, you still feel sluggish while riding a 39×21 during your afternoon workout. For many years, it was thought that you just went too hard in the race and may not have had enough training miles in your legs to recover. We know better now.

Your muscles and liver have not completely refilled themselves with glycogen. Training rides or races that last 60 to 90 minutes or more can put severe demands on your body's glycogen stores. If the ride was long and hard enough, your muscles may even "bonk" during the event.

Only in the past few years, however, have we begun to investigate the role of nutrition in helping muscles recover from exercise lasting 60 to 90 minutes or more, generally referred to as long-term exercise. Because most of your muscles' adaptations for increased strength and endurance occur in the interval between exercise sessions, your ability to perform at a high level day after day is limited by the extent of muscle recovery and repair after strenuous training. Therefore, it's no longer enough to train long and hard— you have to train smart.

"Take rest and recovery nutrition as seriously as you take your training," says Jay T. Kearney, PhD, former exercise physiologist at the Olympic Training Center in Colorado Springs, Colorado. "For the most part, strength and endurance capacity are developed not during the training session, but instead during the rest phase, when the muscle tissue grows stronger." Providing the right nutrients in the right proportions after exercise ensures your muscles' health and increases endurance capacity and strength, all of which lead to improved performance.

Restoring Lost Fluids

Everybody knows that sweating is a natural consequence of riding your bike for long periods of time, and most cyclists take some measures, during and after riding, to replenish the fluids they sweat out. The problem is that a lot of cyclists aren't fully aware of the consequences of fluid loss during exercise. As we have already discussed, dehydration of as little as 2 to 3 percent of body weight impairs performance. But diminished capacity for exercise isn't all there is to worry about. Because water is essential for body temperature regulation and cardiovascular function, increased dehydration means increased risk of overheating and circulatory collapse. And, along with the water lost through sweating, your body also loses electrolytes, which are important for muscle contraction and relaxation.

Unfortunately, the human body is not well equipped to replenish the fluids that are lost through sweating and evaporation. We simply lack the capacity to take in and retain fluids at the rate with which they are lost during heavy exercise. This phenomenon is known as involuntary dehydration. The good news is that, by paying careful attention to what you drink and when you drink it, you can take steps to minimize dehydration and restore electrolytes.

To understand how your body replenishes lost fluids, you should first understand what causes thirst. The thirst drive is dependent on two factors: your body's blood volume and the concentration of salts, or electrolytes, in your blood. When you lose fluids during cycling through sweating, your blood volume decreases. This results in a corresponding increase in the concentration of electrolytes in your blood, which stimulates thirst.

Drinking plain water is fine for events lasting less than 60 minutes. It's certainly better than not drinking fluids at all. However, when you drink plain water, you usually satisfy your thirst before you consume enough liquid to return blood volume and electrolyte concentrations to pre-exercise levels. In addition, rehydrating with plain water during exercise lasting more than four hours can cause hyponatremia, or "water intoxication," as described in chapter 6.

Recent research has shown that your body absorbs more fluid when electrolytes such as sodium are added to water. In one study, six volunteers underwent two exposures to heat and then engaged in an exercise regimen that caused a mild dehydration, resulting in a 2 to 3 percent decrease in body weight. Each volunteer then drank either water or a water-and-sodium solution to replenish fluids. During the three-hour rehydration period, subjects who drank water alone restored 68 percent of the fluid they lost; subjects who drank the sodium solution replaced 82 percent.

The subjects who drank plain water satisfied their thirst quickly for two reasons. First, water intake caused blood volume to increase, which eliminated the volume-dependent element of thirst. Second, plain water diluted sodium in the blood, resulting in a decrease in sodium concentration within 15 minutes. In this case, the body "shuts off" thirst to keep sodium concentrations within healthy limits. Thus, the dilution of sodium eliminated the salt-dependent element of the thirst drive.

On the other hand, sodium concentration remained significantly higher in subjects who drank water with added sodium. The addition of sodium to water helped to maintain the salt-dependent factor of the thirst drive, prompting the volunteers to continue drinking. This led to a more complete restoration of body fluids within the three-hour recovery period.

So how do you know if your sports drink is a good rehydration beverage? For a sports drink to be effective, it must contain at least 75 mg of sodium for every eight ounces of fluid. This small amount of sodium in sports drinks helps maintain or restore the body's fluid and electrolyte balance. In addition, added sodium improves the flavor of the product, which encourages the athlete to drink more of it.

According to an American College of Sports Medicine consensus conference, carbohydrate should be an ingredient in rehydration drinks in addition to electrolytes. Research has shown that carbohydrate and sodium work together to increase water absorption in the intestinal wall. Carbohydrate's component glucose molecules stimulate sodium absorption, and sodium, in turn, is necessary for glucose absorption. When these two substances are absorbed by the intestines, they tend to pull water with them, facilitating the absorption of water from the intestines into the bloodstream.

CARBOHYDRATE DRINKS BOOST YOUR IMMUNE SYSTEM

It's common knowledge among cyclists that the use of sports drinks before and during long cycling provides an energy advantage. But, recent research also shows that sports drinks can help reduce the long-term stress of hard training. Long rides and intense exercise not only stress the leg muscles and cardiovascular system, but they also suppress the immune system for several hours after the ride. However, recent research by Dr. David Nieman and coworkers from Appalachian State University in Boone, North Carolina, has shown that immune stress can be reduced when a sports drink is consumed every 15 minutes during several hours of hard cycling.

Dr. Nieman's research has shown that one of the markers of endurance cycling is an increase in certain types of white blood cells. Nieman found that the increases in three types of white blood cells were attenuated when the subjects in the study drank a sports drink versus an artificially flavored placebo drink.

The research team also investigated the exercise response to cortisol, a hormone that when released in excessive amounts after hard exercise can lead to muscle soreness and stress on the immune system. Nieman's research found that cortisol's release was lower after activities such as hard cycling when the subjects consumed a carbohydrate sports drink during exercise.

"Our research shows that sports drinks not only provide carbohydrate energy during exercise, but support the link between sports drinks and less stress to the immune system," says Nieman. "Carbohydrate drinks of about 6 to 10 percent carbohydrate [most commercial energy drinks are within this range] consumed during cycling will not eliminate the stress of cycling, but our research and the work of others show they can reduce the increase of several by-products of stress and hard exercise."

Nieman gives the following recommendations to help support your immune system during and after hard training and to reduce the incidence of sickness, colds, and flu:

- Use a carbohydrate beverage before, during, and after long rides or unusually hard training sessions. Drink about 8 ounces every 15 to 20 minutes while riding to not only provide carbohydrate energy but to help support your immune system.

- Eat a balanced diet to help insure adequate vitamin and mineral levels in your body. The intake of up to 600 mg per day of vitamin C for several days before a long ride or century may benefit cyclists. Vitamin C may help reduce the oxidative or free-radical stress to your immune system.

- Ensure that you get adequate sleep during periods of hard training. Lack of adequate rest and recovery has been linked to a suppressed immune system.

- Avoid overtraining and chronic fatigue.

- Try to lower other stresses in your life. Mental and emotional stress from work, family matters, and other forces in your life has been linked to a suppressed immune function and increased risk of respiratory tract infection.

- Avoid rapid weight loss while training hard. Decrease in body weight is another stress that has links to negative immune changes.

- Consider getting a flu shot if you will be training hard or competing during the winter months.

- While training hard or tapering for an important event, limit your exposure to individuals with illness. Hard training over extended periods has been linked to a chronic suppression of specific white blood cells (neutrophils), which are part of your body's first line of defense in fighting infection.

Rebuilding Muscle Glycogen

In addition to restoring fluid and electrolyte balance after time spent on the bike, you need to begin replenishing your muscle glycogen stores. Because glycogen supplies energy in the form of glucose to keep muscles working, restoring its quantities in the liver and muscles is an important factor in optimal recovery from hard cycling. How fast glycogen is manufactured and stored determines how quickly you will be ready to compete or train again at peak capacity. Stimulating insulin is the key to rapid and complete replenishment of depleted glycogen.

Insulin is a hormone released by the pancreas in response to carbohydrate consumption. One of its main functions is to help transport glucose into liver and muscle tissues, where it is stored as glycogen. Insulin also stimulates the enzyme glycogen synthase, which aids in manufacturing glycogen from glucose.

Timing is key in replenishing muscle glycogen. Your muscle cells are most sensitive to insulin during the first two hours following exercise. Assuming that enough carbohydrate is available, elevated levels of insulin in the blood after exercise speed up the transport of glucose to your muscle cells, and this accelerates the rate of glycogen manufacture. After two hours, muscle cells become more resistant to insulin and remain so for several hours.

"Recovery. That's the name of the game in cycling. Whoever recovers the fastest does the best."

Lance Armstrong, three-time Tour de France winner

Clinical studies have proven that athletes who consume carbohydrate within two hours after exercise are able to more completely restore their muscles' glycogen levels. Athletes who waited more than two hours to consume carbohydrate restored about 50 percent less muscle glycogen than did athletes who consumed carbohydrate during the period of maximum insulin sensitivity. The most striking results were observed in soccer players who drank high-carbohydrate beverages between successive games. The players who had taken in carbohydrate were able to cover more yards in the next game, compared with players who did not supplement with carbohydrate. The lesson here is very clear: If you do not consume carbohydrate immediately after exercise, you will not be able to fully restore your muscles' glycogen stores, and depleted energy stores mean less energy for training or competition the next day.

During my work with the U.S. Cycling Team, as coordinator of sport sciences, I tested this concept by having a group of cyclists consume carbohydrate immediately after the end of a training session. I found that in their next training session, performance improved and the cyclists did not feel as if they worked as hard. Clearly, replenishing muscle glycogen is of the utmost importance for optimal performance.

Enhancing Insulin Response

Because insulin is essential in replenishing muscle glycogen after exercise, researchers have focused on enhancing insulin release during recovery. Studies have shown that protein when combined with carbohydrate almost doubles the insulin response and increases the rate of glycogen synthesis by 30 percent. So it seems logical that any sports drink containing protein in addition to carbohydrate would offer an advantage in recovery.

However, more is less in this case. Protein stimulates a substance called cholecystokinin, or CCK, which slows the rate of gastric emptying, the rate at which stomach contents are emptied into the intestines. Therefore, too much protein slows fluid and electrolyte replacement during recovery because fluids must first leave the stomach and enter the intestines to be absorbed into the bloodstream. Delayed gastric emptying slows fluid absorption and, as a result, rehydration.

The challenge, then, is gaining the benefits of supplemental protein while avoiding the negative effect on gastric emptying. You can achieve this by carefully balancing carbohydrate and protein according to a ratio of 4 grams of carbohydrate to 1 gram of protein. When the ratio of carbohydrate to protein is 4 to 1, the protein does not seem to interfere with rehydration. For instance, if you consume 56 grams of carbohydrate after exercise, supplement with 14 grams of protein in order to enhance the insulin response without affecting the rate of gastric emptying.

Recently, John Ivy, PhD, of the University of Texas conducted research on the effect of the amino acid arginine on postexercise recovery. Arginine helps stimulate the pancreas to release insulin and is also known to be important for muscle metabolism. Dr. Ivy studied the effects of carbohydrate supplements that contained arginine on the rate of muscle glycogen synthesis after exercise. Carbohydrate-arginine supplementation increased muscle glycogen replenishment by 35 percent more than carbohydrate alone. Ivy concluded that arginine, when added to carbohydrate, makes more glucose available for glycogen production. It produces this effect by increasing the use of fat rather than glucose as an energy source after exercise. Simply put, arginine makes glycogen replenishment more efficient.

The results of these studies are meaningful for any cyclist in hard training. In order to rebuild glycogen stores, maximum insulin stimulation is essential right after exercise. The addition of protein in the correct ratio with carbohydrate along with arginine can improve performance by enhancing the insulin response, thereby promoting a faster recovery.

Assuming that you work out once a day for about 2 to 4 hours, you have approximately 20 to 22 "free" hours during which your body can replenish your muscle glycogen stores. Stimulating insulin without disturbing your body's other biological processes requires careful attention to your nutrient intake and balance. It must be noted that a high-carbohydrate intake above a threshold of 5 grams for every pound of body weight will not accelerate the rate of glycogen manufactured following exercise. An ideal diet to replace glycogen and levels of essential nutrients involves moderate consumption of carbohydrate and protein. Fat intake should be minimized in the first two hours after exercise, because fat, like protein, stimulates CCK, a hormone that blunts appetite.

Eating After Exercise

Completely replenishing glycogen requires careful attention to your nutritional intake in the hours following exercise. Because your body responds to nutrients in different ways after exercise, it's important to balance carbohydrate, protein, and fat in the right proportions. And, when you eat is just as important as what you eat.

First Two Hours After Exercise

The type of carbohydrate you consume plays a key role in stimulating insulin response. Some foods and drinks cause a rapid rise in blood sugar level, allowing you to take better advantage of the increased period of insulin sensitivity during the first two hours after training or competition. Select your postexercise carbohydrate according to its glycemic index, which is an indicator of how quickly your blood sugar will rise after consumption.

If you're like most cyclists, however, you may find that hard training or racing suppresses your appetite. Even though you know how important it is to consume carbohydrate immediately after exercise, you may be unable to eat solid foods to replenish glycogen rapidly after a workout. Fortunately, if you find that your appetite is suppressed following activity, drinks containing carbohydrate and protein, in addition to their beneficial effects on rehydration, can help you to replenish your stores of glycogen in liver and muscle tissues.

Whether you choose solid foods or liquids, consume your post-ride meal or snack as soon as possible after training or competition in order to maximize glycogen synthesis. According to the optimum recovery ratio, about 1 gram of protein for every 4 grams of carbohydrate seems to be most effective in replenishing muscle glycogen. Try to consume 1 gram of carbohydrate for every pound of body weight, and include some protein in the proper 4-to-1 ratio. For a 150-pound athlete, this means supplementing with roughly 150 grams of carbohydrate and about 40 grams of protein during the first two hours of postexercise recovery. Remember to minimize fat intake because of its negative effect on gastric emptying.

Two to Four Hours After Exercise

Consume another meal or a recovery sports drink with the optimum recovery ratio of carbohydrate to protein two to four hours after exercise. Once again, whether the carbohydrate is in solid or liquid form does not seem to be important in terms of glycogen resynthesis. A high- to moderate-carbohydrate meal will lead to a rather rapid increase in your blood sugar level, usually within an hour. The meal should be composed of 60 to 65 percent of calories from carbohydrate, 20 to 25 percent from fat, and about 15 to 20 percent from protein. This will increase available glycogen for exercise the next day. After this meal, however, you'll want to consume mostly low- to moderate-glycemic-index foods until your pre-exercise meal the following day.

THE GLYCEMIC INDEX

The glycemic index measures the effect of carbohydrate on blood glucose levels. It compares the rise in blood sugar after a certain food is ingested with the rise in blood sugar after an equivalent amount of pure glucose, with a 100 percent glycemic index, is ingested. When you eat any food with a high glycemic index, you experience a rapid rise in blood sugar level, which causes your pancreas to secrete a greater amount of insulin. This is beneficial during recovery because high-glycemic-index foods replenish glycogen more rapidly than low-glycemic-index foods. Table 7.1 categorizes some common foods according to their glycemic indexes when compared with pure glucose.

TABLE 7.1 Glycemic Indexes of Common Foods		
High (< 85)	**Medium** (60 to 85)	**Low** (> 60)
Bagels	Baked beans	Apples
Baked potatoes	Bananas	Applesauce
Bread, white and whole wheat	Bran cereals	Cherries
Corn syrup	Corn	Chickpeas
Cornflakes	Grape Nuts	Dates
Crackers	Grapes	Figs
Glucose	Melba toast	Fructose
Honey	Oatmeal	Ice cream
Maple syrup	Orange juice	Kidney beans
Molasses	Pasta	Lentils
Raisins	Pineapple	Milk
Rice, white	Potato chips	Peaches
Rice Chex	Rye bread, whole grain	Peanuts
Soda (sweetened with sugar)	Sucrose (white sugar)	Plums
Sport drinks (sweetened with sugar)	Watermelon	Tomato soup
	Yams	Yogurt

The glycemic index is important because it indicates the effect different foods will have on blood sugar levels. Many simple sugars, as well as breads and cereals, have high glycemic indexes. These foods replenish muscle glycogen stores rapidly because they cause an immediate rise in blood glucose, which stimulates insulin to speed glycogen synthesis and storage.

During and after workouts and competition, it's better to eat foods that cause a rapid rise in blood glucose and an immediate insulin response because they

(continued)

supply quick energy to working and recovering muscles. Other foods, such as fructose, dairy products, and some beans, have low glycemic indexes. You would probably not want to choose these foods immediately following exercise because your blood sugar level will not rise as rapidly, making the conversion of glucose to glycogen less efficient.

Remaining 18 Hours

During the remaining 18 hours after training or racing, and before your pre-ride meal, you should eat enough carbohydrate to equal a total intake of about 3 to 5 grams for every pound of body weight. In other words, a 170-pound male would want to consume between 510 and 850 grams of carbohydrate during this period. A 125-pound female, on the other hand, should consume carbohydrate totaling 375 to 625 grams. Again, the meals should include approximately 60 to 65 percent of calories from carbohydrate, 20 to 25 percent from fat, and about 15 to 20 percent from protein.

 ## The Final Spin

Taking the proper steps to rehydrate will reduce the chances that you'll overtax your circulatory system as well as lower your risk of developing heat-related illnesses. This will dramatically increase your ability to cycle at peak performance during training sessions or races. An important factor in rehydration is adequate intake of electrolytes. The addition of these mineral salts to many sports drinks not only helps ensure healthy muscle function but also stimulates thirst and aids in the absorption of water by your body. Clearly, restoring fluids and electrolytes is critical during and after exercise not only for performance but for overall health.

Whether you train or compete once or several times a day, muscle and liver glycogen stores must be rebuilt quickly. The speed with which your body synthesizes glycogen determines the amount you will be able to store. Simply put, the more glycogen stored in your liver and muscles, the more energy you will have during subsequent training sessions or events. Insulin, a hormone released by the pancreas, increases the transport of glucose into muscles and stimulates glycogen synthesis. This enhances the rate at which your body increases its energy stores.

There is a narrow window of time during which the glycogen replenishment process is most efficient. You should balance your postexercise carbohydrate and protein according to the optimum recovery ratio, 1 gram of protein for every 4 grams of carbohydrate. This enhances the insulin response without adversely affecting gastric emptying and rehydration.

EXPLORING PERFORMANCE ENHANCERS

The desire to win leads cyclists to look for nutritional supplements and other ergogenic aids to improve performance and aid recovery. For many years, claims made for nutritional supplements often were not appropriate. Many products claimed everything from immediate recovery after endurance events such as long road races to increasing muscle mass more effectively than steroids. While this practice is still popular today, in recent years more and more companies are now supporting independent research and/or developing products based on sound research published in legitimate scientific and medical journals.

Sports nutritional supplements can be divided into four categories:

1. Products representing metabolic fuels, such as carbohydrate, branched-chain amino acids, and, more recently and controversially, fat

2. Products representing cellular components that might be limited, such as creatine, L-carnitine, ribose, and various vitamins

3. Anabolic substances that may enhance performance by changing body composition, such as protein, chromium, and beta-hydroxy beta-methylbutyrate

4. Substances that may enhance recovery, such as sports drinks, glucosamine sulfate, and herbal products

To evaluate such products, you should consider the physiological sense of the claims, the supporting evidence provided, the research articles quoted, and the legal and health implications of use. This chapter will discuss some specific supplements used by athletes and also will focus on the methods of evaluating claims made regarding performance improvement.

The problem in evaluating nutritional supplements is that we often first learn about a product or a supplement from popular magazine advertising and product sales literature. You only have to pick up a sports, health, or nutrition magazine to learn about the newest supplement on the market. In 1993, Gunewald and Bailey evaluated more than 600 nutritional supplements and ergogenic aids positioned toward the bodybuilder and found more than 800 performance claims for those products. Many performance claims advertised were not supported by published research studies. In some instances, they found no research to validate the claims; in other cases, research findings were extrapolated to inappropriate applications.

Understanding Product Claims

An understanding of the methods used in marketing supplements should help you objectively evaluate performance-enhancing claims. Use the following guidelines to evaluate the claims, advertising, and statements presented about a particular supplement or product combination:

• Does the nutritional claim(s) make sense? Assess the supplement or product to see how it fits into cellular metabolism and biochemistry at rest or during exercise. Are you knowledgeable not only in nutrition, but in exercise physiology, metabolism, and biochemistry? If not, find someone who can help you evaluate claims.

• Has the research been published in a peer-reviewed journal or at least as an abstract from a scientific meeting? Is there more than one published paper that supports the claim? Poorly controlled research refers to only one published preliminary report that has not been verified by other, better-controlled studies with appropriate methodology.

• If the research is yet to be published, check the methods and how the study was controlled. Did the study use appropriate methods and statistics?

• How is the research represented? Make sure the research has not been taken out of context, the conclusions have not been extrapolated beyond what was presented in the research, or the conclusions have not been applied in an unproved manner. You should be able to request a copy of the research paper or abstract.

• Be careful of a claim that the product has been university tested. If the supplement has been legitimately researched and approved by the university, a specific professor or university director will be named. Having the strength coach at a particular university use or endorse the product does not necessarily mean that university or laboratory research has been conducted. Research should be conducted by an independent source that can publish the results whether or not the product produced positive results for the supplier or company selling the product.

• Watch for claims stating the product is patented. Just because a product has received a patent does not mean the product is effective. Most of the time the company has applied for a use patent, which says nothing about the research conducted. Patents do not have to demonstrate efficacy and can be obtained with only a theoretical model rather than objective research. Patents do not mean the product has passed any research standards.

• Evaluate the testimonials. Rarely does an athlete endorse a product out of the kindness of his heart. Is the athlete being paid for all or part of his endorsement? If a medical doctor or scientist is giving the testimonial, find out to what extend the testifiers are involved with the company. Do they own the patent(s) on the product?

In addition to evaluating these issues, try to obtain a copy of the published paper, abstract, or "white paper." When evaluating the research paper, here are some additional issues to address in the review process:

• The researcher and laboratory performing the work must be evaluated. Of concern are the reputation of the investigator as a rigorous and fair scientist, the experience of the investigator in the field, the reproducibility of the work, and any possible conflict of interest between the scientist and the company making the product.

• Of equal concern is the appropriateness of the experimental design. It must be based on physiologically understandable concepts (scientifically valid information) and adhere to classic forms (case study, double blind, placebo controlled). Subjects selected should be appropriate for the study, they should be randomly assigned to treatments, and all confounding variables (prior diet, diet during the experiment, prior exercise, body composition, experience with testing procedures) should be controlled as completely as possible. The subject sample size should be large enough to get a biologically significant effect. A dose-response relationship should be sought where appropriate.

• Methods used to assess outcomes must be appropriate (specific for the product, vitamin, herb, etc.) and reliably performed in the investigator's laboratory. They must be sufficiently referenced so that the work can be repeated. Statistical analyses should be specified and appropriate.

• Results should be complete and clearly presented with understandable graphs and tables, all of which should be clearly labeled. Statistically significant differences should be reported. Associations claimed must be temporally feasible and physiologically plausible.

• The discussion of the work should be objective and should address and attempt to discuss conflicting data from other investigators. Method limitations should be discussed, and the implication of those limitations on interpretation of results mentioned. References other than those of the author should be included, and final conclusions should follow directly from the data; the author should not speculate or interpret the data to any great extent. Are the conclusions specific to the study?

Many companies conduct research at reputable universities by knowledgeable researchers. Once the research is conducted, it then is presented at scientific meetings and published in peer-reviewed journals. Then, objective claims can be made about the nutrient, supplement, or product mixture. We can only gain from this process.

Now let's take a look at some of the supplements and dietary products that have become popular with athletes over the past few years and review the science that has been shown to make these products effective for sports performance. We also will look at some of the ethical issues and dangers involved with the use of erythropoietin and other performance-enhancing drugs by competitive cyclists.

10 QUESTIONS THAT PUT SUPPLEMENTS TO THE TEST

Here are 10 questions to ask when purchasing a nutritional supplement, evaluating its advertising, or reviewing literature:

1. What scientific evidence is available to support the claim?
2. Where were the scientific studies conducted?
3. By whom? What were the researchers' and laboratories' qualifications?
4. Do the researchers have commercial or financial interest in the company?
5. Where was the study published? Was it a reputable scientific journal or a magazine?
6. Was the study peer-reviewed?
7. Are there any other studies to support or deny the claims?
8. What do recognized experts in the field say about the research?
9. Who are the experts? What are their credentials?
10. Do the experts have financial interest in the product?

Caffeine: A Stimulating Topic

In his popular book *Eat To Win*, Robert Hass states, "Caffeine provides endurance athletes with an unquestionable, scientifically demonstrable advantage over opponents of roughly equal athletic ability." This and other statements in the popular press have convinced cyclists that ingesting caffeine will improve performance. But what dose of caffeine is necessary to gain an ergogenic effect? And when is its use justified in cycling?

Caffeine is one of a group of compounds called methylxanthines that occur naturally in more than 60 species of plants, including coffee beans, cocoa beans, cola nuts, and tea leaves. It is naturally present in coffee, tea, cola soft drinks, cocoa, and chocolate. The amount of caffeine per serving varies with the type of product. Caffeine content per 5-ounce cup is about 60–150 mg for drip or percolated coffee, 40–110 mg for instant coffee, 2–5 mg for decaffeinated coffee, 10–50 mg for brewed tea, and 10–30 mg for instant tea. Soft drinks range from 0 to 60 mg of caffeine per 12-ounce serving.

Caffeine stimulates the central nervous system and can reduce a variety of effects elsewhere in the body. Depending on the dose, caffeine can increase metabolic rate and heart rate and can step up the production of urine. Caffeine also affects the central nervous system by enhancing perception and alertness and possibly reducing fatigue during muscular work.

Caffeine has received mixed reviews in research studies looking at increased performance. In athletes, the primary findings have focused on the ability of caffeine to increase endurance. Caffeine increases fat metabolism by raising the levels of free fatty acids in the blood; fat stores are used for energy production rather than limited stores of carbohydrates (glycogen). Caffeine prolongs endurance by enhancing fat use and sparing glycogen. When released into the blood from body stores, fat—of which there is almost always an ample supply (even in highly trained athletes)—can power your body's muscles during prolonged running, cycling, or swimming. Caffeine also may influence performance by reducing perceived effort or acting as a stimulant on the central nervous system.

While many scientists question the ability of caffeine to improve performance outside of laboratory research, a recent field research study has shown that caffeine can help in actual race conditions. In the study, conducted at Christ Church College in England, 18 runners of various abilities were asked to run a 1,500-meter time trial on two separate occasions. In one trial, they ran after drinking two cups of strong coffee containing 150 to 200 mg of caffeine each. The other run was completed following two cups of decaffeinated coffee. Of the 18 runners, 14 ran on the average of four seconds faster after drinking the caffeinated coffee, a statistically significant finding.

In a second test, 10 runners were asked to sprint the final 400 meters of a 1,500-meter time trial. In this trial, runners were asked to cover the first 1,100 meters at a fixed pace, then sprint the final 400 meters. All 10 runners ran the final 400 meters faster after consuming caffeine and also had lower blood lactic acid levels. The researchers concluded that the caffeine improved muscular power and reduced mental sense of exercise fatigue.

While the majority of research extols the use of caffeine, several studies have found caffeine to have no effect. This probably means that everyone is different, and the dosage of caffeine needed to improve performance is unknown. Research shows that individuals differ greatly in their responses to caffeine.

Caffeine has some detrimental effects. It is a powerful diuretic (as is apparent from the inevitable need to visit the bathroom after a coffee break). This can be a serious problem in hot weather when hydration is imperative. Some athletes also complain of nausea when they use caffeine in hot weather. Caffeine may cause dehydration, stomach distress, irregular heartbeats, and other discomforts, especially in those who don't usually consume it.

Endurance athletes and researchers have mixed opinions about the timing and amount of caffeine to ingest to improve performance. For long-distance events, drinking one to two cups of coffee 30 to 45 minutes before the race and ingesting some caffeine periodically during the race seems to be the recommended practice to increase performance. The amount of caffeine ingested is crucial. If you ingest too much, you will experience gastric upset and espresso nerves, and you will begin to dehydrate because of excessive urine production. About 5 mg of caffeine per kilogram of body weight (2.2 pounds equals 1 kg) seems to be the appropriate dosage. People who take over 7 mg per kilogram of body weight may get headaches and not feel well. Bear in mind, though, that caffeine affects everyone differently.

Some scientists have stated that the difference between taking caffeine (coffee, cola, Vivarin, No-Doz) and taking amphetamines in competition is a matter of ethics. A similar matter of ethics could be questioned in the use of carbohydrate loading or excessive vitamin supplements. These also can be considered forms of doping. To make matters worse, the International Olympic Committee has been changing its mind on the matter of caffeine for years. At one time it was illegal, then for a period of time it was legal, and then levels over 15 micrograms of caffeine per milliliter of urine became grounds for disqualification. Now the level has been changed again, and an amount greater than 12 mcg/ml is considered doping. To reach this limit you would have to consume approximately six to eight cups of coffee in one sitting and be tested within two to three hours. However, other sources of caffeine, such as colas, aspirin, and Vivarin, may cause excessive levels in the urine. During the course of a day's competition, an athlete may inadvertently take too much caffeine and show up positive on testing.

Caffeine is a legal nutritional supplement when used in moderation, and cyclists are free to experiment with it—but use caution. While it most likely will increase endurance performance, its improper use could have detrimental side effects. The excessive use of caffeine could lead to disqualification in competition, if you take enough to raise urine levels higher than 12 mcg/ml.

If you are a habitual consumer of coffee, cola, tea, cocoa, or chocolate, then the extra caffeine before competition may not help. Because caffeine is present naturally in so many foods, drinks, and medications, you probably do get some caffeine every day.

Here is some age-old advice: If you use caffeine, moderate amounts of it are advisable; if you do not use caffeine, don't start using it to boost performance.

Ribose for Increased Power

Sometimes cyclists can train their bodies so hard that the amount of energy stored in their muscle cells drops and can't be restored efficiently before their next workout. When this happens, they can wind up with a long-term reduction in the vital energy compound adenosine triphosphate (ATP).

ATP provides virtually all the energy needed by the body. The energy released from the breakdown of the ATP molecule is used to power all bodily functions, which is why ATP is considered the "energy currency" of the cell. We need ATP to make our hearts beat and to give our muscles power when we demand it.

A new dietary supplement available helps stimulate natural ATP production. D-ribose, also called ribose, is an essential ingredient in the ATP rebuilding energy equation. Ribose is a simple sugar that forms the carbohydrate portion of DNA and RNA, the building blocks of life. This unique, five-carbon sugar occurs naturally in all living cells, including all the cells in the body. Ribose is also the sugar that begins the metabolic process for production of ATP.

As glucose is metabolized, part of it goes directly to energy production through a whole series of metabolic reactions requiring oxygen supplied by the bloodstream. Some also is sent through other reactions for production of compounds used to manufacture molecules necessary in ATP generation, called nucleotides. Ribose is made in this series of reactions and is a necessary compound in nucleotide production. Without ribose, nucleotides could not be produced, and your body would not be able to generate ATP.

Although ribose is found naturally in all cells in the body, heart and muscle cells cannot make ribose very quickly. In fact, during times of metabolic stress, such as during repeated hard efforts or sprints on the bike, cells are not able to form enough ribose to rapidly replace nucleotides as they are used. Furthermore, there is no known food source that supplies a sufficient amount of ribose to be metabolically significant.

In theory, supplemental ribose acts as an ergogenic aid for high-power exercise by improving recovery time of ATP. Since ribose is a precursor to adenosine, ribose supplementation theoretically could increase the de novo synthesis and regeneration of ATP from other nucleotides such as adenosine diphosphate. Recently, several human studies have investigated ribose as a potential sports supplement.

In one study by John Berardi, BS, and Tim Ziegunfuss, PhD, at Eastern Michigan University, eight young men participated in a double-blind, placebo-controlled, crossover pilot study to evaluate the effects of ribose supplementation on repeated sprint performance. Sprint tests involved six 10-second sprints on a bicycle ergometer with 60 seconds of passive rest between sprints. In a double-blind and randomized manner, subjects ingested four 8-gram doses of ribose or a placebo over a 36-hour period. The final dose was ingested two hours prior to post-supplementation testing.

Subjects then performed the post-supplementation sprint test. After a five-day washout period, subjects repeated the experiment ingesting the alternate supplement. Results revealed that changes in peak power (2.2 to 7 percent) and mean power (2 to 10 percent) when taking the ribose were nonsignificantly higher in four of the six sprints. At face value, these findings don't support the potential ergogenic value of ribose supplementation. However, the authors also reported that effect size calculations revealed a strong treatment effect (greater than 1.0). This basically means that results were not significant because the study had too few subjects. These findings suggest that additional research using larger sample sizes may be able to detect a significant impact in healthy subjects.

An additional study by Janson Witter, MS, and Scott Trappe, PhD, at Ball State University investigated the effect of ribose supplementation on performance and energy recovery during and following high-intensity exercise. In this pilot study, two subjects were given ribose and two were given a placebo (glucose) for three days prior to three days of sprint ergometer exercise, two sessions per day (six sessions total). Exercise sessions consisted of 15 10-second sprints with resistance set at 7 percent of body mass, with 50 seconds of rest between sprints. Muscle biopsies were taken before the first exercise session, immediately following the final exercise session, and after 48 hours of rest.

The results show that power per kilogram of body weight, peak power per kilogram, and total power per kilogram were all consistently higher in the ribose subjects than in the placebo subjects. On average, increased power output was 9 to 9.9 percent higher with ribose administration. Analysis of adenine nucleotides in thigh muscle of each subject showed that ribose subjects were able to more effectively utilize their energy stores and recovered more quickly following exercise. Following supplementation, ribose subjects began exercise with higher nucleotide pools, finished with lower nucleotide pools as the result of greater energy utilization, but recovered to a higher level than placebo subjects after 48 hours of rest.

By now, enough research has been completed to make me confident in advising two points for the use of ribose with athletes. One point is that ribose needs to be present when the body's muscles and cells need it to salvage ATP. In other words, using ribose during and immediately after exercise will be the most efficient. Taking it one-half to one hour after exercise is expected to have little effect. I recommend using 3 to 5 grams at the start of exercise and 3 to 5 grams right after exercise. During long-term high-intensity exercise, 3 to 5 grams can be taken every hour with a sports drink.

The second point is that the exercise needs to be very intense, long, and have anaerobic bouts in order for ribose to have a significant effect. A person doing routine exercise would not expect to see a benefit. When trying to train intensely in order to move to a higher level of fitness or when performing in competition, cyclists are running their energy stores down enough to benefit from the power of ribose. In these situations, ribose enables the cells to salvage and recycle the adenine nucleotide precursors to ATP.

"I've been bicycle racing professionally for the last four years. The attitude toward racing and toward doping ranges from your typical Swiss rider, who thinks it's just terrible that anyone would actually cheat, to other racers, who think that if you don't get caught, you're OK."

Andy Hampsten, Tour of Italy and Tour of Switzerland winner,
during a medical symposium on the use of erythropoietin in sports

EPO: A DANGEROUS FORM OF BLOOD DOPING

Erythropoietin (EPO) is a hormone made mostly in the kidneys. From there it travels to bone marrow to stimulate the production of red blood cells. A continuous supply of EPO is essential to maintaining red blood cell mass, and thus the oxygenation of all body tissues.

EPO was first isolated and purified in the 1970s, enabling scientists to determine the exact sequence of amino acids that forms its unique structure. They then used recombinant DNA technology to produce the synthetic form of EPO, Epoetin-alpha, which was approved by the Food and Drug Administration in 1989. Commercial forms in the United States are Epogen, made by Amgen, and Procrit, made by Ortho Pharmaceuticals.

This drug is used by a variety of athletes worldwide. Numerous tombstones bear witness that many of them are unaware that it comes with a potentially lethal sting in the tail.

Developed to treat patients with kidney failure and some types of anemia, EPO originally was injected intravenously. This hazardous procedure causes a rapid, dose-dependent, and unstoppable rise in hematocrit, the percentage of the total volume of blood made up of red cells.

This may be OK for patients whose blood is really thin from lack of red cells, with hematocrits of only 20 to 30 percent. The jump caused by EPO brings them back up to normal blood thickness. (Normal hematocrit for males is 42 to 52 percent, for females 36 to 46 percent.) But for athletes with already normal red cell mass, it can turn their blood as thick as molasses, raising hematocrit to 60 percent or higher. That puts a huge load on the heart to keep the blood pumping. With intense exercise, even the strongest heart may collapse under the strain. There are reports that intravenous use of EPO led to the deaths of more than 18 European cyclists in the early 1990s.

As you might expect, a significant increase in the oxygen-carrying capacity of a cyclist's blood benefits performance in multiple ways. EPO achieves this athletic edge by raising anaerobic threshold and maximal oxygen consumption capacity.

Athletes in longer endurance events benefit the most because these events are done at or below the anaerobic threshold (apart from the final sprint). In an EPO-charged athlete, a given level of effort represents a lower percentage of total aerobic power. The benefit can be enormous.

Take a five-mile run, for example. One well-controlled study of elite middle-distance runners showed that artificially increasing red cell mass improved times by 2 percent. That doesn't seem like a whole lot, but in elite runners it's the difference between first and last. For a runner with a best time of 25:00 minutes, for example, EPO could lower his time to 24:30.

For longer endurance events, the benefit increases accordingly. In one recent study of recreational athletes, EPO improved time-to-exhaustion by 17 percent. For someone who reaches total exhaustion at 35 km of a 40-km time trial, a simple injection of EPO could easily get him through the last 5 km at a higher intensity.

On the near horizon is an EPO pill. Scientists at Johnson & Johnson have succeeded in making a tiny molecule that mimics the action of EPO. This molecule is small enough and simple enough to survive the digestion and liver mechanisms that destroy oral forms of complex proteins such as EPO. The same technology lends itself to development of oral forms of all hormones.

Harness the Power of Glutamine

Everywhere you turn these days, it seems someone is touting the benefits of glutamine. You see it in advertisements for many sports nutrition products. Manufacturers have added it to a number of sports supplements, from protein drinks to bars to recovery drinks. Athletes ask for it by name. But what exactly is glutamine (also referred to as L-glutamine)? Is it important to those of us who put in the miles on the bike? And can it help you perform better?

If you were to believe everything you read, you'd be convinced that glutamine could build muscle, accelerate recuperation, regulate protein synthesis, and provide fuel for your immune system. You'd be right.

To understand how a single amino acid can accomplish so much, let's take a closer look at what glutamine is and how it works. Glutamine is the most abundant amino acid in the body, constituting approximately 60 percent of the free amino acid pool. To describe glutamine as a nonessential amino acid would be technically correct, but that description can't be taken literally.

Individuals frequently misinterpret the distinction between essential and nonessential amino acids to mean important and unimportant. Nothing could be further from the truth. Somewhere during our evolutionary process, our bodies prioritized amino-acid needs into two categories: amino acids the body can't manufacture and must therefore be provided via diet (essential); and amino acids the body can manufacture from miscellaneous components, such as other amino acids, various dietary constituents, and by breaking down its own tissue (nonessential). Essential amino acids you either get in what you eat or not at all. With nonessential amino acids, it's only preferable (not essential) that they be provided through diet.

Glutamine is one such nonessential amino acid. It fuels some of the body's major systems such as the brain, intestines, kidneys, lungs, and immune system. The body will literally break down its own muscle tissue to get glutamine if not enough is ingested. For most people, the thought of breaking down muscle tissue simply to get glutamine would not make much sense.

Glutamine is the main fuel for the immune system. Glutamine levels fall after exhaustive exercise. Low glutamine levels may be partly responsible for the increased risk of illness during periods of heavy training and after endurance competitions. Research is being conducted on whether feeding the body more glutamine in times of heavy endurance training and competition strengthens the immune system and prevents athletes from getting sick.

In a 1996 study, the consumption of a glutamine supplement immediately and two hours after a marathon and ultramarathon reduced the incidence of infections during the week after competition by 32 percent when compared with a placebo. However, a follow-up study was unable to show a positive effect of glutamine supplementation on immune function in a group of marathon runners. A study of competitive swimmers taking a glutamine supplement during a season reported fewer symptoms of chest congestion and frequency of coughing. Current research suggests that adequate glutamine helps the immune system in times of increased stress or hard training.

Glutamine also may help preserve muscle mass; however, less research has been conducted in this area than in the area of immunity. A recent study on wrestlers examined the effects of 14 days of high-dose (0.18 grams per pound body weight per day) glutamine supplementation in wrestlers consuming a low-calorie diet. After two weeks, the glutamine group maintained a positive nitrogen balance, a sign that muscle was not breaking down. The placebo group had a negative nitrogen balance, indicating muscle was breaking down.

Research also has shown that taking branched-chain amino acids (BCAAs) and glutamine prior to exercise may help maintain amino acid pools in the body, minimize exercise-induced muscle breakdown, and delay the onset of fatigue.

In a 1995 study, glutamine had a stimulatory effect on glycogen accumulation in human skeletal muscle. This suggests that the availability of glutamine after exercise promotes muscle glycogen accumulation by mechanisms possibly including diversion of glutamine carbon skeleton to glycogen.

Many nutritionists suggest that individuals in hard training ingest a carbohydrate-protein snack or meal replacement supplement prior to exercise in order to reduce muscle breakdown and help protect the immune system. I also suggest individuals ingest carbohydrate and protein following exercise in order to promote glycogen and protein synthesis. The particular carbohydrate-protein supplements should contain 6 to 10 grams of glutamine and/or BCAA per serving. Fortunately, most carbohydrate-protein supplements on the market today contain glutamine and BCAA.

While very large doses of glutamine have been given to humans (0.1 to 0.3 grams per pound of body weight) for several weeks with no side effects, the safety and long-term (more than two years) effects of glutamine supplementation for athletes are unknown. Anecdotal reports from bodybuilders who have consumed high doses of glutamine for several years reveal no problematic effects.

Glutamine can be a useful supplement for cyclists interested in optimal performance. However, more is not necessarily better. Keep your dosages moderate. If used appropriately, glutamine may help you make the performance gains you've been looking for in your program.

HMB Increases Muscle Size and Strength

Beta-hydroxy beta-methylbutyrate (HMB) was introduced in late 1995 and almost overnight became one of the hottest supplements on the market. You might say it was the supplement equivalent to the movie Titanic—it was a blockbuster. But, in the sports nutrition arena, fads come and go. What's hot today is often not tomorrow. However, HMB has now been on the market for more than five years, and it's even more popular now than when it first came out.

HMB is actually a metabolite (a by-product of metabolism) of the amino acid leucine. Leucine is one of three amino acids known as the BCAAs (isoleucine and valine are the other two). It has been known for a long time that the BCAAs play a critical role in the turnover of lean body tissues (muscle) and are muscle sparing in a variety of muscle-wasting states. Of the three BCAAs, leucine appears to be the most important for preserving hard-earned muscle mass and intense exercise.

The main drawback of leucine is the fact that you must use large amounts of this amino acid to get a positive effect, making it both expensive and impractical. In many studies that showed benefits, doses were in fact given intravenously and were as high as 5 grams per hour of leucine.

It was theorized that a metabolite of this important amino acid might be responsible for many of the positive effects of leucine and could be taken in far lower doses by mouth. That metabolite appears to be HMB.

Dr. Steven Nissen and his research team at Iowa State University of Science and Technology at Ames conducted a study to determine if HMB would prevent muscle breakdown in humans undergoing resistance training and whether differing levels of protein intake would affect muscle mass or strength. Furthermore, they assessed the effects of training and HMB administration on body fat and lean body mass levels.

In the first set of studies, untrained male subjects ages 19 to 29 who weighed an average 180 pounds were given either none, 1.5, or 3 grams of HMB and two different levels of protein (117 or 175 grams) per day. They lifted weights three times a week, five lower- and upper-body exercises each, three sets of three to five reps at 90 percent of one repetition maximum, for three weeks.

The researchers found that HMB supplementation decreased muscle breakdown and that levels of the enzyme creatine kinase used to measure muscle damage were lower in the group that took 3 mg of HMB per day. This would suggest that less muscle damage occurred in individuals taking the supplement.

Consistent with this increase in muscle mass, HMB-supplemented subjects showed an increase in strength to a similarly proportional degree. The placebo group displayed increases in combined upper- and lower-body strength of only 8 percent, the 1.5-gram group increased 13 percent, and the

3.0-gram group increased total strength by 18.4 percent! The level of protein intake did not seem to affect responses to HMB.

The Iowa State scientists found that lean body mass increased in a "dose-responsive manner with HMB supplementation." That is, the more taken, the more lean body mass gained. After three weeks, the placebo, low-HMB, and high-HMB groups gained 0.88, 1.76, and 2.66 pounds, respectively. According to the authors, the major finding is that "HMB supplementation resulted in an enhancement of muscle function and lean body mass in humans undergoing resistance exercise."

A basic question used when evaluating nutritional ergogenic aids is, does a plausible mechanism of action exist? That is, is there a physiological basis for the effectiveness of the supplement, a reason why it could work?

With HMB, this is where the problem is, and this is also where the ensuing research should focus. No one really knows the mechanism by which HMB exerts its purported anabolic effect. Nissen believes HMB gets in the way of enzymes that normally break down muscle protein. This is certainly possible, but it is also possible that HMB plays a secondary role and is a mediator in another primary anabolic process stimulated by HMB.

If that's true and if we identify this process, we might be able to stimulate the process to a greater degree in different ways or with different supplements. The point is, when you don't know exactly how a physiological mechanism works, you can never know if you're maximizing its function.

For now, it seems reasonable to state that HMB may help muscle cells undergoing exercise-induced physical and metabolic stress ward off the normal breakdown of muscle tissue protein that occurs when encountering these stressors, and HMB facilitates the intramuscular repair of these cells following exercise.

I believe that these studies, along with HMB's safety as a supplement, are enough to recommend the use of approximately 3 grams per day for cyclists looking to increase strength and power.

Does Glycerol Increase Hydration?

Maximizing hydration is important because dehydration carries with it two big negatives for cyclists. First, each 2 percent drop in body weight can significantly lower a cyclist's ability to produce power during a long workout in a hot and humid environment. This is an amount that can be lost easily during one hour of working out in the heat. Second, excessive dehydration also increases the risk of heat exhaustion and even heatstroke.

Performance and strength during training and competition decline primarily because dehydration reduces the water portion of the blood (plasma) and, subsequently, blood volume. Less blood is sent to the muscles to provide fuel and oxygen and to the skin to help with cooling. With the quantity of blood reduced, heart rate and body temperature climb, and exercising at a fast pace is more difficult. Although drinking fluids during competition helps prevent dehydration, the emptying of fluids from the stomach often cannot keep pace with high sweat rates.

Glycerol is an essential component in body cells. Cell membranes are composed of a group of substances known as phospholipids. Each phospholipid molecule consists of a polar head, made up of glycerol, and a nonpolar tail. Since glycerol itself is nonpolar, it has the ability to travel freely across cell membranes.

Glycerol is also hydroscopic, or water loving, which means it is a powerful magnet for water. Because glycerol moves in and out of the various compartments of the body and brings water with it, the medical community has found myriad uses for it in medicine. Some research suggests that glycerol can be used for hydration in athletes. Let's review some of the recent findings.

For the past 10 years scientists have been investigating ways to prevent or at least limit the negative effects of dehydration. Dr. Paul Montner and coworkers at the University of New Mexico Veterans Hospital have found that glycerol is a safe and natural chemical that can do the job. Their research has shown that when glycerol is ingested prior to cycling, blood volume remains high, heart rate remains lower, and performance improves.

In their original study, 11 trained cyclists drank a glycerol-water drink before one ride and an artificially flavored, plain water drink before another. During both rides the cyclists rode at a moderately high intensity under laboratory conditions for as long as possible. When water was ingested, the cyclists were able to ride only 77 minutes, but when glycerol was ingested along with water, they were able to ride for 94 minutes. During the glycerol trial, blood volume was preserved and body temperature and heart rate were lower compared with the water trial.

These preliminary studies showed that glycerol acts like a "sponge" when assimilated into the blood, absorbing water into the blood and holding it there. More water in the blood allowed for more moderate heart rates and for more blood to be sent to the skin for cooling and to the muscles to help with energy production.

Work continues on the use of glycerol. The results show that glycerol can be used during and after exercise to maintain body fluid volume and help with rehydration after strenuous exercise.

At the national meeting of the American College of Sports Medicine, Dr. Montner reported on continued research his group at the University of New Mexico is doing. Dr. Montner stated that glycerol can induce fluid retention and reduce heart rate during exercise. He showed that glycerol taken during exercise (previous work had focused on consumption before exercise) increased fluid retention and increased stroke volume (amount of blood pumped by the heart per beat) and was the likely mechanism for reduced heart rates during the exercise session.

At the same meeting, a group from Western Illinois University completed some work on glycerol's effectiveness as a rehydrating agent after exercise. In their study, subjects exercised for a period of time that required them to lose 3.4 pounds of body weight on two separate occasions and then either consumed water or a water-and-glycerol solution over a three-hour recovery period. The results of this preliminary study suggest that glycerol and water may facilitate rehydration after dehydration in the heat by increasing plasma volume significantly after the third hour of rehydration versus just rehydrating with water.

This research is encouraging and shows that glycerol has the potential to serve as a pre-event, event, and post-event hydrating agent. Dr. E.W. Askew, former director of medical control for the United States Olympic Committee, in an article detailing the use of glycerol stated that soon we may be seeing sports drinks on the market that help athletes achieve a state of optimal hydration. Dr. Askew recommended that the dose of glycerol taken with fluid not exceed 1 gram per kilogram (2.2 pounds) of body weight every six hours.

A loading program may include taking glycerol with adequate amounts of water or a sports drink about 90 minutes before competition or training. The athlete also should continue to hydrate every 30 minutes leading up to the start of the race. This gives the glycerol a chance to move out of the stomach and into the bloodstream before the athlete begins exercising. During a very long race (three or more hours), an athlete may consider taking additional glycerol along with fluids at about the three-hour mark.

Some athletes testing relatively higher doses of glycerol have reported symptoms of nausea, bloating, and lightheadedness after consuming glycerol. As with any drink or food, glycerol may be tolerated differently by each individual. An athlete should try hydrating with glycerol in practice several times before trying it on race day. None of the subjects in the New Mexico study reported problems; it may be assumed that they were using the right amount of glycerol and if they had consumed larger amounts they may have experienced these symptoms.

While glycerol may not make a camel out of a cyclist, it can help optimize hydration when ingested with fluids. Thanks to recent research, you may see glycerol-containing sports and energy drinks soon, but athletes also must remember to consume drinks that contain 6 to 10 percent carbohydrate before and during competition to ensure that blood glucose levels are maintained and that muscles are recharged with glucose. Competitive road cyclists need to maintain blood volume and blood glucose levels during exercise. Glycerol- and carbohydrate-containing sports drinks can help prevent fluid losses and the lowering of blood glucose, which can impair judgment, aerobic efficiency, reaction time, and performance.

While glycerol is a safe food additive, athletes should use a source suitable for human consumption. You can find glycerol, also called glycerine or glycerin, in many pharmacies. Most products contain 99.5 percent pure glycerol, making it a snap to measure and mix in proper dosages.

MCT: A Fat That Metabolizes Like a Carbohydrate

A fat that is metabolized like a carbohydrate could be a boon to all cyclists desiring a high-energy food during racing or training. The fat, medium-chain triglyceride (MCT) oil, now sold in health-food stores and catalogs for about $10 a pint, quickly became the energy food of the 1990s.

MCTs are saturated fats composed of 6 to 12 carbons; long-chain triglycerides (LCTs) are saturated and unsaturated fats with 14 to 24 carbons. Palm oil, cocoa butter, corn oil, dairy fats, and tallow are examples of LCTs. Kernel oils and coconut oil contain MCT, with coconut oil containing about 15 percent 8-to-10-carbon chain fatty acids. MCT oil is essentially 100 percent 8-to-10-carbon fatty acid triglycerides. MCTs don't naturally occur in nature; they are processed from oils.

MCTs are absorbed differently by the body than regular fats. They are absorbed rapidly and can become a more immediate source of energy (like carbohydrates), but they are not as readily stored as body fat because they burn quickly. They can be used directly by the liver where they are readily burned as energy. It also has been speculated that MCTs can improve endurance performance because they can enter mitochondria (the aerobic powerhouse of muscle cells) easier than LCTs. Your muscles produce most of their energy during exercise by breaking down fat and carbohydrate inside the mitochondria. Since MCTs are able to enter the mitochondria rapidly, they should increase energy production and help conserve the muscles' stores of carbohydrate.

In addition, unlike carbohydrates, which supply 4 calories per gram, MCTs supply 8.3 calories per gram (slightly less than some other forms of fat). Athletes seeking a ready source can take advantage of MCT's ability to deliver more calories per gram than carbohydrates.

Until recently, scientists have only speculated on how MCTs may improve performance. That all changed when a group of researchers led by Tim Noakes in South Africa showed improved performance during a 40-km time trial. Six trained cyclists completed three endurance rides on separate days, beginning with a two-hour ride at about 70 percent of their maximum heart rate. Each ride was followed by a 40-km time trial, which they were instructed to complete as quickly as possible. During the three rides, the cyclists consumed either a 4.3 percent MCT beverage, a 10 percent carbohydrate beverage, or a beverage containing both 4.3 percent MCTs and 10 percent carbohydrate. In all three rides, the cyclists consumed 14 ounces of the drink at the beginning of the ride and then about 3.5 ounces every 10 minutes of the ride.

After all the tests were completed, the MCT-carbohydrate drink produced the best performance in the 40-km time trial—just 65:00 minutes versus 66:45 minutes with carbohydrates and a slow 72:00 minutes with just the MCTs.

The researchers suggest that MCTs added to the carbohydrate drink improved performance by decreasing carbohydrate depletion in the cyclists' legs during the first two hours of the ride by replacing the carbohydrate as the primary fuel source during the two hours of riding. As a result, when the subjects increased their intensity during the time trial, the combined beverage spared more carbohydrate for the high-intensity effort.

Owen Anderson, PhD, in an issue of Running Research News, suggests that a MCT drink alone may conserve glycogen (stored carbohydrate), but it cannot replace carbohydrate that has already been used by the muscles—only a carbohydrate beverage can do that. But a beverage with MCTs and carbohydrates can have a double effect. It can decrease the use of glycogen by the muscles and substitute for the used glycogen. Drinks with only MCTs can only slow glycogen depletion.

Before you start adding MCTs to your sports drink, take note that Anderson cautions that MCT-carbohydrate drinks may only be of benefit in road races or training rides lasting more than two or three hours. In shorter events, during which intensities are usually higher, muscles prefer to only use carbohydrate. Only during long-endurance events can MCTs benefit performance.

On your next long ride try mixing your own MCT-carbohydrate drink. A good mix would be 4 to 5 percent MCT and 8 to 10 percent carbohydrate. This would be 4 to 5 grams of MCTs and 8 to 10 grams of carbohydrate power in every 100 ml (3.4 ounces) of water. If entering an event lasting more than two hours, give this MCT-carbohydrate cocktail a try; you may or may not see dramatic improvement in your performance.

L-Carnitine: The Energy Nutrient

In 1984 L-carnitine first gained widespread public recognition with the publication of Carnitine: The Vitamin BT Phenomena. It was reported that L-carnitine played an integral role in the Italian soccer team's successful bid for the World Championship in 1982.

Since then, a grassroots interest in L-carnitine has blossomed, and a number of L-carnitine-containing formulations is now available. Is there evidence that exercise will increase the need for L-carnitine? Does L-carnitine supplementation alter physiological responses to exercise? And, most important, does L-carnitine supplementation enhance performance?

L-carnitine is supplied to the body both via food intake and through synthesis from various other nutrients. Dietary sources of L-carnitine are confined mainly to animal foods, particularly red meat. (This obviously has important implications for vegetarians.) Dietary L-carnitine is absorbed in the small intestine. Internal synthesis requires six other nutrients, including amino acids, vitamins, and iron. Because synthesis takes place primarily in the liver and kidneys, the skeletal muscle and the heart, which depend on fat breakdown for energy, are highly dependent on L-carnitine transport from the site of synthesis.

Many of us may have heard of L-carnitine, but how many of us really know what it is and what it does? L-carnitine is an amino acid-like and vitamin B-like substance that can exist in two forms, the D- and L-isomers. (Isomers are compounds that have the same chemical makeup but are mirror images of each other, like one's left and right hand.) Only the L-isomer, that is, L-carnitine, is found in nature and is biologically effective. In fact, the D-form is biologically inactive and because of its potential negative effects, the sale of D-carnitine and D, L-carnitine (a mixture of the two isomeric forms) is banned in the United States.

As a cofactor for several enzymes in the muscle cell, L-carnitine may influence the metabolism of fatty acids and energy substrate for cellular energy production in several ways that could have important implications for sports performance. L-carnitine supplementation may influence fatty acid metabolism, facilitating the transfer of long-chain fatty acids into the mitochondria for energy production. Increased oxidation of fatty acids could decrease the use of carbohydrate as energy, sparing muscle glycogen for the latter stages of prolonged aerobic endurance events.

Additionally, other metabolic effects of L-carnitine could facilitate the entrance of pyruvate (a by-product of glucose breakdown) into the mitochondria for energy production. Theoretically, L-carnitine supplementation could decrease the accumulation of lactic acid and improve anaerobic power endurance. Physiological studies show that L-carnitine supplements inhibit the decline in free carnitine in muscle caused by maximal exercise and completely prevent the decline in free carnitine during endurance exercise.

Acute bouts of exercise result in a significant drop in muscle carnitine levels and a concomitant increase in the urinary excretion of this nutrient. In normal human subjects, for example, 40 minutes of exercise on a bicycle ergometer at 55 percent $\dot{V}O_2$max lowered total muscle carnitine levels by 22 percent. Moreover, a significant increase in the plasma level of carnitine-fat complexes (called acyl-carnitine) also was observed, which indicates a substantial loss of acyl-carnitines from muscle to plasma during acute exercise. These plasma acyl-carnitines are rapidly excreted, which accounts for the rise in urinary L-carnitine during exercise. These results, taken together, indicate that acute periods of exercise increase carnitine turnover, which underscores the importance of carnitine in athletic performance.

J. Arenas and his team of researchers examined the effect of either an L-carnitine supplement (2 grams per day) or a placebo on muscle stores of L-carnitine during a six-month training period. The subjects were 13 long-distance runners and 11 sprinters. In the placebo group, there was a reduction in free and total carnitine fractions in muscle biopsy samples. This effect was greater in the endurance athletes. In contrast, the athletes who took the carnitine supplements showed an increase in these fractions after six months of training. It should be noted that the differences were small, about 6 percent. The fall in total and free carnitine in exercised muscle was suggested to be due to an increased output of short-chain acyl-carnitine in the urine. The authors concluded that the oral L-carnitine supplementation stabilized the muscle L-carnitine pools, thereby preventing a loss of L-carnitine from the muscle into the plasma-urine compartment.

Much research points to the benefits of carnitine in endurance sports. L-carnitine also increases the maximum use of oxygen in athletes, allowing them to exercise longer without fatigue. Another study showed that a group of trained runners given 2 grams of L-carnitine per day increased their peak running speed by almost 6 percent.

A study of more than 100 trained athletes showed that carnitine helps improve endurance. The dose that appears to be the most helpful is in the range of 1 to 4 grams per day. Carnitine is most effective when taken for a few weeks prior to competition. Some studies even show that L-carnitine increases muscle strength in endurance athletes. This may be because carnitine helps burn fat for energy, sparing the muscle tissue that is sometimes broken down and used for fuel during intense aerobic sports.

While the studies mentioned have shown that L-carnitine supplementation can alter muscle fuel usage and physiological responses, other studies have not. In addition, studies have not adequately examined the effect of L-carnitine.

Take carnitine daily to keep muscles primed, and extra carnitine before an endurance event to keep the body optimally able to release energy. In his book The Carnitine Miracle, Robert Crayhon states that L-carnitine peaks in the blood plasma 30 to 60 minutes after it is taken. Blood levels are not as important, however, as the amount of carnitine inside muscles and the amount in the carnitine-dependent enzymes in cells. This can take weeks to build up.

To help enhance performance, start with 1 gram of carnitine per day in divided doses before breakfast and lunch. Increase your dose, if needed, by an additional gram every week until you see a difference in performance.

Most athletes find that between 1 and 4 grams is helpful. Do not take carnitine too late in the day or it may keep you awake at night!

Glucosamine and Joint Distress

Many cyclists are familiar with the discomfort of joint pain. In the knee, for example, excessive trauma from a crash or malposition of joints from poor positioning of the cycling shoe cleats can cause damage to the cartilage.

Cartilage is a plasticlike tissue made up of thick bundles of collagen. Like a tapestry, collagen fibers are woven in many directions within the joint to form the shape and size of cartilage. As cartilage begins to merge with bone, it becomes more calcified or hardened, forming a seamless bond to bone. Cartilage in a joint such as the knee helps cushion joints every time the knee moves, as part of the body's shock-absorbing system.

In the knee, much of the pain, discomfort, inflammation, and eventual osteoarthritis occur because of damage to the cartilage, which leaves the heads of the leg bones, the tibia and femur, in contact with each other, causing pain and increased inflammation.

A study of athletes looked into the action of taking a supplement that has helped relieve the pain of osteoarthritis inflammation. A total of 68 athletes with cartilage damage in their knees were given 1,500 mg of glucosamine sulfate daily for 40 days, and then 750 mg for about 90 to 100 days. Of the 68 athletes, 52 enjoyed complete disappearance of their symptoms and resumed full athletic training. After 4 to 5 months, athletes were able to train at preinjury rates. A follow-up 12 months later showed no signs of cartilage damage in any of the athletes.

To understand how glucosamine works in supporting joint health, take a look at the structure of collagen and it components. In the cartilage, glycosaminoglycans (GAGs) make up the tissue framework onto which collagen holds. Collagen and GAGs together continuously construct and reconstruct cartilage.

This is where glucosamine comes into play. Glucosamine is the major precursor of GAGs. But even more important, the making of glucosamine from glucose and glutamine is the body's rate-limiting step in GAG production, and hence a rate-limiting step in building and rebuilding cartilage after trauma.

Following cartilage trauma or tearing, the limit does not allow the body to make sufficient GAGs for optimal healing. In addition, as we age, the ability to convert glucose to glucosamine declines because of a reduction in the level of a converting enzyme, glucosamine synthetase. This is where oral glucosamine comes in. Taking glucosamine supplements can increase GAG levels significantly.

"SHOW ME THE MONEY"

As drug testing gets more sophisticated, so does cheating. In fact, scientists fear that one day, testing for the 100-plus banned stimulants, narcotics, anabolic agents, diuretics, and hormones will include not only blood and urine but also genes. As genetic research and manipulation become more commonplace, cyclists may find ways to reprogram their genetic codes to become stronger and faster. For now, cheaters have to settle for less futuristic methods that simply keep them one step ahead of the latest drug-testing technology.

Willie Voet, the French Festina cycling team masseur whose arrest by customs officers in 1998 spawned a drug scandal at the Tour de France, described some tricks that cyclists used to beat urine tests. In his recent book Chain Massacre: Thirty Years of Cheating, Voet admitted that cyclists stuffed condoms filled with "clean urine" up their anuses with a rubber tube hidden by pubic hair to provide an untainted, body-temperature urine sample.

Voet also admitted that the testing protocol left enough time for the cyclists to regulate their own hematocrit levels when tests for EPO were announced. Almost every rider he "coached" in the Tour de France owned a German-made, pocket-sized centrifuge. When the test was announced, a rider had enough time to prick his finger and test his own hematocrit level. If it was over the allowable 50 percent, all a rider had to do was hook himself up to an intravenous drip of sterile saline for 20 minutes or so and dilute his blood enough to pass the test. The centrifuge allowed the riders to know they would pass the test before they took it!

I've also seen cyclists use concentrated forms of caffeine administered as a suppository (to avoid stomach upset) just before a race, giving them a large advantage in their event. By the time the race is over and a test administered, the caffeine has dissipated from the system and is not detected.

Before the invention of EPO, athletes stored their own red blood cells and reinfused them a day or two before competition. This original form of blood doping is fraught with risk of infection and other complications. Drug experts also have alluded to the use of a mimetic, a drug that acts like a banned drug but isn't yet detectable. As scientists perfect tests for detecting the use of supplemental EPO, other scientists are developing a drug that acts like EPO and a hormone that releases more of the body's natural supply of EPO.

Antidoping research has been vastly underfunded for years, which explains the almost remarkable lack of progress in developing reliable, modern drug tests. The International Olympic Committee (IOC), with assets of more than $350 million for 1998, pledged one-hundredth of that amount—$3.5 million—to drug research in the time leading up to the 2000 Sydney Olympics.

The IOC has pledged to take the lead in creating an independent drug-testing agency to oversee international testing. However, even this plan is fraught with an inherent scam that might play well on the public relations machine but leaves athletes willing to cheat with a back door. The IOC's vision of the antidoping agency uses $25 million in IOC funds to conduct unannounced tests and contribute to drug research. A major flaw, one even de Merode, director of the IOC Medical Commission, acknowledged, was that the agency would not interfere with or revise the long-criticized established systems of drug testing. So, what's the difference?

The bottom line is that the ticket-buying public wants to see better and better performances each time the Olympics or major sporting events are conducted. We want to see world records shattered and gold medals won for our respective countries. The majority of people tuning into the games and supporting the sponsors who support the games really don't care how their favorite star wins, they just want to see her win.

As Jerry Maguire says, it's all about money and as long as it is, winning is everything. No matter how sophisticated drug policing becomes, the carrot dangled before cyclists is far too enticing for many of them not to cheat. The important thing for some cyclists is getting away with it.

A Critical Look at Androstenedione

The admission of Mark McGwire, record-breaking batter for the St. Louis Cardinals, that he takes supplemental androstenedione to improve his athletic performance spurred unprecedented sales of the bottled testosterone precursor. Purported to increase muscle mass and strength, androstenedione remains controversial for its hazy relationship to steroids and the associated stigma. Here's a look at what is known about androstenedione and what remains to be studied.

Androstenedione's popularity with athletes and bodybuilders is easily understood. It is a metabolite of the well-known "youth" hormone dehydroepiandrosterone (DHEA) and a hormone precursor to testosterone, the hormone responsible for making the male body masculine. Androstenedione has about one-seventh the activity of testosterone and is directly converted to the hormone by a single reaction. It is naturally produced in the body.

No scientific evidence supports using androstenedione to improve athletic performance. Athletes used it in the former German Democratic Republic program as an anabolic, energy-enhancing supplement, but few details are available on the program. Androstenedione has a short half-life (the amount of time it takes for the body to degrade it to half its concentration). The shorter a substance's half-life, the less time it spends in the body. Androstenedione thus, in my opinion, does not lend itself to a long-term regimen. An athlete would need to take supplements several times a day on a near-continuous basis to maintain substantial blood levels.

Athletes should use anabolic-androgenic supplements such as androstenedione cautiously. A review of the "doping" program used in the former German Democratic Republic details a litany of adverse effects in male and female athletes who used other androgenic-anabolic supplements including anabolic steroids and growth hormone. Anabolic, or tissue-building, steroids are synthetic analogs of testosterone. Side effects included muscle tightness and cramps, increased body weight, acne, gastrointestinal problems, changes in libido, amenorrhea, liver damage, and stunted growth in adolescents.

Another review of anabolic steroids in the journal *Clinical Chemistry* adds to the list of side effects decreased high-density lipoprotein (HDL) cholesterol and an increased risk of prostate disease, liver cancer, and psychological problems, including dependence on the steroid. The review author stresses that the therapeutic index—the ratio of dosage required for supposed beneficial effects to toxic doses—is unclear, adding, "The long-term consequences and disease risks of androgenic-anabolic steroids to the sports competitor remain to be properly evaluated."

In fact, Richard Weindruch, MD of the University of Wisconsin at Madison, stated in a prostate cancer research grant proposal to the National Institute of Aging that "epidemiologic data suggest that diet and serum androstenedione levels may influence the progression of latent forms of prostate cancer into more aggressive prostate cancer." He further states, "One prospective study linked high androstenedione levels with the later development of prostate cancer." He concludes that selling androstenedione may be irresponsible because of the potential risks associated with its long-term use.

Excessive testosterone naturally present in some people or produced from the conversion of androstenedione in others may be further metabolized to dihydrotestosterone (DHT). There is no benefit to high levels of DHT as it has no muscle-building effect. It is, however, linked to male-pattern baldness, lowered HDL cholesterol, increased facial and body hair, and abnormal prostate growth. Researchers hypothesize that taking large amounts of androstenedione could certainly trigger such side effects. High DHT levels also may cause enlargement of breast tissue in males, called gynecomastia, through a process known as aromatization, during which testosterone is converted to the estrogen estradiol.

Although it has been noted that many instances of adverse effects from androgenic and anabolic agents are reversible and that few severe incidents occur with moderate use, men who use androstenedione for extended periods of time should confirm their prostate health with regular prostate-specific antigen blood tests. They also should discuss the therapy with their primary-care physicians, as is often suggested for DHEA users.

After many years of use, the efficacy and mechanisms of action of androstenedione and other androgenic-anabolic supplements remain unknown. Until scientific evidence supports its long-term safety, androstenedione should not be sold under the assumption that it is either an effective or safe athletic ergogenic aid. Clearly, adolescents and women of childbearing age should not use it. The ethics of using androgenic-anabolic supplements in sports also are debatable. In 1998, androstenedione was added to the list of substances banned by the International Olympic Committee, and it has been banned by the Union Cycliste Internationale, the international governing body of cycling.

The Final Spin

The bottom line regarding nutritional supplements is *caveat emptor*—let the buyer beware! Most of us like to believe that we're too well informed to fall for the latest miracle supplement. But when you're training hard and the performance gains are not coming as quickly as you'd like, the temptation to try something in a bottle or capsule is great. Some will help performance, but at the same time some may be harmful.

During hard training, you may look favorably on a product claim if a well-placed advertisement suggests that taking the product may produce gains in muscle mass. But, until proven otherwise, remember that eating a diet high in carbohydrate with moderate protein and fat, and training hard are still the best ergogenic aids. Most supplements should be used only as insurance policies against inadequate diets, to enhance energy metabolism, or to aid in recovery.

PART III

Planning

Generally when cyclists first start training, they think training means simply riding as hard as they can until they get in shape. These athletes soon find that they are not gaining fitness but actually are riding themselves into the ground as they get more tired after each workout. What these cyclists are missing is an understanding of how training progression works and how to build a well-structured training program. They know little about how to prepare both physically and mentally to reach their full potential in racing, often leading to overtraining and an extended time off the bike before returning to structured training.

These cyclists could be using workouts to their benefit by using periodization to construct their training programs. Some coaches, such as Chris Carmichael, believe that many athletes are in a chronic state of overtraining. This often occurs because many athletes spend a tremendous amount of time doing group workouts. These workouts generally turn into mini-races and training intensities are high, often above lactate-threshold levels.

As you work your way through this section of the book, you will find a more structured approach to training with more easy recovery days than you normally have built into your training program. If this is the case, don't be surprised to find increased energy and a new sense of motivation in training and races.

With periodization, long-term training plans are broken into smaller segments. These smaller segments focus on specific training tasks and target increased fitness and performance while reducing the risk of injury, over-training, and illness. You will learn how to divide the training year into smaller periods of training, alternating sessions of heavy training load with recovery sessions of lower intensity and volume. Manipulating these and other training components over the course of a week, month, year, or even longer is referred to as training periodization. As you meet your short-term goals in these individual training sessions, you also will gain long-term fitness to help you meet larger, broader, midterm, and even your dream goals.

The peaking process includes workouts that tie together the development of your aerobic energy system with the exact demands of racing. Key racing needs to be combined with recovery periods and workouts that target race or event-specific demands. This is the time for you to pull together all of the aspects that will bring you to peak athletic performance. Have confidence in your ability and all the hard work you have performed, along with the knowledge that your training has guided you hand in hand along the way. Many times psychological peaking is more important than the physiological or training aspect of peaking. Since your overall training time will decrease as you are in the peaking phase, you will have more time to sit around and think about all the possible options. Sit back and get ready for your targeted event. Hitting a peak correctly with great form is more like a liberation of energy than a forced expulsion of it.

Top performances occur after maximum conditioning has been achieved. Translated, this means you can't peak if you haven't done the work beforehand or if you have pushed yourself too hard and become overtrained!

9

PLANNING FOR THE YEAR

Exactly five days before the 1999 Tour de France, coach Chris Carmichael knew that Lance Armstrong was prepared for the greatest performance of his life. He knew this based on the data Armstrong produced while performing some key field testing designed by Carmichael. The key to success was all the preparation Armstrong had done prior to the Tour. His victory was 10 years in the making, built on all the work Armstrong did while on the National Team, all the work and guidance he received on the Motorola Team, and finally, his preparation with the U.S. Postal Cycling Team.

As a cyclist, you know how hard it is to design a training program. In addition to evaluating physiological capabilities, you also must consider other training principles, such as tapering (gradually reducing training mileage and intensity), peaking (attaining maximum potential before major competitions), and recovery (resting between sessions and seasons). How do you incorporate all these elements into a useful training program? The answer lies in periodization.

Periodization is the long-term planning and scheduling of training. Each period prepares the cyclist for the next, more advanced training period, until the cyclist peaks at the most important competition of the year. Carmichael has used periodization for several years with his athletes. This planning led to Armstrong's peaking to win the Tour de France on several occasions. By systematically varying the volume, intensity, and recovery of various periods, you can maximize your performance while reducing the risk of overtraining and injury. This chapter will show you how.

A Yearly Plan

To create a yearly training schedule, first look at your yearly competition calendar. Try to determine some specific training periods and phases, such as general preparation, specialization, competition, and transition. Establish the peak point in your competition season (e.g., the regional championships, National Championships, or World Championships). You will want to peak physically, mentally, and tactically during this period.

Many cyclists refer to the annual training cycle as the macrocycle. A macrocycle is a complete training cycle, from the start of training to a peak at a major competition and then through the concluding transitional or recovery period. You may have to modify the macrocycle if you live in an area where the competitive season does not match up with the schedules illustrated in this chapter. Also, you may have to adjust the mileage or the time you wish to peak to fit your competition or fitness goals.

"I used to train too much, too many hours. In my first year as a pro I trained 35 hours per week, which was too hard."

Tony Rominger, three-time Tour of Spain champion and one-time Tour of Italy winner

Periodizing the Training Cycle

The advantage of a yearly training schedule is that if you have solid information about your strengths and goals, your time to train will be well planned. A yearly training schedule enables you to work in certain time frames of specific training. To reach your best training and competition results, you will have to divide the annual training cycle into various periods.

The annual training cycle for cycling is conventionally divided into three main periods of training: preparation, competition, and transition (or active rest). Some cyclists refer to these intermediate- or medium-length cycles as mesocycles. Within each period, you try to control the training volume, intensity, frequency, and skill work to direct yourself toward a peak performance.

Some periods are further divided into phases. You can divide each period into as many phases as necessary as long as these parts all lead to your main competition goal. Road cycling in the United States can mean competing from March to October. That means that your general preparation phase will have to begin four or five months prior to your competition period. The transition period usually starts when the competition period is over, usually around the beginning of October. Readers from other countries will have to adjust the months to fit their seasons of training and competition.

Table 9.1 is an example of a model similar to the one used in previous years by the U.S. Cycling Team's senior men. It shows training and competition miles logged at each stage of the season. Their yearly cycle begins with general preparation in November, and they peak at the World Championships. This yearly schedule is for senior men who are competing on the elite international level or are close to turning professional. Training starts out rather slowly in November, but more racing miles are added to the program as they get closer to competition and to the predetermined peaking points of the National Championships and World Championships.

Table 9.2 shows a sample yearly schedule for senior women who are competing at the elite national and international levels. These women also peak in the late summer months. If you have been racing for only a few years or want to compete at only the national level, then you can cut the training and racing miles and hours of general body conditioning by about 25 to 35 percent across the season to fit your program.

Table 9.3 shows the yearly schedule for national-class junior men (ages 16 to 18), who have a later seasonal peak because the World Championships are held in late September. Again, juniors who are just beginning to race or who want to race only on the regional level should cut the suggested mileage and hours of training by 25 to 35 percent.

Table 9.4 shows a yearly schedule that may be used by a serious college student or working individual who is peaking for a major competition in

TABLE 9.1 — Training/Racing Schedule (Senior Men—Road)

	Month	Training miles	Racing miles	Training and racing miles	Body exercise hours
Preparation period: general preparation phase (11 weeks)	Nov.	400		400	40
	Dec.	800		800	45
	Jan.	1,000		1,000	45
Preparation period: specialization phase (13 weeks)	Feb.	1,400	300	1,700	30
	Mar.	1,500	400	1,900	20
	Apr.	1,200	600	1,800	
Competition period (22 weeks)	May	400	700	1,100	
	Jun.	500	700	1,300	
	Jul.	800	700	1,300	
	Aug.	800	700	1,500	
	Sep.	500	400	900	
Transition period (6 weeks)	Oct.	300	100	400	
	Nov.	200		200	
Total		9,800	4,600	14,500	180

General preparation: November 16 through January 31
Body exercise: mostly aerobic training, running, swimming, skiing, hiking, cyclo-cross, resistance training, road training, and indoor cycling. Build mental and physical performance.

Specialization: February 1 through April 30
Training and races only for training. Work on endurance, power, speed, speed endurance, sprints, technique, and tactics.

Competition: May 1 through September 30
Races: national and international, World Championships, and Olympics.

Transition: October 1 through November 15
Move from racing to regeneration. Rehabilitate the body for the general preparation phase.

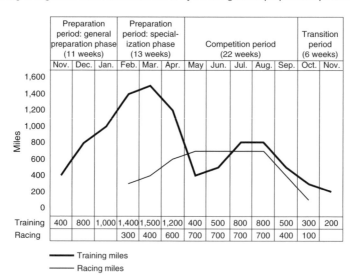

TABLE 9.2 Training/Racing Schedule (Senior Women—Road)

	Month	Training miles	Racing miles	Training and racing miles	Body exercise hours
Preparation period: general preparation phase (11 weeks)	Nov.	500		500	40
	Dec.	500		500	50
	Jan.	800		800	50
Preparation period: specialization phase (13 weeks)	Feb.	1,000		1,000	30
	Mar.	1,000	200	1,200	20
	Apr.	800	400	1,200	
Competition period (22 weeks)	May	600	400	1,000	
	Jun.	500	400	900	
	Jul.	550	450	900	
	Aug.	500	450	950	
	Sep.	400	300	700	
Transition period (6 weeks)	Oct.	300		300	
	Nov.				
Total		7,450	2,600	9,950	190

General preparation: November 16 through January 31
Body exercise: mostly aerobic training, running, swimming, skiing, hiking, cyclo-cross, resistance training, road training, and indoor cycling. Build mental and physical performance.

Specialization: February 1 through April 30
Training and races only for training. Work on endurance, power, speed, speed endurance, sprints, technique, and tactics.

Competition: May 1 through September 30
Races: national and international, World Championships.

Transition: October 1 through November 15
Move from racing to regeneration. Rehabilitate the body for the general preparation phase.

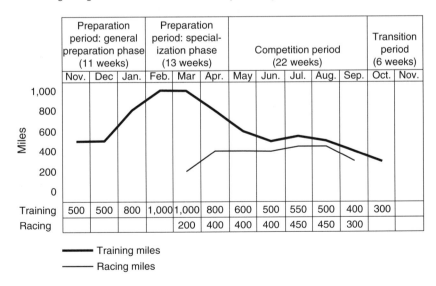

TABLE 9.3	Training/Racing Schedule (Junior Men—Road)				
	Month	**Training miles**	**Racing miles**	**Training and racing miles**	**Body exercise hours**
Preparation period: general preparation phase (11 weeks)	Nov.	330		330	26
	Dec.	680		680	30
	Jan.	740		740	30
Preparation period: specialization phase (13 weeks)	Feb.	850		850	30
	Mar.	900	100	900	20
	Apr.	900	200	1,100	
Competition period (22 weeks)	May	900	200	1,100	
	Jun.	1,000	300	1,300	
	Jul.	700	300	1,000	
	Aug.	550	300	850	
	Sep.	800	200	1,000	
Traisition period (6 weeks)	Oct.	100	50	150	
	Nov.	200		200	
Total		8,850	2,050	10,200	156

General preparation: November 16 through January 31
Body exercise: mostly aerobic training, running, swimming, skiing, hiking, cyclo-cross, resistance training, road training, and indoor cycling. Build mental and physical performance.

Specialization: February 1 through April 30
Training and races only for training. Work on endurance, power, speed, speed endurance, sprints, technique, and tactics.

Competition: May 1 through September 30
Races: national and international, World Championships.

Transition: October 1 through November 15
Move from racing to regeneration. Rehabilitate the body for the general preparation phase.

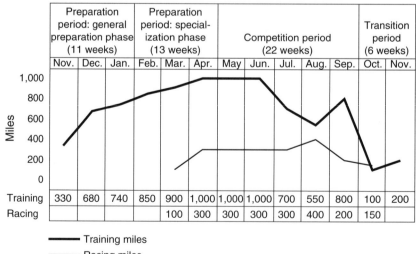

TABLE 9.4 Training/Racing Schedule (College Student—Road)

	Month	Training miles	Racing miles	Training and racing miles	Body exercise hours
Preparation period: general preparation phase (15 weeks)	Nov.	200		200	40
	Dec.	450		450	45
	Jan.	650		650	45
	Feb.	650	100	750	30
Preparation period: specialization phase (9 weeks)	Mar.	800	200	1,000	20
	Apr.	700	200	900	
Competition period (18 weeks)	May	600	400	900	
	Jun.	600	400	900	
	Jul.	600	450	900	
	Aug.	500	450	900	
Transition period (10 weeks)	Sep.	350	200	550	
	Oct.	180	100	280	
	Nov.	120		120	
Total		6,400	2,100	8,500	180

General preparation: November 16 through February 28
Body exercise: mostly aerobic training, running, swimming, skiing, hiking, cyclo-cross, resistance training, road training, and indoor cycling. Build mental and physical performance.

Specialization: March 1 through April 30
Training and races only for training. Work on endurance, power, speed, speed endurance, sprints, technique, and tactics.

Competition: May 1 through August 31
Races: National Championships.

Transition: September 1 through November 15
Move from racing to regeneration. Rehabilitate the body for the general preparation phase.

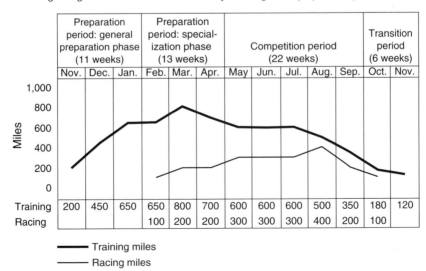

August. This schedule is for the senior male cyclist who wants to race seriously on the regional level but is not committed to international racing. As you can see, the mileage has been reduced because of other time constraints, but it is still very serious mileage.

From these schedules you can see that properly planning conditioning, training, and racing is crucial to peaking during a specific time of the year. You may have to adapt the periods and phases to your particular climate and competitive season. Again, if you are new to the sport, you may want to reduce the schedules by 25 to 30 percent your first year. You also can easily see how a yearly schedule employs the concept of periodization, or training according to prescribed periods. The purpose of periodization is to divide the annual cycle into three distinct periods, allowing for the development and improvement of the physical, technical, and psychological aspects of cycling. Let's examine each period so that you can better plan your season.

The Preparation Period

The preparation period of the yearly program is the longest, lasting up to six months. Because of its length and the different tasks that need to be accomplished, this period is divided into two phases. The first phase consists of general conditioning through weight training, off-road riding (mountain biking or cyclo-cross training), and cross-country skiing. The second phase is marked by specialized training on the bicycle. Work on endurance, speed, and power, and begin racing.

During the general preparation phase of the preparation period, you begin with activities of relatively low intensity and long duration. Train five to six days a week for two to four hours each day. Toward the end of this phase, training intensity increases and more miles will be put on the bicycle.

Engage in activities that will build your overall body conditioning. To build general endurance, for example, go on long, hilly hikes or cross-country ski for several hours. The intensity during these efforts should be 60 to 80 percent of your maximum heart rate. Keep the intensity below anaerobic threshold for the majority of these workouts.

Cross-country skiing, snowshoeing, running, hiking, and in-line skating are useful for developing endurance. Resistance training should now switch from the transition phase to the foundation and basic-strength phases (see chapter 4). You will begin using slightly heavier weights while decreasing the number of repetitions.

Around December, you also will need to start putting in miles on the bicycle. During this month, on-the-bike training becomes increasingly important, and supplemental training starts to taper off in January. Consider riding your road bike (indoors and outdoors) and mountain bike during this phase. The following is an example of a "typical" week—of course, there really is no such thing as a typical week at this time of year because of weather and daylight considerations. Cycling may have to be done indoors and broken up into several sessions to relieve boredom.

Monday: morning—one hour of easy endurance training; afternoon—resistance training

Tuesday: easy endurance training for two hours, one jump, and one three-minute effort at anaerobic-threshold pace

Wednesday: resistance training and 60 to 90 minutes of endurance training

Thursday: an easy day of very little effort (30 minutes maximum) or a day of total rest

Friday: morning—one to three hours of endurance training

Saturday: endurance training off the bicycle for two to four hours with a few short efforts of one to five minutes at anaerobic-threshold pace

Sunday: a long bicycle ride for two to three hours with one or two jumps

In the specialization phase, racing enters the program. General exercises come to an end. Resistance training enters the power phase, and once racing begins you will continue into the peaking phase of resistance training (see chapter 4). Some cyclists may consider continuing with one to three sets of 6 to 10 resistance exercises once a week to maintain the strength developed in the off-season.

The physiological requirements for this phase increase in intensity. You begin doing intervals, power work, sprints, and anaerobic-threshold training. Heart rates climb to between 85 and 95 percent of your maximum. Allow adequate rest between hard training or racing sessions. You can now add short stage races of three to four days to your program. As the season comes closer, your mental preparation has to become increasingly competition related.

During this phase, keep your racing program within the goals of the preparation period: to develop endurance and increase speed and power. Consider participation in races only when they do not interfere with these goals. In other words, you do not want to compete in races that are too difficult. Races during this phase can be used as "training races." Training races are entered not necessarily to win but to get in miles on the bike and to occasionally test yourself in breakaways and sprints.

Training intensity should increase steadily along with duration. March will be the biggest month in terms of training and racing miles. In the specialization phase, a week's work may go like this:

Monday: an easy, flat ride of two to three hours; heart rate at 60 to 65 percent of maximum

Tuesday: a good warm-up and two hours of long intervals (use small gearing); heart rate up to 95 percent of maximum

Wednesday: two to three hours of jumps, sprints, and anaerobic-threshold riding—five or six sprints of 400 to 500 yards, 20 to 30 minutes of riding at anaerobic-threshold pace, and two jumps of 150 to 200 yards

Thursday: two hours of mixed long intervals and one long climb of 20 to 40 minutes; heart rate at 70 to 95 percent of maximum

Friday: a day of rest or an easy ride of one hour; heart rate at 60 to 65 percent of maximum

Saturday: a club or team ride of three to four hours (heart rate up to 80 percent of maximum) or a local road race

Sunday: a club or team ride of two to three hours (heart rate at 60 to 95 percent of maximum), one hill effort, and six to eight sprints; or a local road or criterium race

The Competition Period

The specialization phase leads directly into the competition period. You should be in top form as your competitive season begins, and later in this period your physical, mental, and tactical training must come to a peak. Your main concern now, besides producing results, is to maintain your racing performance as long as the competition period lasts. Because a season can last from May until the end of September, this may be difficult to accomplish. For this reason, you should schedule small rest or recovery phases into the competition period.

Top performance and optimal fitness are variable, and it is difficult to maintain optimal fitness for five months. Top performance may escalate and decline; if you observe your race results dropping, you may have to adjust your training program immediately. First determine whether the decline is due to mental or physical factors. If the problem is mental, reevaluate your goals as outlined later in the chapter. If the problem is physical, you may have to take some time off the bicycle—usually one or two days is enough—then gradually add intensity back into your program. You may consider entering a shorter race or one in which you have less competition to allow yourself to perform well again. If your performance is down because of illness, make sure to recover adequately before your next hard training session or race.

Tapering for Optimal Race Performance

Training provides long-term fitness improvements but produces short-term fatigue. In the time leading up to an important race, the challenge is to find the optimal balance between maintaining the best possible racing fitness and resting to reduce the fatigue of training and possible overtraining. This is referred to as a well-planned taper.

To achieve your best when it counts, you can only do a full taper before a few key races each year. If you were to race often and taper thoroughly for each race, you would have little time left for hard training. So you learn to "train through" some races. But for the big ones, you will want to go all out to achieve your best.

A paper published in the International Journal of Sports Medicine reviewed more than 50 scientific studies on tapering to find out whether tapering betters performance and how to go about it. The review showed that there is no question that tapering works. Most studies found an improvement of about 3 percent when athletes reduced their training before competition. This translates to more than five minutes for a three-hour road race or more than a minute for those racing a 40-km time trial.

Several of the studies concluded that the optimal length of taper is seven days to three weeks, depending on the distance of the race and how hard you've trained. Too short a taper will leave you tired on race day, while tapering for too long will lead to a loss of fitness. How do you find the right balance? Consider that any one workout can give you far less than a 1 percent improvement in fitness, but a well-designed taper can provide a much larger improvement in race performance. Therefore, it is probably wiser to err on the side of tapering too much than not enough.

Frank Pyke, PhD, of the Australian Sports Institute also has examined specifically the effect of a taper on cycling performance. During a taper by the Australian National Cycling Team, an improvement in cycling performance did occur. However, no change in isokinetic (strength at a set velocity of movement) leg strength occurred when tested in the laboratory on an isokinetic strength testing machine. In a second project, an increase in cycling performance occurred after a two-week taper period along with an increase in isokinetic leg strength at slow velocities (30 and 120 degrees/second) of movement. However, cycling performance increased most after only one week of the taper; leg strength increased most after the whole two-week taper.

Increases in leg strength and cycling performance were related but at relatively low statistical levels. Since cycling performance peaked one week into the taper and leg strength two weeks into the taper, the low relationship between the increase in cycling performance and leg strength is not surprising. However, both of these studies on cycling do indicate that an increase in strength during the taper period does occur, though it may not be strongly related to the increase in cycling performance.

These studies do clearly indicate that a taper can improve performance. However, the increase in performance may not be strongly related to an increase in strength or power. So, if an increase in strength and power does not explain the increase in performance, what does? All of the following changes do occur with training and could continue to occur in a brief taper period and so contribute to an increased performance after the taper:

- Muscle stores of carbohydrate could be increased because of the lower volume of training during the taper.
- The muscle's ability to use oxygen could be increased (increased aerobic enzymes).
- The muscle's ability to tolerate by-products of intense anaerobic activity, such as lactic acid, could be improved.
- Improved blood flow to the working muscles could take place.
- More efficient recruitment of muscles and their motor units during physical activity could occur and contribute to an improved performance.

All of these changes could contribute to an improved performance in cycling. However, because strength is determined by the performance of several muscle actions, it is unlikely that strength is increased during the taper by increased blood flow, muscle carbohydrate, ability to use oxygen, or tolerance to waste products such as lactic acid. Therefore, the increase in strength when it does occur is most likely due to an increase in the ability to recruit the muscles or their motor units. Although the reasons for an increase in cycling performance after a taper are unclear, it is clear that an increase in performance can take place because of a taper.

The scientific evidence clearly indicates that the key to effective tapering is to substantially cut back on mileage but maintain training intensity. Reducing overall mileage has the greatest impact on lessening accumulated fatigue.

The best way to reduce mileage is to reduce substantially the distance or time of workouts, but to cut back only moderately on the number of rides per week. How much you reduce your mileage depends on your current training volume and the distance you will race.

If you need to prepare for a major event, such as the National Championships, plan a short break of about two weeks without a competition in the training schedule. The two-week period should start with 3 to 4 days of easy riding followed by 9 to 10 days of specialized work in preparation for the event. For example, if the race will have a lot of climbing, you need to spend a few training sessions working on your climbing technique and power.

High-intensity and race-simulated intervals, sprints, motor pacing, and other exercises should be part of your program. At two days to go before the race, you should include only light training of low duration with two or three jumps each day and then prepare mentally and nutritionally for the competition.

Peaking for a Major Competition

Every cyclist needs competition in order to properly prepare for a major peak point in the season. Planned competitions cannot be replaced with hard training and are necessary to reach top physical performance. The amount of competition needed to reach top fitness, however, varies from cyclist to cyclist. If you train and compete with other cyclists, you may not be able to race as often as the strongest cyclist on the team. You have to compete in the right amount of races of the right caliber to ensure your success. Occasionally entering lower-caliber races and having a greater chance of success may be extremely good for you, especially if you find it hard to finish well for a period of time. See the upcoming information on planning your weekly and daily training sessions for an example of a weekly program during the competition season.

Cyclists get too rigid in their routines and just do a weekly schedule. Look beyond seven days. With a four- to six-week cycle, you can do more and gear more toward a major event.

Chris Carmichael

When successful athletes are in top form for the big events, we say they have peaked or are at their peak for an event. Occasionally an athlete goes through the whole season in top form—Eddy Merckx and Bernard Hinault were the last great road cyclists able to accomplish this feat for several cycling seasons—but such an optimal level of performance is rare. Whether optimum peaking rarely occurs because the season is too long for most athletes to perform at their peak or because so few know how to stay at their peak is an ongoing argument.

Peaking for a race does not just happen. Months, even years, of preparation are required for events such as the World Championships. Peaking at the right time requires setting goals for yourself, and it requires the discipline to establish the priorities needed to achieve those goals.

Self-discipline is enhanced and priorities are more easily established if you have goals to work toward. One goal may be to set a personal record on a course you have raced before, another to win your age category at a particular race. You should establish goals early in the season. Choose goals based on your past performances, your body's physical capabilities, your bike's mechanical capabilities, and input from other athletes and coaches. Goals are not absolute and may be adjusted as your training progresses.

This peaking concept need not be restricted to one season but can be approached on a much broader scale. For example, you may peak for a few regional events during the upcoming season, add longer events to your schedule the next year, and have as your goal for the third year to place well in your age group at the National Championships.

Peaking is often difficult to plan for because of the crowded race schedule and the variety of events offered. It's one thing to peak at a specific event such as the district championships; it's another thing to peak for a series of races spread out over two weeks. Now throw the National Championships into your program, and you begin to appreciate the difficulty of scheduling for peaks. Add to this the pressure of sponsors, press, and coaches—you may begin to wonder if peaking is even possible during the season. Many times you will have to decide which events you must train through in order to prepare for your next major race.

Most cyclists, coaches, and sport scientists say that you can peak only two or three times a year. You need to allow a minimum of four to six weeks between events to perform well. For example, you may peak for an event in late spring, again for a race in midsummer, and a final time for the National Championships in the fall. Between the events you will need to recover and rebuild, and you will enter races for the purposes of training and fine-tuning your performance.

Prior to a major event you should cut down on distance work and add speed and last-minute technique training to your program. All hard training should end a few days before the event and be replaced with easy or moderate rides with a few short bursts of speed when you feel good.

In order to peak effectively to attain your goals, use the following guidelines throughout the season to ensure success:

- Emphasize consistency in your training program. Have a program that plans for the whole season.
- Realize that a sound, successful training program is your best source of self-confidence.
- Rest sufficiently after all races to restore energy levels.
- Don't train hard when sick.
- Identify your nutritional needs and nourish yourself properly. (See chapters 6 and 7 for information on proper nutrition.)
- Do not consider any one aspect of training more important than another. Off-season training and in-season training are integral to your total program.
- Avoid injury. Don't do anything foolish in training or racing that could lead to a serious crash or overuse injury.
- When possible, train in an environment that promotes a concentrated effort.
- Maintain a strong commitment to being fit and healthy

What I've outlined here is a systematic approach to planning your season and peaking for important events. Remember that although the annals of cycling are filled with stories of outstanding athletes who succeeded at big events, other stories tell of the individuals who lined up at the start as leading contenders and failed. It should have been their time, but they were not prepared because in many cases they had not properly peaked for the competition. The secret to success in any sporting event is being prepared for optimum performance at the right time.

DOES ALTITUDE TRAINING IMPROVE PERFORMANCE?

Although there seems to be debate among sport scientists concerning the value of altitude training as preparation for sea-level competition, there is no doubt about its value among some of cycling's most famous coaches and athletes. Charlie Walsh, the former coach of the Australian Cycling Team for many years, often took his athletes "to altitude" in both Mexico and the United States several times each year to enhance their performances.

Most athletes see coming to altitude as a way to stimulate the body to produce more red blood cells, which, upon returning to the oxygen-rich environment of sea level, enables them to transport more oxygen to the working muscles.

Many cyclists used to think they had to move to towns such as Boulder, Colorado, to take advantage of the physiological effects of altitude. But published scientific research and practical evidence from world-class coaches seem to show that several three-week stays at moderate altitudes also may have physiological benefits. These three-week stays at altitude seem to be beneficial for endurance athletes because research demonstrates that three weeks is long enough to raise red blood cell concentrations but short enough so that overall fitness does not deteriorate, which has happened with stays lasting a few months.

In an issue of Running Research News, Owen Anderson, PhD, pointed out that athletes may want to adjust their training programs at altitude during these three-week stays to provide short-interval, high-intensity exercise combined with distance training to achieve the most out of their stays. He based his recommendations on research conducted on seven elite Norwegian cross-country skiers who lived and trained at a moderate altitude of 6,200 feet for three weeks. Training durations ranged from two to four hours a day, and on several days the training program included many high-intensity efforts. Before and after the three weeks of training at altitude, the athletes were asked to run on a treadmill at sea level for six minutes at a 10-km race pace. Blood lactates were measured at one and three minutes after the run. Hemoglobin, $\dot{V}O_2$max, and hematocrit (the ratio of red blood cells to total blood volume) also were measured before and after the three weeks at altitude. The control segment of the study was to train the same subjects a year later at sea level at their previous altitude intensity.

(continued)

After three weeks at altitude, the group's average for hemoglobin increased from 15 to 15.8 grams per 100 ml of blood, and hematocrit increased from 46.3 to 48.6 percent, but $\dot{V}O_2$max did not change. Blood values returned to pre-altitude values after about two weeks at sea level.

Although $\dot{V}O_2$max did not change, there was a significant change in the athletes' lactate profiles: a decrease in blood lactate at the 10-km pace after returning from altitude. Prior to altitude, the group's lactate profiles rose to about 4.8 mmol/L during a six-minute run; after three weeks at altitude and returning to sea level, lactate profiles rose only to 4.0 mmol/L. Interestingly, the athletes who improved their lactate profiles the most were those with the biggest gains in hemoglobin and hematocrit.

F.W. Dick of the British Athletic Federation shared similar information at the 1991 European Athletics Coaches Association Endurance Congress in his lecture on when to use altitude training relative to target competitions. He gives the following recommendations to athletes wishing to use altitude training for improved performance.

First, stay at an altitude of about 6,200 feet for about three weeks twice a year. The first stay should fall at the end of winter training and at the commencement of preseason training. In our yearly training schedule, this would be during the month of January. The second ascent to altitude should be in the final preparation period prior to a major championship.

Schedule the second stay so that the competition is about 15 to 24 days after the return from altitude, because many athletes feel quite fatigued after three weeks of hard training at altitude and need time to recover. Dick reported that it takes many athletes about 8 to 11 days to feel as though they have reacclimated to sea level and that peak performance will be within 15 to 24 days.

If you plan to experiment with this method of altitude training, realize that the range of days that are best for performance varies among athletes. You should practice this procedure several times before using it for a major competition. Experiment with the amount of days needed for you to reach top form once you return to sea level.

For the past 10 years, the Australian cycling track team has been one of the most dominant teams at the World Championships. Walsh feels that his team's short exposures to altitude have improved the athletes' abilities to perform their best at this competition. They return to sea level with fortified blood and with leg muscles that have a large capacity for oxygen utilization.

The Transition Period

The transition period is the end of the competition season and serves as your transition time to the beginning of the preparation period. After a season of competing and peaking for major events, you need a period of reduced training to emotionally and physically recover from the bike.

However, according to Steve Johnson, PhD, national master's champion and operations manager of U.S.A. Cycling, total time off the bike is not good. "Cyclists should gradually reduce their cycling mileage. It is important to keep in touch with the bicycle. Off-season training usually consists of low-volume, low-intensity workouts." Johnson also emphasizes the importance of psychological recovery: "It is important to replace the stress of training with things you enjoy." Many coaches encourage athletes to participate in other recreational activities.

In this period of active rest, your goal is to maintain a specific performance level and a training condition of medium to high fitness. It is important to continue to exercise during this period because passive rest will make it difficult for you to start training in the general preparation phase.

The transition period should not be longer than eight weeks. Cross-training in other activities should be a part of your program, and if you choose to compete in cyclo-cross or mountain bike races during this period, the psychological pressure of performing should be as low as possible. You also should begin resistance training now.

Planning Weekly and Daily Training Sessions

Weekly training sessions often are referred to as microcycles, though microcycles can be as short as three days. The daily training program or session is a single workout, such as an afternoon workout on sprinting tactics. You may have up to two training sessions per day.

Weekly Training Plan

This is where you focus in on daily training variations of intensity, mileage, and exercise selection. Here is an example of a weekly training plan during the month of July in the competition period:

Monday: a recovery ride of one to two hours at low intensity

Tuesday: two hours of training with a few jumps and short intervals, a local night race, motor-pacing, or lactate criss-cross training

Wednesday: morning—endurance riding for three to four hours on mixed terrain at varying tempos; afternoon—weight training, six to eight exercises for the lower back, shoulders, arms, and abdominals

Thursday: two to three hours with jumps and short sprints

Friday: an easy ride for one hour

Saturday: morning—an easy ride for 30 minutes; afternoon—a criterium

Sunday: a 75-mile road race or long group ride

Daily Training Plan

A typical daily training session includes a warm-up, the body of the training session, and a cool-down. Organize your daily training session for the optimal value of the workout. You may deviate from your daily training session because of weather conditions or if you have not recovered from the previous day's efforts. Here is an example of a training session designed for the middle of July, about four days before a local race:

- A warm-up of about 10 to 15 miles
- Two 200-meter sprints
- Three two-minute intervals
- 20 minutes of lactate criss-cross training
- A cool-down of 10 to 15 miles

Designing a Training Diary

Every cyclist is an individual and responds differently to training, so every training method cannot satisfy the training needs of every cyclist. What is good for Lance Armstrong may not be good for Jan Ulrich or for you. Rather, every cyclist must develop his own training methods and yearly training schedule. The guidelines in this book will give you direction, and then you must monitor how your body responds to the various training methods. The only way to do this is to keep a detailed training diary.

The basis of your training diary is your daily record (see figure 9.1). On this record you enter the details of your physical condition: your waking and exercising heart rates, your sleeping patterns, your morning body weight, how you feel during training and racing, and how you perform in races. Training diaries are available through bookstores or catalogs, or you may want to design your own using a standard notebook. For an example of a completed diary entry, see figure 9.2.

Here are some important points to record in your diary:

- As specifically as possible, describe the training session. Did you work on long, slow distances? What type of intervals did you do? Record whom you rode with, on what routes, and what the weather and wind conditions were.

- Record the time you went to bed the previous night and the number of hours you slept. Record any naps you took during the day. Research has shown that athletes who are overtraining start going to bed later at night, sleep less, and wake up tired in the morning. So sleep patterns are a vital indication of whether you are overtraining.

- Record your body weight in the morning after you have emptied your bladder. If you have lost several pounds since the day before, you are dehydrated and need to drink plenty of fluids before your next training

Day: _____ Date: _____

Last night's bedtime:_____ Hours slept: _____

Body weight: _____ Waking heart rate: _____

Feeling rating: _____

Long-term goal:_____

Short-term goal: _____

Today's goal: _____

Training/race session notes:

_____

_____

_____

_____

_____

_____

_____

_____

_____

_____

_____

Figure 9.1 A sheet from a cyclist's diary.

session. A continual fall in body weight over a few weeks is an ominous sign and indicates progressive overtraining.

• Record your heart rate upon waking. Count your pulse for 15 seconds, multiply by 4, and record this number. A sudden rise of more than five or six beats per minute in the early morning may mean that you have not recovered from the previous day's training or that you are getting ill. You should not train hard that day. A persistent elevation of five or six beats in your morning pulse rate indicates a more serious form of overtraining. It may be wise to take a few days off until your waking pulse returns to normal.

• Each morning record how you feel. Use a scale from A to F, A for "feeling great" and "cannot wait for the day's training session," and F for "feeling terrible" and "don't want to even see a bike."

• Besides recording your feelings, you can train and track your mental toughness by focusing on motivation. Most riders neglect this form of

---

Day: _Monday_   Date: _May 6, 20XX_

Last night's bedtime: _10 pm_   Hours slept: _8 1/2_

Body weight: _157_   Waking heart rate: _49_

Feeling rating: _B+_

Long-term goal: _Break 1 hr. in the 40 K Natl. Championships Time Trial_

Short-term goal: _Win Geneva 10 mile trial on Memorial Day_

Today's goal: _Work on Sprint Technique_

Training/race session notes:

Weather was cool — 60's — a little windy.

Easy ride 20 miles with 2 jumps of 200 yards.

Felt good after the hard race yesterday.

Knee problem seems to be going away.

Figure 9.2 A sample entry from a cyclist's diary.

mental training because they fail to verbalize their goals. Don't make this mistake. Recording your long-term, short-term, and daily goals and their achievement should be an integral part of your training diary. Meeting your daily goals is a tremendous confidence builder.

• Create a comments section. Record any minor ailments such as colds, influenza, muscle soreness, or injuries. Record your general state of well-being. Are you enthusiastic, positive, or lethargic? Write about how motivated you were for the practice or competition. If you were psyched up, record the thoughts and feelings that helped you. Record training or race results. On race days, record the conditions of the race: size of field, gears used on climbs, sprints, tactics, mistakes, who was in the break, and your final placing. And keep records of any medical tests or physiological tests completed that day.

In cycling, as in any sport, you can't know where you are going if you don't know where you have been. A training diary is a map and record of where you've been and a guide to where you want to go. In addition to your diary, you occasionally may want to summarize your data. Figure 9.3 is an example of a blank page from one rider's weekly summaries of physiological and psychological variables.

COUNTING THE MILES TO RACE DAY

Data from your daily training log can be summarized on a yearly mileage graph (see figure 9.4). Then you can compare these summary data with your yearly racing and training mileage schedule that you drew up at the beginning of the season. This will give you a quick estimate of how you are living up to your yearly plan and if you are reaching your mileage goals for racing and training. Your yearly mileage graph also can help you compare your present mileage achievements with a previous year's. Every year as you become stronger and fitter you will see an increase in your mileage and intensity. This information, along with the summary information on physiological and psychological factors (figure 9.3), will help you evaluate your program and make necessary short-term adjustments. For example, a continued rise in your waking pulse rate may be a sign that you are fatigued and on the verge of becoming overtrained. You may need to decrease your mileage and intensity for the next few days (or a week) to allow for recovery.

Results of your yearly races can be recorded on a summary chart (see figure 9.5). You can use information you recorded first in your training diary. Then you will have a running commentary on your races, placings, and how you fared against the rest of the starters. Under the "Comments" column you can record the terrain of the course, gearing used at various points in the race, details of the finish area, and any other particulars important to this race. Then next year you can use this information to train for and select equipment for this particular event.

Summary Data						
Week	Waking pulse rate (beats/minute)	Sleep (hours)	Cycling time (km)	Cycling distance (hours)	Effort rating (points)	Body weight
1						
2						
3						
4						
5						
6						
7						
8						
9						
10						
11						
12						
13						
14						
15						
16						
17						
18						
19						
20						
21						
22						
23						
24						

Figure 9.3 Summary data sheet.

25					
26					
27					
28					
29					
30					
31					
32					
33					
34					
35					
36					
37					
38					
39					
40					
41					
42					
43					
44					
45					
46					
47					
48					
49					
50					
51					
52					

Yearly mileage graph

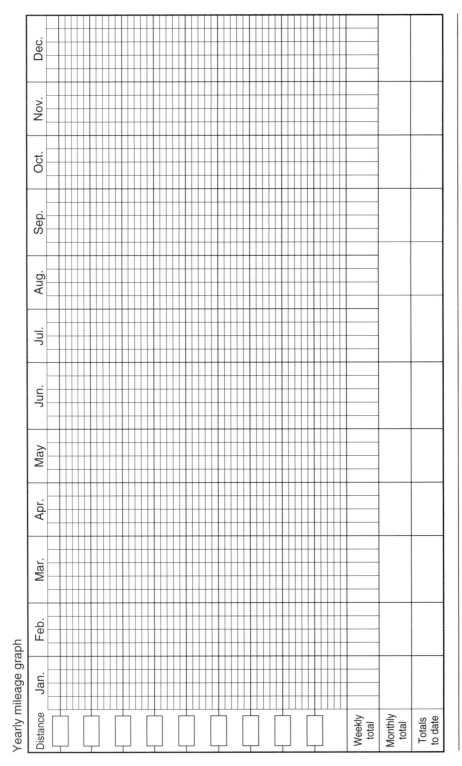

Figure 9.4 Complete a yearly mileage graph to compare actual miles ridden to the goals you set. Set distance goals along the left-hand side of the chart and color in a bar each week to reflect your mileage.

Races of the Year				
Date	Event	Distance time, pace	Place, starters	Comments

Figure 9.5   Use a races-of-the-year chart to track your performance in competition.

The Final Spin

Planning at the yearly, monthly, weekly, and daily levels will provide you with clear goals and objectives for the season. By keeping both the plan and your daily training diary, you will be able to review your training plan to determine what may have been a deciding influence in the success or failure of your season.

A well-planned yearly training program, supplemental resistance training, stretching, and a training diary are a cyclist's best friends for continued success. A well-thought-out plan and a complete training diary are continued sources of motivation and provide essential clues as to which training methods have been successful or not so successful. Many great cyclists, such as Miguel Indurain, Lance Armstrong, and Mari Holden, attribute a large measure of their success to developing a sound yearly training program and keeping detailed logs.

Steve Johnson emphasizes the importance of planning and keeping detailed records. "Training is all about setting performance goals and, most importantly, reaching them," says Johnson. "Periodization provides a cyclist with a methodical, organized approach to scheduling the training year so preseason goals can become medal-winning realities."

COMMITTING TO A WINNING SEASON

Being successful in cycling is being the best you can possibly be—finding and expanding your limits. Your potential in cycling is limited by three things: training, psychological readiness, and talent. These three qualities, in combination, make a good cyclist better.

But, regardless of fitness, strength, or skill, it is one's psychological state, particularly motivation and determination, that makes the difference between winners and losers. Stand at the start of any world-class time trail and you can see in the faces of the riders who is ready to race and place mind over matter.

Every person has a certain amount of talent and athletic potential. Part of it is genetic, a gift from your parents. Another part is improvement from training. But, regardless of the inherited and developed levels of ability, the "most athletic" cyclist will not always win the race.

Why? Eddie Borysewicz, former Olympic cycling coach, once said, "75 to 80 percent of your physical potential is inherited; the remaining 25 to 30 percent comes from your mind." You need to consider the mental side of training and competition because winning is an act of the will as much as of the body. Tough, motivated cyclists often can outperform more talented cyclists.

Developing Commitment

Commitment is the attribute that brings all qualities into focus for competitive cyclists. Commitment is what you "do" with your talent. It is the answer to questions such as, "What amount of training am I willing to do to qualify for the National Championships?" and, "How hard am I willing to train during the off-season?" Commitment is how badly you want to win.

The following ideas can help you enhance your sense of commitment to cycling:

- **Set goals and targets for yourself.** What do you want to achieve during this cycling season and the next? How are you going to get there?

- **Be tough on yourself.** What are you willing to give up to become a better cyclist? Are you willing to go out on those long road rides in the middle of winter? If you get dropped in a race, are you willing to chase until you get back to the pack?

- **Know yourself.** Acknowledge strengths and weaknesses. If you are a poor sprinter, are you willing to spend some time on the track to improve speed? What keeps you going when the times are tough? Do you set realistic goals?

- **Have a plan.** Use your strengths in cycling to carry you from one level to the next. Do you have a training diary? Know where you are going and how to get there.

To be a good rider, you must think like a Texan: 'I am the best.' You have to be tough and tough on yourself. You must want success so badly that you're willing to take 105 percent out of your body to get it.

Eddie Borysewicz, former USA National coach

One example of a cyclist with commitment is Andy Hampsten. He had a normal quota of inherited talent but also had a great capacity for commitment. He improved gradually as a junior and senior, eventually winning the Tour of Italy and Tour of Switzerland. When a cyclist is committed, no coach can predict what levels of performance he will eventually reach.

Start now, not tomorrow. Start with today's workout—what are you waiting for? What kind of support system do you have to improve your performance? Use as many resources as possible in your quest to be the best: coaches, equipment, family, and so forth. How can they aid you?

Be efficient. Besides training hard, train smart. What is the quickest, smartest, and most efficient way to reach your goals? If you plan properly, you will succeed. Enjoy your successes and learn from your failures. When you fail, analyze what happened and learn why you did not reach your goal, and work to not let it happen again.

Talent and commitment to the sport are the combination that can take you to your goals in cycling. Remember, you determine how good you want to be at this sport.

Going for the Goal

Cyclists have always found that goal setting contributes to performance and confidence in training and competition. Training is not an end in itself but an activity with a purpose. To win more races than the cyclist just above you in the club program, to qualify for the state championships, or to help your team win the team time-trial competition at a stage race—these are specific goals. In the absence of goals, either small or ambitious, it is virtually impossible to persevere long enough to see a training program bring results. What is the purpose of pushing yourself so hard, after all, if you cannot measure what you have accomplished? One cyclist's goal may be to win five races this season; another to break one hour for a 40-km time trial. To keep motivated you cannot let yourself be satisfied—you have to keep raising your goals.

Whatever your personal program, however, it will not bear fruit unless its goals are likely to be attainable. Dr. Jerry Lynch, director of the Center for Optimal Performance, notes, "In my work with elite athletes at the U.S. Olympic Training Center, one major difference I have seen between those who reach their goals and those who fall short can be attributed to their level of commitment to reaching their goals. The stronger the commitment, the better the chances for obtaining objectives. This holds true for the recreational cyclist as well. Many set unrealistic goals, complain of the difficulties of reaching their goals, or are most likely not committed to reaching their goals. Most likely there are other major commitments in their lives. If their profession or family are more important, then cycling will (and should) take a back seat. Knowing this exists when you develop your goals will help you set more realistic goals and reach them successfully. Cycling must fit into the priorities of your lifetime goals."

Obviously, the first and easiest step toward successful performances is understanding and using the techniques of effective goal setting. Specific goals direct activity more effectively and reliably than vague or general goals. A cyclist whose goals are vague, who wants to "do better," probably always will be dissatisfied. Is finishing in the top 10 a good performance or not? What about losing a major road race, but by less distance in the sprint than expected? What is needed are clearly recognizable goals: a top-three finish in the National Championship road race; partial squat 250 pounds by the end of March. A quantitative or numerical goal is a specific goal.

Using short-term, intermediate, and long-term goals will aid performance more than using long-term goals only. Use short-term goals as steps to help you reach your long-term goals. Do not expect to make major jumps in performance levels right away. Use short-term goals to show progress toward your long-term goals. Table 10.1 lists some examples of short-term, intermediate, and long-term goals.

The more challenging or compelling the goal, the better the performance. Goals should not be so difficult that you fail to take them seriously. However, goals that are too easy to attain will not improve performance. If you have the ability to attain the goals you select, a challenging goal will greatly enhance motivation. You may consider talking with your coach and teammates for their input into what may be challenging and realistic goals for you.

Goals work best if there is prompt feedback showing progress in relation to the goal. You must be able to check how well you are doing in relation to the goals that you've set. You must measure performance.

Show patience and persistence in reaching your goal. After his shooting accident in 1987, Greg LeMond set a long-term goal of winning the Tour de France again. Although there were some setbacks along the way, he eventually reached his goal in 1989. There will be setbacks along the way; they are a normal consequence of trying to improve. Use your setbacks as opportunities to learn and reevaluate your goals and your training or race strategy.

TABLE 10.1   **Examples of Short-Term, Intermediate, and Long-Term Goals**

Short-term goals	Intermediate goals	Long-term goals
1. Ride as well as I can in each workout.	1. Average 900 to 1,000 miles per month between April and October.	1. Break one hour for a 40-km time trial.
2. Improve sprinting ability at the end of long road races.	2. Win State Road Championships.	2. Win National Road Championships.
3. Improve climbing ability to crest hills in the top 10% with the lead group.	3. At end of the season, receive a sponsorship offer from a well-sponsored team.	3. Turn professional in three years.
4. My legs will remain loose during long road races.	4. Finish in the top three in three-stage races this year.	
5. Purchase the best equipment available to me within my budget.	5. Attend a winter training camp at the Olympic Training Center.	

When you overtrained, did you go out too fast? Did you eat enough during the race? You can use this information to accomplish your goals, but it may be in the next race.

As Kay Porter and Judy Foster mention in The Mental Athlete, "The effects of a goal-setting system are cumulative. As you achieve your first goals, you become more certain of what you want from yourself and your sport and how to accomplish it. Learning to set short-term, intermediate, and long-term goals is one of the most powerful tools any athlete can use to increase measurably the level of his or her performance. Your goals become the framework that guides your training and competitions. Your goals, whatever they may be, and the desire to achieve them, are the motivation that pushes you through the rain and snow, through the pain and injuries, and through the times when you feel stuck at a certain competitive level or plateau."

PSYCHING UP

Arousal is a term used by sport psychologists to describe a state of eager readiness to play. Cyclists who are aroused before and during a race usually perform better than those with low levels of energy. But too much arousal can be just as harmful to performance as too little arousal. Your best performance comes when you reach your optimum level of arousal. Learning to manage a proper amount of arousal before your competition is key to your success in racing.

Figure 10.1 shows three broad ranges of arousal: underarousal, overarousal, and a zone of optimal arousal. As we have all experienced in competition, as arousal increases, performance improves up to a point, then performance decreases. Each of us has a unique arousal-performance curve that depends on a variety of factors besides the complexity of the task at hand. These include stress level, self-confidence, motivation, attention, experience, and thoughts.

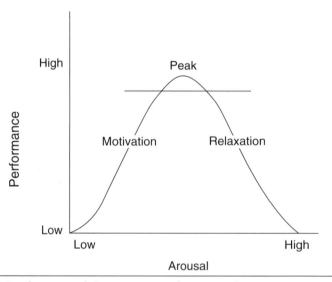

Figure 10.1 As arousal increases, performance improves to a point, then decreases. The arousal-performance curve is unique to each cyclist.

From "Sport Psychology and Cycling" by Andrew Jacobs. In *Science of Cycling* (p. 207) by E.R. Burke (ed.), 1986, Champaign, IL: Human Kinetics. Copyright 1986 by Edmund Burke. Reprinted by permission.

Signs that you are underaroused are feelings of low energy or tiredness or a lack of motivation or endurance. Signs of overarousal might be feelings of tightness or tension, headaches, high heart rate or breathing, or the feeling that the race is going hard when the pace is slow. During a long road race you may have to "cycle" through various levels of arousal to ensure optimal energy output at key times during the event.

To ensure an adequate state of arousal before or during a race, practice these arousal guidelines:

- Spend a few minutes each day thinking about how you want to perform in your next race. Do not wait until the morning of the race.
- Before competition, stick to as normal a routine as possible.
- Try to stay away from conflicting situations or quarrels in the days before or the day of the race.
- Look forward to racing. Competition should be fun.
- During a long road race, make sure your level of arousal increases along with the activity of the race.
- Avoid emotional talks or warm-up sessions that cause arousal to peak several hours before competition.

Before a time trial you may want to practice the following routine:

1. Check equipment and gearing.
2. Eat sensibly and plan your eating schedule properly for race start time.
3. Know where the start is and arrive early.
4. Check wind and other weather conditions.
5. Warm up properly.
6. Relax. No need to be aggressive before the event.

Remember, however, that your optimal arousal level is unique and may not fit these general guidelines. Do whatever works for you in order to reach your physical and emotional high before a major training session or race.

Concentration

Many coaches and cyclists agree that the most important psychological factor during competition is concentration. Being able to focus on the race, the changing tactics, the environment, and your competitors is a key to success in racing.

Several years ago, Bill Morgan, PhD, and a sports psychologist conducted a study on marathon runners and what they thought about during a race. As he talked with athletes of all levels, from elite to novice, Morgan began to notice a consistent distinction. Almost without exception, the top runners spent their time monitoring what they were doing and how they felt at each stage of the race. (During a race, a successful cyclist will check his inner dials, his fuel supply, his speed, his pedaling revolutions per minute (rpm), how his legs feel, and other parts of his body machinery.) In contrast, the less accomplished runners, wanting to escape the discomfort and pain of the event, tended to think about other matters while racing—school, work, family, and the like. The less successful cyclist consciously strives to ignore the distress signals his body is sending to his brain by keeping his mind otherwise engaged away from the task at hand.

This, and other psychological research, has determined that the most successful athletes are best at narrowing their attention under pressure. For example, in the time trial you will need to concentrate on pushing hard, keeping your rpm up throughout the race, and focusing in on a goal of a specific time or of catching your opponent. Andy Jacobs, former sport psychologist working with the U.S. Olympic Cycling Team, has reported these same traits, showing that elite cyclists have the ability to narrow their focus of attention when necessary under the pressure of competition. Some cyclists refer to this process as tunnel vision.

_____

"The bicycle racer, no matter how gifted, is a colossus with feet of clay if his psyche is not doing its part, in training or the heat of competition."

Bernard Hinault, five-time Tour de France winner

The following procedures may help you focus or recapture your diverted attention before or during an event:

• Become more attracted to what you are trying to concentrate on during the race. If you are trying to keep form while time trialing, look at your shadow on the road if the sun is in the right position. When trying to hold your pedaling cadence, concentrate on a rhythmical beat. When trying to hold a rider's wheel while climbing, keep up pedal stroke for pedal stroke.

• It may be how you view a distraction that makes it so distracting. Riding in the wind may be a distraction for many, yet those who ride well under that condition do not see the wind as a problem.

• If you begin to doubt yourself or feel excessive fatigue during a race, focus on the race and your opponents. This will focus your attention toward external factors and take your mind off your pain and suffering. Try relaxing your upper body, breathe deeply, and remember to eat and drink.

• Do not let course conditions, such as hot weather or a hilly course, hinder your performance. Visualize that these conditions will work to your advantage against less prepared opponents.

• Before the race starts, stay away from the start line for as long as possible. Arrive just before the start. This will keep you away from the confusion that often precedes the start of a stage or road race.

Mental Training Log

Most cyclists have probably kept some form of workout diary. The training diary is a way to chart your physical training and progress. The mental training log is a way to chart the mental factors that affect your performance. The training diary includes information such as the type of workout you performed that day, total miles ridden, training intensity, sleep, and diet. A mental training log could include information such as goals, arousal levels, and motivational statements.

Why keep a mental training log? For the same reason you keep a physical training diary. You keep track of your physical progress as a cyclist. You record race times, weight loss, and strength gains. However, most cyclists rarely chart their mental progress. If mental training is so important, why is it so often neglected? The answer is that most cyclists have never bothered writing their goals down and keeping track of other psychological skills.

The first thing to do is to expand your training diary to include the short- and long-term goals you have in cycling. For example, a long-term goal may be to break the hour in the 40-km National Championships Time Trial, and a short-term goal may be to win the first 10-mile local time trial of the season. A workout goal may to be to tell yourself that you will not get dropped on the long climb today.

Instead of setting these goals only in your head, it is a better idea to write them in your training diary. Writing goals motivates you to complete your workout plan so that your goal will be attained. Here are some guidelines for keeping mental goals in your daily training program:

- Write goals and expectations for each workout and race.
- Record your positive thoughts and feelings and what they did for you.
- Write how motivated you were for each practice or competition.
- Report on how energized you were for each workout or race. What was your state of arousal?
- Write a brief statement on how you mentally prepared for each workout or competition.

Keeping track of your mental training goals will give you that mental edge. Most cyclists already keep a training diary of physical adaptations and stresses of training. You also should log the mental aspect of training in your diary. Including what you do mentally, as well as physically, is important in making you a better cyclist.

The Final Spin

Most people, from cyclists and spectators to coaches and sport scientists, recognize that the mind plays an important role in performance. Psychological preparation and the use of mental skills or strategies during training and racing are often crucial to optimal performance. Terms such as motivation, drive, commitment, and mental toughness are commonly used to describe this factor. Research and practical work completed with cyclists at all levels show that training the mind is as important as training the body to make the champion. If you enter a competition in the same physical shape as another racer, most often the one who finishes first will be the one who is stronger mentally.

11

PREVENTING OVERTRAINING

Do you ever have days when your legs feel so heavy you wonder how you'll ever find the energy to ride? Sure you do—every cyclist does. Fatigue is a normal part of training, and it helps provide the stimulus needed to reach new levels of fitness. There is a threshold, however, beyond which the stimulus overwhelms your ability to recover and you enter the domain of overtraining.

The problem results when you work harder and more frequently than your body can handle. When more buildup (anabolism) than breakdown (catabolism) occurs, you increase fitness. With overtraining, however, all that repetitive, high-intensity work outpaces your ability to recover, leading to performance declines rather than advances.

Symptoms of overtraining vary; you may have trouble sleeping, frequent colds, increased resting heart rate, weight loss, impaired racing times, slow recovery, or a loss of enthusiasm for cycling. Also, overtraining can lead to immune-system suppression, resulting in increased susceptibility to infections. In women, it's associated with amenorrhea (loss of menstrual periods).

Exactly what overtraining does to the body isn't clear. It may contribute to overstimulation of the sympathetic nervous system, which happens when the sum total of life's stresses is too great. In response, the body releases an excess of adrenaline and noradrenaline, leaving you unable to fully relax and incapable of performing your best.

Burnout

The phenomenon of overtraining, also known as staleness, burnout, or fatigue, is very real. Considering the length of the cycling season, family responsibilities, and the demands placed on today's athletes in school, cyclists have good reason to watch out for staleness and symptoms of overtraining.

When you train, it is an essential and difficult task to find your optimum training thresholds and not exceed the limits of your stress and adaptation capacities. Because of the scope of this topic, we will not attempt to cover all the factors and possible mechanisms thought to contribute to overtraining. But we will look at specific physiological and psychological variables that have been shown to be related to the deterioration of athletic performance due to overtraining.

In *The Lore of Running*, Dr. Timothy Noakes gives examples of several nationally ranked athletes with symptoms of overtraining. One athlete noted that his morning pulse had increased by 10 beats per minute and he complained that he was lethargic, was sleeping poorly, and had less enthusiasm for training and competition. He expressed concern that his legs felt sore and heavy and that the feeling had lasted for several training sessions. Another distance runner reported that three weeks after a marathon he was still sleeping poorly, had a persistent sore throat, and had low energy levels.

These two athletes were exhibiting some of the classic physical and psychological signs and symptoms of overtraining. Both were in urgent need of complete rest from hard training.

The symptoms of overtraining may be seen in the athlete who is eager to excel and begins to train frequently and intensely. At first the athlete improves, but after a while his times become stationary and below his set goals. Anxious to pass the dead point, the athlete begins to train even harder. Instead of improving, his times become worse, and he begins to feel inadequate and frustrated. Besides a decline in performance, some changes in personality and behavior can be detected. The athlete has developed a state of staleness.

In the early 1980s, Dick Brown, who at the time was an administrator and physiologist at Athletics West (a world-class running club), conducted a study to try to identify potential indicators of overtraining among athletes. Of the several dozen indicators monitored, three were found to be helpful to athletes in their daily training and could be recorded in their training diaries without expensive monitoring equipment. These were morning body weight, morning heart rate, and hours of sleep.

Brown's research found that if an athlete's morning heart rate was 10 percent above normal resting heart rate, if she received 10 percent less sleep, or if her weight was down 3 percent or more, then her body was telling her that it had not recovered from the previous hard workout or that some form of illness was plaguing her. Brown's research points out that an athlete should cut back on that day's workout if she has two abnormal indicators and should take the day off and nap if she registers in the red on all three indicators.

If the signs of staleness or overtraining are present, you may have to suspend training for several days or decrease the intensity and duration of the sessions. If strong signs or symptoms prevail, it is possible you will have to spend days or weeks at a decreased level of training before you recover and can return to hard training.

Causes of Overtraining

Cyclists who fail to adapt to the stress of sustained, long-term, high-intensity training can push themselves into overtraining. The condition also may have a rapid onset if high-intensity training takes place too early in the training cycle before athletes have had time to adapt to the stress of training. In the late 1980s, researcher Dave Costill, PhD, from the Human Performance Lab at Ball State University, showed that as few as 10 days of increased training may result in overreaching in some athletes. Lack of recovery also may contribute to overtraining.

The chief cause of overtraining, however, is a poorly conceived training program. For example, rapid increases in training volume and intensity and protracted schedules of high-volume training, along with inadequate recovery and rest, will put many athletes at risk of developing overtraining. Failing to consider other stresses that the athlete is experiencing also increases the risk. But even the most carefully planned training program can cause problems with some athletes. Research has shown that standardized assessments of training and secondary sources of stress may not be useful in predicting the risk of staleness in groups or teams. This variability underscores the importance of regarding your personal limitation for increases in volume and intensity of training.

Overtraining is a complex condition whose primary cause is prolonged overload training without proper recovery. Other types of stress—competition-related, monotony and tedium, medical conditions, diet, environment, psychosocial issues, and travel—can compound the stress of training and contribute to overtraining.

The primary feature of overtraining is an unexpected drop in performance that cannot be attributed to factors such as illness or injury. This drop-off may be preceded by a period when performance is maintained but at greater cost. Other symptoms of overtraining include mood disturbances (depression, anger, anxiety), general fatigue and malaise associated with a loss of energy and vigor, and feelings of heaviness in the limbs. Changes in sleep patterns and appetite also have been commonly noted and may be useful in diagnosing overtraining.

It is imperative to identify overtraining at its early stages when short-term interventions may still be effective. You could be on your way to a serious state of exhaustion unless you heed the warning signs. How can you keep from becoming a victim of overtraining? Check the rundown of overtraining symptoms listed in table 11.1 (from the work of Timothy Noakes), and if several apply to you, cut down on training and rest for a while.

Prevention and Recovery

The risk of overtraining can be reduced if not eliminated through careful periodization of training. Adequate rest and recovery, especially during the heaviest training periods, is crucial. You may have to enforce rest in your program even when you are unwilling to reduce training for fear of becoming detrained. Similarly, you may need to be cautious about trying to train back into shape too quickly after a layoff. Proper nutrition and hydration is also especially important during peak training.

For severe cases of overtraining, a complete break from training is necessary. You must learn to listen to your body and be alert to signs of overreaching. Rest need not mean total inactivity, which can be a significant source of stress for cyclists accustomed to training daily. Active recreation can be effective as a recovery aid and help deter monotony. Proper nutrition is important even when you are not in training.

TABLE 11.1 Symptoms of Overtraining

Emotional and behavioral changes	Physical changes
• Loss of enthusiasm and drive; generalized apathy	• Impaired physical performance; inability to complete training
• Loss of joy in, and thirst for, competition	• Gradual weight loss
• Desire to quit	• Looks drawn, sallow, and dejected
• Lethargy, listlessness, tiredness	• Early morning heart rate increases by more than 5 beats per minute; abnormal rise in standing heart rate and during and after a standard workout; slower recovery in heart rate after exertion
• Feeling peevish; easily irritated, anxious, ill-humored, bored	• Heavy-leggedness; sluggishness that persists 24 hours or more after a workout
• Inability to concentrate at work; poor academic performance	• Muscle and joint pains; persistent muscle soreness from session to session
• Changes in sleeping patterns; insomnia; sleep does not refresh	• Swelling of lymph glands
• Loss of appetite	• Gastrointestinal disturbances, in particular diarrhea
• Loss of libido	• Increased susceptibility to infections, allergies, headache
• Poor coordination; general clumsiness	• Minor scratches heal slowly
• Increased fluid intake at night; feeling thirsty	• In women, loss of menstruation (amenorrhea)

If overtraining is suspected, a medical examination should be conducted to rule out illness or disease. If other factors can be ruled out, then a training break is necessary. Recovery from overtraining may take a minimum of two weeks of rest, but much longer breaks may be needed in more severe cases. Resumption of training is an individual decision because there is no universal indicator of when recovery from overtraining is complete.

A medical illness resulting from overload training (e.g., upper respiratory tract infection) also requires appropriate treatment. Proper nutrition is an important concern as overtraining often results in reduced appetite.

An unexpected, unplanned drop-off in the capacity to train or compete at customary levels often indicates that overtraining has hit, but it is crucial to first rule out other conditions that also affect performance. Early warning signs that may precede a loss of performance include mood disturbances, excessive fatigue, changes in sleep and appetite patterns, and excessive difficulty and perceived effort in completing normal training bouts.

"To be a champion you need firstly, before anything else, the physical capabilities that come from birth. It is vital to have a strong character or courage. Finally, you have to have the ambition to always push yourself."

Eddy Merckx, five-time Tour de France winner

Planning and monitoring are the keys to preventing overtraining. You must periodize training and recovery programs while taking into account external stressors. Testing and evaluating your training progress on a regular basis can help prevent any unexpected performance drop-offs and facilitate prompt intervention should a drop-off occur.

What can be done to prevent overtraining? Take the following measures into account:

- Sleep at least eight hours a night when you are training hard.
- Eat a balanced diet that includes all the basic nutrients.
- Do at least 8 weeks of endurance work to build up a good base. Do not increase the frequency, duration, or intensity of training sessions too quickly.
- Gradually build up the quantity and quality of training so that you are prepared both physically and mentally for increasing volume.
- Many coaches recommend taking a 15- to 30-minute nap before the afternoon workout.
- When training hard, the intensity of your work should correspond to your level of fitness and experience, not someone else's.
- Know yourself and how you react to stress. Continually review your mental training log to monitor your stress and training goals.
- Use a training diary and record morning pulse rate, body weight, sleep patterns, medical problems, and all your training sessions on a daily basis.
- Schedule days of rest into your training program on a periodic basis. They will make you stronger.

Every discussion of burnout usually ends with the same, and rather indefinite, definitive statement: Too little stress, physical or psychological, does not bring about desired changes; too much stress is harmful. By being aware of your body's warning signals and by knowing the stages of adaptation, you can progress safely through training and steadily improve your fitness.

Are You Overtraining or Undereating?

If you're experiencing the classic symptoms of overtraining, the problem may not be too much activity, but too little fuel. The problem may simply be not enough carbohydrate to fuel your muscles.

Check your weight. If you've lost weight unintentionally, the first thing you should do is have a checkup with your doctor. Sudden weight loss can be the first sign of illness. If your doctor finds nothing wrong, your weight loss probably means you're not eating properly.

If you check your energy needs and match them against your average diet, do you come up short? Try to eat more complex carbohydrates. You may need extra whole-grain breads and cereals, rice and pasta, fresh fruits and vegetables. As long as an increase in carbohydrates doesn't make you sneak over your normal healthy weight, you're probably on the right track. If you have trouble estimating your energy needs and planning an appropriate diet, talk to a registered dietitian or a nutritionist.

If your average daily calorie count seems to be about right, are you matching your eating pattern to your activity level? You probably don't need the same number of calories every day and every week. Many cyclists taper during the winter and then build toward spring races. How about midseason training? For three or four months, your training might push up your calorie needs by a factor of two or even three.

After a long ride, your carbohydrate stores will be at a fairly low level. It takes extra fuel to refill your tank. An average calorie intake just may not be enough to allow you to bounce back. Remember, a 50- to 100-mile ride by itself takes several thousand calories. You'll need more carbohydrate after that, compared with an easy day. Similarly, a 300-mile week will use twice as many calories as a 150-mile week, and the extra calories should come from carbohydrate.

In addition to eating extra carbohydrate, you also may want to try one of the energy replacement drinks available at sporting goods stores. For long ride, choose a drink containing a small amount of protein and glucose polymers rather than simple sugars.

On the whole, your body will tell you what it needs. During the evening after a 100-mile ride, you may feel like eating everything in sight. But sometimes a very hard effort may depress your appetite, so you need to be thoughtful about your training and eating.

If you've been having problems that feel like overtraining, make sure you're eating enough carbohydrate. If the average seems about right, make sure you match your intake, day by day, to your training load. Your car won't run on empty, nor will your body. Put those carbohydrates back in your muscles at the same rate you use them.

The Final Spin

Overtraining is individual. A program that's just right for your partner may be too much for you. Effective training means knowing how to manage your body's ability to recover and adapt. Overtraining represents poor management. You can train hard and not become overtrained if you build in breaks between hard workouts to let your body recover.

The best prevention? Know thyself. Pay attention to your body's signals. Keep a detailed training log so that you can learn from your previous responses. Use a proper tapering program before big races to rebuild energy stores before big events. By stepping back and analyzing what you've done, you can avoid the pitfalls of overtraining.

PART IV

Racing

It often is argued that road racing is something of a lottery, that the best person doesn't always win. I disagree, because sheer physical ability isn't the only factor that should be considered in evaluating a victory. Bike handling, position on the bike, pedaling mechanics, tactical sense, ability to suffer, and sheer luck all play a part, and rightly so. The best rider almost always does win because he is the one who has turned all these factors, luck included, to his advantage.

So how do you narrow the odds and improve your chances, given that physical strength and fitness have already been assured? In this section, you will discover how to improve your bike position for optimal aerodynamics and power output; learn ways to improve pedaling mechanics for efficient and effective pedaling; and, finally, learn how to put all this together for improved riding techniques, from riding in a pace line to sprinting at the end of a hard-fought road race.

All the various tactics and techniques involved in road racing are best learned "hands on" by actually taking part in as many different types of competitions as possible. However, knowing what skills need to be learned and recognizing the difference between planned tactics and tactics forced on riders by circumstances does require a little guidance.

Even Lance Armstrong learns something new every day, but, after all, that is one of the great attractions of our sport. At least, I hope to give you enough insight on the basics to enable you to learn the rest from your own experiences and observations.

PERFECT
POSITIONING

For the cyclist interested in performance, proper positioning on the bicycle is paramount. A properly fitted cyclist will be efficient, powerful, comfortable, and injury-free on the bike. An efficient and powerful position is one that enables the cyclist to pedal the bicycle effectively without wasted energy or improper pedaling mechanics. Proper positioning and comfort on the bicycle allow for the athlete's weight to be distributed over the saddle, pedals, and handlebars so that the skeletal system bears the weight instead of the muscles of the back and arms.

A good bike fit, then, is imperative not only for comfort but also for minimizing the risk of injury. Improper positioning often leads to overuse injuries and premature fatigue while riding. For the past 15 years, Andy Pruitt, EdD, director of the Boulder Center for Sport Medicine, has described cycling as "a marriage between the human body, which is somewhat adaptable, and a machine that is somewhat adjustable." In fitting, one needs to adjust the bicycle to the cyclist so that the cyclist has to adapt as little as possible.

Sitting Pretty

The importance of a proper fit between you and your bicycle can be seen in increased economy of oxygen consumption. Mark Hodges at the Olympic Training Center conducted a study that measured the oxygen consumption of elite juniors before and after they were positioned properly on bicycles. After a proper fitting, the group was able to reduce its average oxygen consumption by 8 to 14 percent at a given workload.

The most important angle on a bicycle is formed by the seat tube with the ground. A good fit requires your knee to be over the pedal spindle when the crank arms are horizontal. The angle of the seat tube with the ground usually is designed to accomplish this. The typical range for all bicycles is 70 to 75 degrees, although some triathletes' seat tubes are at 90 degrees. The most common angles are 72 to 74 degrees, which will allow an average-sized cyclist to position the knee over the pedal spindle with only minor adjustments in fore and aft movement of the saddle.

The seat–tube angle is related to the length of the femur (thigh bone). The longer the femur, the smaller the angle and the farther back the cyclist tends to sit on the bicycle. If you have a short femur, the seat–tube angle has to be larger to position your knee far enough forward. In general, the smaller the bicycle, the larger the seat–tube angle. Professional cyclists who ride long road races with many climbs increasingly opt to ride bicycles with a 72-degree seat–tube angle.

Seat–tube length, which is determined by leg length, allows for proper positioning of the saddle in relation to the pedals. At his School of Champions clinics, John Howard recommends allowing one to two inches of space between the rider's crotch and the top tube when the rider is standing barefoot over the bicycle. An acceptable frame will have four to five inches of seat tube showing when the seat is properly adjusted.

The latest trend is to choose the smallest frame size that will allow proper biomechanical relationships. A smaller frame will be stiffer and lighter and will handle better because of its lower center of gravity.

The top-tube length is determined by the relationship of the upper body to the lower body. Mark Hodges, former director of coaching for the U.S. Cycling Team, recommends the following formula for determining top-tube length: First divide height in inches by pants inseam in inches. If the answer is greater than 2.2, you have a long torso compared with your legs. A value less than 2.0 means that your torso length is disproportionately short. Average values fall between the two. If you are at either extreme, selecting a frame with proper top-tube length is crucial.

According to Hodges, if you have short legs and a long torso, you need a frame with a closer relationship between the seat-tube length and the top-tube length (commonly measured from the center of the seat tube to the center of the head tube). A "long" frame, for someone with a long torso, might have a 58-cm seat tube and a 59-cm top tube; a "short" frame, for someone with a short torso, might have a 54 × 52 combination.

Average frames normally have top tubes 2 to 3 cm shorter than their seat tubes. Selecting a frame with the inappropriate ratio for your body type may adversely affect breathing, steering, and weight distribution and eventually strain the muscles that support the torso. Do not believe anyone who says that you can compensate for an incorrect tube length by adjusting the stem extension or the position of the saddle on the rail. That approach just messes up many other adjustments on the bike.

Women generally have proportionally shorter torsos and longer legs than men have, which often makes it difficult for some women to ride frames built for men. As the awareness of women's needs grows, we see more and more bikes being designed specifically for women.

Saddle Height

Changes in saddle height affect the muscle activity of your legs. Michael Desipres in France conducted research that studied muscle-activity patterns using electromyography (EMG). Three male cyclists were asked to ride their own bicycles at three different intensities and two saddle heights. EMG measurements of eight leg muscles were sampled at 95 percent and 105 percent of inseam length (measured from the ground to the crotch). Desipres concluded that as saddle height increased, the leg muscles turned on earlier in the pedal cycle and stayed on longer. The magnitude of muscle action did not appear larger; the EMG activity was just recorded for a longer period.

Saddle height does seem to make a difference, and cyclists and coaches all seem to have their own methods for achieving the optimum. But if you look at a few of the most popular methods, you will see that the saddle heights they produce end up fairly similar.

The John Howard Method

John Howard, former Olympian and Iron Man champion, recommends having a 30-degree bend in the knee when seated on the saddle, with the ball of the foot on the pedal and the pedal in the 6 o'clock position. The 30-degree bend is measured with a goniometer. You can buy one at a medical supply store or make one of your own using a ruler and protractor. The goieometer is lined up with the femur and tibia, with the axis being the midpoint of the femur (see figure 12.1). Your foot must be in its natural pedaling position to properly take the measurements.

Rocking of the hips is a sign that the saddle position is too high. Excessive upper-body movement and frequent saddle standing are signs that it is too low.

Figure 12.1 John Howard recommends a saddle height that yields a 30-degree knee bend when seated with the pedal in the 6 o'clock position.

The Greg LeMond Method

Greg LeMond says that you should multiply your inseam length in centimeters (measured in stocking feet from floor to crotch) by .883. Measure yours by standing with your back against a wall and your feet about 15 cm apart. Put a carpenter's square or record album snug against your crotch, exerting the same pressure as your saddle would. One edge should be flat against the wall. Have a friend measure from the top to the floor.

The product of this equation should equal the length from the center of the bottom bracket axle (point A) to the top of the saddle (point B; see figure 12.2). If you have clipless pedals, LeMond recommends subtracting 3 mm from this measurement to get your saddle height.

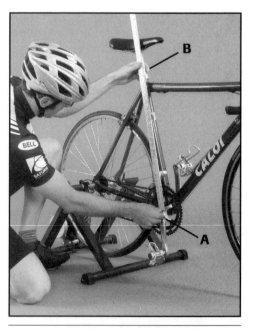

Figure 12.2 Greg LeMond recommends multiplying inseam length in centimeters by .883. The result should equal the length from point A to point B.

The Andy Pruitt Method

Andy Pruitt is a certified athletic trainer and physician's assistant who has treated many of the top cyclists in the United States. He has experimented with a riding position that puts minimal pressure on the knee and allows for a powerful pedal stroke. His method of setting saddle height is similar to John Howard's and also uses a goniometer. He uses the greater trochanter (hip) to the lateral condyle (bump on the outside of the knee) to the lateral malleolus (bump on the outside of the ankle) as reference points for selecting saddle height (see figure 12.3). The angle formed from these points should be between 25 and 30 degrees.

By using this seat height, you can reduce knee injuries and also avoid the dead spot at the bottom of the pedal stroke. But you should be careful in determining the anatomical landmarks because if you do not hit the right places, you can be off by a great deal.

Figure 12.3   Andy Pruitt recommends the saddle height to be such that the angle formed by the three points shown is between 25 and 30 degrees.

Common Ground

If you complete all the measurements properly, you will notice that all methods yield similar saddle heights. Whatever method you use, make sure that your saddle is level or pointed up slightly at the nose. A horizontal saddle allows you to move back and forth across the saddle to change position as the terrain dictates. And if there is anything that all the opinions on saddle height have in common, it is that you'll have to change your position slowly. If you are currently accustomed to riding at a saddle height that is off by a lot, you should move the saddle up or down only 2 mm every two weeks.

RIDING IN THE DIRT

When you're on a mountain bike, your body position will be different, mainly because of the upright bars. Upright bars hold your upper body more erect, putting more weight on the saddle and rear wheel. This allows for better traction and enables a seated cyclist to push a larger gear. Because many of today's mountain bikes have the same seat–tube angles as road bicycles, cyclists often use the same saddle height and fore/aft dimensions as on their road bikes.

The top tube of a mountain bike should be 2 to 4 inches lower than that of a road bike. But if you ride a 24-inch road bike, don't assume that a 20- or 22-inch mountain bike will be the right size. As with road bikes, mountain-bike sizes usually are determined by seat–tube length, and some models have sloping top tubes that result in extremely short seat tubes. In these cases, smaller frame sizes fit larger cyclists. The clearance between the crotch and top tube should be 3 to 6 inches.

Stem extension is important because you often will ride out of the saddle, shifting your body. If your knees hit the bars, consider changing to a longer stem with a higher rise. Pro racers usually use low-rise stems, sometimes as low as a 90-degree angle, that are around 135 to 150 mm for a 5-foot-10-inch to 6-foot rider.

On a mountain bike, your upper body in most cases will be more extended. As on the road bicycle, the top of the stem should be one to two inches below the imaginary horizontal line extending from the top of the saddle. A frame that is too small will force you to lean over too far because the handlebars are so far below the saddle. Too large a frame also will stretch you out too far. A comfortable reach on a mountain bike is one that gives you enough room for lots of "body English" on climbs and descents and allows no overlap of knees and elbows. Too high a position will raise your center of gravity and unevenly distribute your weight between the front and rear wheels.

Fore/Aft Position of Saddle

One of the longest-standing recommendations for achieving horizontal saddle position is commonly called KOPS, for "knee over pedal spindle." Complete this check while your bike is mounted on a wind-load simulator and with the top tube leveled with a carpenter's bubble level (figure 12.4 shows you how). First, get seated comfortably, with the crank arm in the 3 o'clock, or horizontal, position. Locate the bony protrusion below your kneecap. Drop a plumb line from this point; it should bisect the forward pedal's axle. Slide on the saddle until the string and axle line up, then dismount and move the saddle forward or backward along its rails as needed. Repeat this process until your knee lines up with the pedal's axle. Make sure your foot is located in its normal position. Dropping or raising your heel can change the position of your knee. The rails under the saddle allow it to be moved about two inches.

After this adjustment, recheck your saddle height. Moving the saddle forward is the same as lowering the saddle slightly; moving the saddle backward raises the saddle. A midsize bicycle frame with a seat–tube angle

Figure 12.4 When your fore/aft seat position is proper, a plumb line dropped from below your kneecap will bisect your pedal axle when you have the crank arm at a 3 o'clock position.

of 73 or 74 degrees allows for sufficient fore/aft saddle adjustment to accommodate most riders. If you ride a bike with a 75-degree seat–tube angle and have a long thigh, you may not be able to put the seat back far enough.

The position of the knee over the pedal's axle is just a starting point. You will need to personalize your fore/aft position to accommodate your physique and meet your riding needs. A road cyclist usually will ride with the knee 1 or 2 cm behind the axle, and a sprinter will ride with the knee 1 or 2 cm in front of the axle. A triathlete, too, usually rides in a more forward position, with the knee in front of the pedal's axle. This allows her to get into a more aerodynamic position and lay out over the bike without her knees hitting her chest. And because most triathletes come from a running background and have strong, flexible hamstrings, they feel more comfortable in this position.

Again, the saddle should be set either level or with a slightly elevated nose. You can check saddle tilt by placing a carpenter's level along the longitudinal axis of the saddle. Some women prefer the nose of the saddle to be angled slightly downward to prevent pressure on the perineal area. Some men will opt to have the saddle tilted more upward, but this may lead to urologic and neuropathic problems.

Stem Height and Extension

The top of the stem should be no more than 5 cm below the top of the saddle. Going lower than this may help your aerodynamic position slightly, but it will put more strain on your neck. If your thigh comes in contact with your torso when you ride, it is a sure sign that the stem is too low. Keep in mind that a higher stem will be more comfortable and a lower stem will be more aerodynamic. Do not extend the stem beyond the mark on the side of the stem or you risk breaking it out of the head tube.

The measurement that most affects upper-body position is reach, the combination of handlebar extension and top-tube length. In an off-the-shelf bicycle frame, the length of the top tube (measured from the center of the seat tube to the center of the head tube) is proportional to the length of the seat tube and corresponds to the upper-body measurements of the average-sized cyclist who would need that frame size. As mentioned earlier, only in the past few years have frame manufacturers addressed the needs of female cyclists, who generally have shorter upper bodies and longer legs than men of the same height.

To determine proper stem extension, mount your bike on a wind-load simulator and assume a normal riding position with your hands on the drops of the bars. Have a friend (it's best to have a very close friend) drop a plumb line from the end of your nose while you are looking down at a 45-degree angle to the floor surface. The plumb line should fall about an inch behind the handlebars (see figure 12.5). While maintaining the same position, look at the front hub. If the majority of the hub is obscured from view by the handlebars, the stem is of acceptable length.

Figure 12.5 With your stem properly extended, a plumb line dropped from your nose while you are looking down at a 45-degree angle will fall about an inch behind the handlebar.

After you are in shape, taking a long ride may let you know whether the stem length is correct. If it is too short, you will experience pain in your neck and shoulders. If the extension is too long, you will feel discomfort in your triceps. According to Greg LeMond, your elbow should touch your kneecap or be within an inch of it when your hands are on the drops, your elbows are bent at a 65- to 70-degree angle, and your legs are in the 1 o'clock and 7 o'clock pedaling positions.

Stems come in extensions from 4 to 14 cm to allow for proper fit. If you find yourself needing a much shorter or longer stem, the top-tube length of your bike is the major problem. Never allow very long or short stems to compensate for a poorly sized frame. Your steering and center of gravity will be compromised, and the bike will not be very comfortable to ride.

Handlebars

For a road bike, select handlebars that are straight across the top. They should be as wide as the bony protrusions on the top outsides of your shoulders. If your bars are too narrow, they will restrict your breathing; if too wide, they will leave your chest area too open and increase wind drag.

Adjust the bars so that the bottom of the drops is parallel to the ground. A neutral position for the brake levers is achieved when the tips are in line with the bottom of the drops.

"Aerodynamics cost me the Tour de France."

Laurent Fignon, after Greg LeMond beat him in the 1989 Tour de France using clip-on handlebars

Crank-Arm Length

Biomechanists will be the first to tell you that crank arms influence your cadence and the leverage you can exert on the pedals. Longer crank arms are used for pushing large gears at a low cadence, and shorter arms allow for a higher cadence with smaller gears. You would use short crank arms for track sprints and criteriums, and longer crank arms for time-trialing and climbing hills. On a mountain bike, you would use longer crank arms for better leverage in climbing.

Check your crank-arm length if you feel your knee is flexing too much at the top of the pedal stroke even though your saddle height may be properly set. You may have to switch to shorter arms. You can change the crank arms for comfort and performance just as you can the stem or saddle. When you change the crank arms, you may need to readjust saddle height.

The first coach or biomechanist to arrive at a formula to determine proper crank-arm length may win a Nobel Prize. For the time being, most people agree that crank-arm length should be proportional to your height and leg length. See table 12.1 for an idea of the crank-arm length you should try under most riding conditions.

TABLE 12.1	Finding the Right Crank-Arm Length
Cyclist's height (inches)	**Crank-arm length (millimeters)**
Less than 60	160
60–64	165–167.5
65–72	170
72–74	172.5
74–76	175
Over 76	180–185

Aerodynamic Positioning

Anyone who has raced a bicycle in a triathlon or duathlon has experienced the adverse effects of wind resistance. In the early 1980s, the use of disk wheels and aerodynamic bikes and clothing set a precedent and firmly established the benefits of reducing wind resistance. It was not until the late 1980s and the introduction of the Scott DH handlebars that the next step in aerodynamic efficiency developed: radical changes in positioning on the bike.

Several years ago, I attended a seminar sponsored by Performance Bicycle Shop in which Boone Lennon presented his key points on correctly positioning an athlete on a bicycle that has aero bars. Lennon is a former ski coach and current bicycle-racing enthusiast who holds two patents on aero-bar design and who, with Scott USA, introduced these bars to the cyclist and triathlete mass market. Much of the information Lennon relayed sprang from extensive wind-tunnel testing done at Texas A&M University. He also told of the years he spent field-testing the bars, completing coast-down tests on the roads around his previous home in Ketchum, Idaho.

In all his work on handlebar development, he never wanted to sacrifice the comfort of the cyclist. His mission was to make athletes more aerodynamic while allowing them to ride more powerfully. He mentioned four areas that you should concentrate on to reduce air resistance through body position: keeping your arms narrow, your back flat, your chin down, and your knees in close to the top tube.

Lennon used the analogy of your body being an "open cup" when you ride into the wind with your arms wide apart (see figure 12.6a). By narrowing your arms, you close the opening of the cup and allow for the wind to be directed around your body (see figure 12.6b). Begin by gradually bringing your armrest pads a few centimeters closer on the handlebars until you can comfortably ride with your forearms touching for long periods of time. This may take you several weeks or months. Once you can ride like this comfortably and powerfully, you have accomplished Lennon's first goal of closing the cup.

a   b

Figure 12.6   Closing the cup.

Next, work on riding comfortably with a flat back (see figure 12.7b). You can accomplish this by tipping your pelvis forward on the saddle. Make sure your saddle is level and your stem length is long enough to get the proper stretch in your back. This will eliminate the hump—most obvious from a side view—that you see in many cyclists' backs (see figure 12.7a). Do not practice this movement until you have been able to ride with your forearms touching for long periods of time.

a

b

Figure 12.7 To change from riding with a rounded back (a) to a flat back (b), rotate your pelvis forward on the saddle.

Now you need to lower your chin to fill in the gap between your arms (see figure 12.8). Lowering your chin also will lower your shoulders and make you a more perfect aerodynamic object. Do not drop the chin so low that you cannot safely look down the road. Safety and comfort are your key concerns while time-trialing or riding off the front of the pack.

Figure 12.8   Lower your chin to fill the gap between your shoulders and arms to further close the cup.

Once you have accomplished these changes in upper-body position, learn to keep your knees in while pedaling. If your new upper-body position causes you to throw out your knees to avoid hitting your arms, you may have to raise the stem or your shoulders slightly. Keeping your knees in while pedaling is just as important as keeping your forearms together, your back flat, and your chin low. Research conducted in a wind tunnel has shown no correlation between pedaling rate and a reduction in wind drag.

During the question-and-answer session at the end of his presentation, Lennon mentioned that the tilt of the bars is important in accomplishing one or more of the four steps to positioning yourself comfortably on the bicycle. Most athletes that I have observed in racing keep the tilt of the bars somewhere between 15 and 30 degrees to achieve optimum comfort, performance, and power.

Several seminar participants were concerned about the effect of this aerodynamic position on breathing and oxygen consumption. Research completed by Steve Johnson at the University of Utah and published in Cycling Science showed that using aero bars in this position had no measurable physiological cost on cycling. In the study, 15 highly trained subjects rode a bicycle ergometer in the laboratory under two different submaximal conditions. The ergometer was fitted either with dropped bars or with clip-on bars.

There was no evidence in the study to suggest that the clip-on bars interfered with breathing mechanics. In addition, there was no significant difference in oxygen consumption when the athletes worked at 80 percent of maximum during the 10-minute steady-state ride. Therefore, concerns are unfounded that the severely crouched position that aerodynamic handlebars require interferes with breathing.

As with any new equipment, the more practice you have riding with the aero bars, the more familiar and comfortable you will become with their operation. Not using aero bars or clip-ons is sure to put you at a disadvantage in certain events. And they are certainly much cheaper than disk wheels. With practice, you will be able to ride well in the new position (figure 12.9).

Figure 12.9 A frontal view of an aerodynamic and biomechanically comfortable riding position.

Drafting

In order to be successful in bicycle racing you must know how to draft. Drafting is also the least expensive method of reducing drag. Remember, the area behind a cyclist is a low-pressure area, so when someone passes you, jump in behind him and ride in his low-density space. This effect is called drafting and is more noticeable the closer you ride to the cyclist in front of you. You must learn to ride comfortably within 6 to 10 inches of the back wheel in front of you. Table 12.2 shows the decrease in wind resistance as the distance between cyclists decreases. It takes months of practice to ensure that you can ride safely while drafting in a single pace line or in a pack of cyclists.

While drafting, a cyclist can consume 30 to 40 percent less energy than those leading the pace line or pack. Research completed by Dr. James Hagberg at the University of Florida measured the reduced oxygen consumption (shown as energy savings in figure 12.10) of cyclists who were drafting in various formations on a flat road.

TABLE 12.2	The Effect of Drafting
Wheel gap (ft)	**Decrease in wind resistance (%)**
0.5	−44
1.0	−42
2.0	−38
3.0	−34

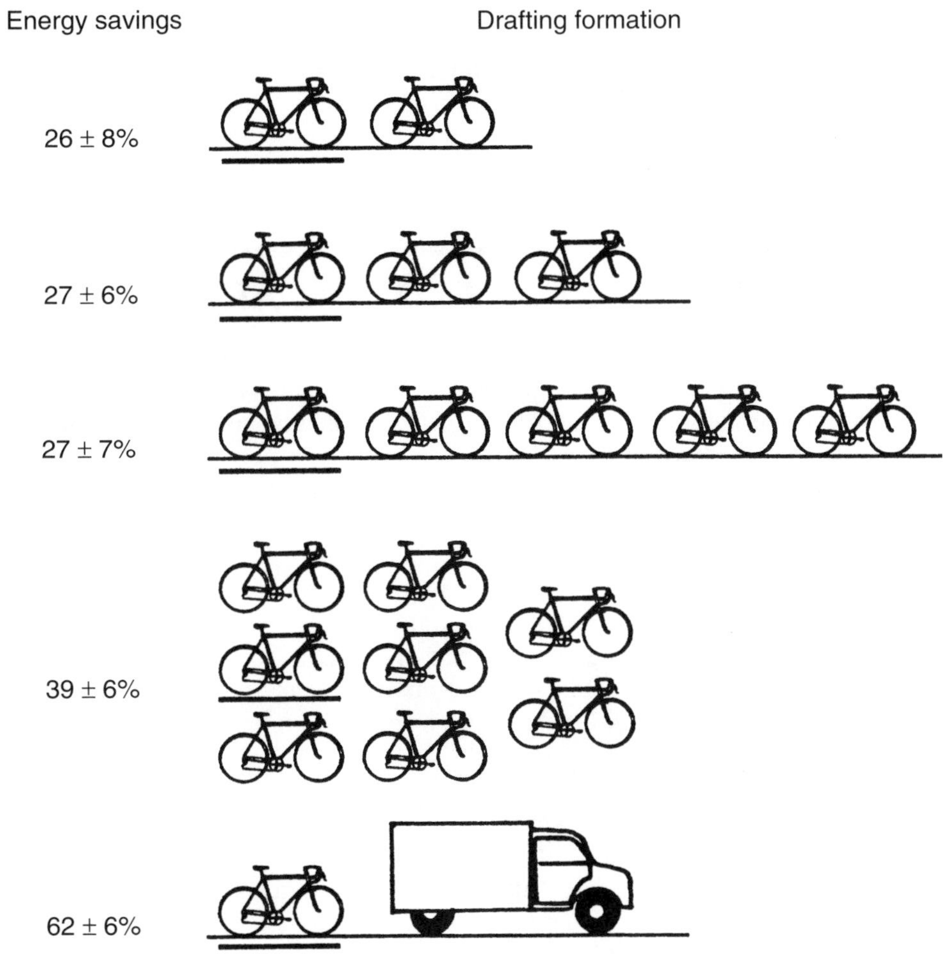

Energy savings   Drafting formation

26 ± 8%

27 ± 6%

27 ± 7%

39 ± 6%

62 ± 6%

Figure 12.10 Reduction in oxygen consumption due to drafting different numbers and formations of cyclists and a vehicle at 25 mph. The underlined cyclist represents the position of the test subject. All reductions are significant compared with riding alone at 25 mph.

From "The Effect of Drafting and Aerodynamic Equipment on Energy Expenditure During Cycling" by James Hagberg and Steve McCole, 1990, *Cycling Science*, 2, p. 20. Copyright 1990 by Cycling Science Publications. Adapted by permission.

When a cyclist was drafting at 20 mph, $\dot{V}O_2$max was reduced by 18 percent compared to riding alone. At 25 mph, the benefit was considerably greater, saving 26 percent. You might think that drafting a line of riders would increase the benefit, but the study does not bear this out. Drafting one cyclist or a line of two or four resulted in about the same reduction in $\dot{V}O_2$max at 25 mph.

With a group of eight riders there was a reduction of 39 percent, significantly more than drafting behind riders in a pace line. This was probably due to the greater frontal area of the leading riders and to the riders on the side deflecting more air. The greatest reduction in energy cost—62 percent—came from riding behind a truck. In fact, in 1985 John Howard went 152 mph riding a bicycle behind a race car using a special enclosure at Bonneville Salt Flats.

The key to riding in a group is to take turns at the front, allowing yourself time to recover while riding in the draft of the other cyclists. Cyclists in a pace line can travel more than 2 mph faster than a lone rider over the same distance.

DECREASING FRONTAL AREA

You are the real aerodynamic culprit on the bicycle. The human body causes about 70 percent of the total drag (the bicycle and wheels about 30 percent), so improvements to your riding position will be the most important factor.

Riding on the drops of the handlebars gives a more aerodynamic shape to the upper body and lowers your frontal area facing the wind. Compared to riding in a touring position, with your hands on the tops of the bars, the crouched racing position lowers wind resistance by more than 20 percent. This could mean more than a three-minute improvement in a 25-mile time trial.

Work completed at the Texas A&M wind tunnel has shown that clip-on handlebars and other models of aerodynamic bars can reduce wind resistance at the typical racing speed of 25 mph. Compared to "cowhorn" bars, aero bars will save one to two minutes in a 25-mile time trial and increase speed by .5 mph or more.

The test showed that as the elbows were pulled progressively inward, drag decreased. When the elbows are spread, the turbulent wake from the arms spins off into space and energy is lost, but when the elbows are drawn inward, air flow around the body is smoother. In other words, the body is drafting in the slipstream of the arms. It takes time to get accustomed to riding with your elbows in, but faster time trials will be your reward.

Oran Nicks, director of the Texas A&M wind tunnel, said that allowing your upper arms to stick out can really slow you down. "The drag on the two upper arms of a cyclist may closely approximate the amount of drag of the rest of the body's frontal area," said Nicks. Review aero positioning to ensure that you put yourself in position to get the greatest advantage from your aero bars.

The Final Spin

The ability to go fast and climb hard while cycling is very important. In addition to strong muscles and proper nutrition, the frame size, gear ratio, pedaling cadence, and your position on the bicycle are crucial to performance. You must consider the bicycle and yourself as one integrated unit.

Even though you may want to develop a position like that of Lance Armstrong, Jan Ullrich, or Mari Holden in time trialing, you must let your own riding style and anatomy dictate your position. Your highest priority should be adjusting your bike and, when necessary, adapting your style to assure pain- and injury-free riding. Improved performance will follow.

13

DESIGNING STRATEGIES AND TACTICS

Of all forms of cycle racing, road racing is perhaps the most glamorous and the one that most readily captures the public's imagination. There's something that goes even beyond the heroic in an athlete pitting himself against not just his human opponents but the vagaries of nature.

Back-breaking mountain climbs, leg-jarring cobbles, fierce winds, rain-soaked roads, and hailstorms all play a part in making this sport as much a battle against the elements as a battle against cyclists who are generally the fittest, most highly trained of all athletes.

Moreover, road racing is a great equalizer. Just look at the greats of the sport and you will find all sorts of physiques represented: tall and lean; short and stocky; and those who look as though they couldn't even lift a heavy bag of groceries.

The great art in road racing is to recognize your strong points and weaknesses and ride appropriately while also exploiting the weaknesses of your rivals.

Remember, in any race, victory is what counts, unless you are riding purely as preparation for a far bigger and more important race, in which case it does not matter if you attack and end up "blowing up" before the finish. It's winners who count, and the way to win is to marshal your own particular resources in the best and most economical way.

Some will argue that the best cyclist does not always (or even in most instances) emerge as the winner of a road race. I disagree. I don't think sheer physical ability in itself is all that should be considered. Knowledge, suffering, technique, strategy, and luck all play a part, and it is right that it should be so.

The best cyclist does win because the winner is the person who turns everything, luck included, to her advantage. She wins because she is a complete person just as an architect who can see broader business considerations will be more successful than one who knows of nothing beyond his drawing board or tools.

This chapter discusses basic racing techniques and strategies in competition. The information in it will, I hope, save the novice cyclist a lot of time and effort wasted through mistakes. But it can't take the place of first-hand experience. Nor can it cater to every individual's needs. The methods described in this chapter have worked well for me, and I believe they will work well for most cyclists. But if they don't suit your style or your ambitions, feel free to adapt them to fit your own racing strengths and weaknesses.

Climbing

For the cyclist whose talent is an ability to climb well, even a small hill is an ideal opportunity for a race-winning move. If the climb is early in the race, it might simply prove an opportunity to reduce the bunch to a smaller, more manageable size, particularly if there are more climbs near the finish. Or it could be used as a springboard to form a breakaway group from a lone break over the crest of the climb.

For the cyclist who climbs badly, a hill can prove to be the effective end of his race. However, even a very poor climber, by dint of a little determination, may be able to hang on to a large group as the field breaks up. If he manages this, he can limit his losses on the descent because a group of a reasonable size will probably organize itself to chase and bring back the climbers who have broken away. Sometimes it becomes necessary to let the better climbers simply ride ahead in order to reserve strength for chasing them when the climb is over and the terrain becomes more favorable.

Try to evaluate the climb as you approach it. Formulate a plan for covering the hill quickly and efficiently. With a bit of experience, you will know when to climb in or out of the saddle (or when to combine these techniques), and you'll know what degree of effort will work best.

Because there is not significant draft from other cyclists, it is very much an individual effort in which you will have to pace yourself and ride your own tempo.

In the Saddle

Climbing in the saddle is generally better for long climbs where a sustained effort is required and you need to conserve energy. The optimum climbing cadence is from as low as 60 rpm up to about 90 rpm. The lower-than-normal revolutions per minute (60 to 75) are recognized on hills because of the nature of the work. What you personally find to be most efficient for climbing will determine the gear and cadence you adopt.

The majority of cyclists prefer to use smaller gears and spin more up hills, as Lance Armstrong has done in recent years. With this choice, concentrate on pedaling smoothly the entire pedal circle. Most cyclists find it more comfortable to sit forward on the saddle while spinning like this, having the pedals more underneath them.

Changing positions on the saddle, forward or back, every kilometer or so on a long climb will work the muscles a bit differently and keep them fresh longer. Experiment and find what cadence is best suited to your muscles. In any case, sit up with your hands on the tops of the bars and breathe deeply. Since the speeds going uphill are much slower than those on the flats, there is no need to be hunched over in a streamlined position. Riding the drops will only restrict your breathing when you most need the air! Also, change your hand position frequently on the tops of the bars to keep your arms and shoulders from tiring.

Some cyclists prefer to use slightly higher gears and lower revolutions per minute. With a lower cadence, a cyclist needs to sit back more on the saddle, concentrating on the power stroke. Upper-body strength is utilized more with a higher gear (slower revolutions per minute). Pull back on the bars while pushing forward and down on the pedals. The lower back muscles are put to hard work here, too. Upper-body movement is inevitable and even beneficial while climbing hard, as you use your weight and upper-body strength to propel yourself uphill.

This doesn't mean you should lug the gear and thrash all over the bike. It just means you require more power on the downstroke.

Out of the Saddle

Getting off the saddle adds power to the pedal stroke for hard efforts up steep or short hills, but it also uses more energy. Most cyclists will find, though, that with the proper technique out of the saddle they can conquer a hill with less effort by using their body weight and upper-body strength. Done properly, it looks like this: Out of the saddle with your hands holding the brake levers, you pull with the right arm as the right leg pushes down on the power stroke. You then shift your weight from right to left and pull on the bars as you push with the left leg. On steep grades, it's almost as if you are walking up the hill. The bike will have a natural sway from side to side as your body weight is shifted. Make sure you have good control over the bars so that you don't zigzag up the hill.

Getting out of the saddle can be valuable for two other reasons. On a long climb it can be a way of stretching the legs and giving them a bit of rest while they work in a slightly different way. Additionally, because it adds more power to the pedal stroke, a cyclist might get off the saddle for a short section of steeper grade where he ordinarily would have to shift to a lower gear. Generally speaking, you can climb in one gear higher out of the saddle than while sitting.

Descending

If climbing a mountain is hard work, descending the other side is the big payoff. The only thing more enjoyable than gliding effortlessly down a mountainside on your bike is maybe going a bit faster.

Downhill racing is an art in itself, requiring a combination of iron nerve and skilled technique. Here are guidelines for some basic downhill techniques:

- Try to keep your weight over the back wheel to prevent bouncing over rough patches in the road.
- Always approach corners from the outside to the inside and try to follow a good line.
- Relax, but keep a good grip on the handlebars.
- Adopt a low, streamlined position.
- If you have to brake, use both brakes, though it is preferable to slow down by sitting up slightly and using your body as a windbreak.

- Take note of traffic signs that might indicate hairpin bends, sharp corners, or potholes.
- Wet roads can make descents very tricky. Be careful of painted lines; they become very slippery when wet.

A final word of advice: Don't risk too much on descents when there is nothing to gain by, for example, leading the pack downhill. Rather relax and merely try to stay with the group. If you have broken away on your own and the finish line is near the bottom of a mountain pass, go for it and descend at maximum speed. Remember, too, that an individual cyclist descends a mountain pass with tricky corners faster than a bunch of cyclists, who will be slowed down by caution.

Riding in Pace Lines and Groups

As a racer, you'll have to feel comfortable with riding in a pack and in pace lines. Except for the individual time trial, most road races take place in a group or in a pace line. You must feel comfortable riding in close proximity to other cyclists. You need to be able to ride closely behind another cyclist's rear wheel to get the full benefit of a draft. If you ride too far behind the wheel of the cyclist in front of you, you won't get the full benefit of the slipstream created by her. You'll do a lot of extra work fighting wind resistance, sacrificing your chances to win the race.

Single Pace Line

The single pace line is the most basic riding formation, with all the other pace lines being variations of it. Simply put, this is one straight line of cyclists, each drafting closely behind the next. The cyclist at the front "breaks the wind" for a time and then moves off to the side and "soft-pedals" until he can swing in at the back of the line.

For the majority of training and racing situations, this is the most efficient way to travel in groups of two or more cyclists. With skilled racers, as many as 15 cyclists may use a single pace line effectively; for cyclists new to the technique, 4 cyclists make a good-sized learning group. Almost always in racing, breakaway groups use this straight pace line. This is also the safest pace line when there is traffic with which to be concerned.

Double Pace Line

The best way to socialize on the bike is in the double pace line. Riding two abreast, cyclists can carry on a conversation, talk shop, or whatever. This riding formation works the same as the single line. When the two cyclists have finished their turn at the front, they pull off, one to the right, the other to the left.

Cyclists at the Olympic Training Center log a majority of their early-season miles riding in this tight formation in groups of 18 to 24 cyclists. This is good practice for racing, too. Not only can you work on drafting closely behind someone, but also you practice riding elbow to elbow with the cyclist next to you.

Before touring or training two abreast, you should be aware of your local traffic laws, as it might not be legal. If it is permissible to ride two abreast, make sure you drop back into the line quickly after taking your pull at the front. Motorists definitely don't like to see people riding four abreast.

Circular Pace Line

The circular pace line is a bit more difficult, requiring more skill in controlling and handling your bike. The formation is like that of the double pace line, but now the group rotates in a circle.

This formation is best applied when there is a strong wind and it's too tiring to stay on the front for a long pull. It also works well for large groups riding at a faster pace. For this pace line, the cyclist on the front swings off, for example, to the left, then eases off the pedals a bit to drop back as a fresh cyclist begins to pull through. As soon as this cyclist has pulled ahead of the cyclist dropping back, he too swings off and begins to decelerate. This creates two lines, with the one on the right going a bit faster than the one on the left. When the cyclist in the slower lane reaches the back end of the line, he swings over to the right and reaccelerates to speed.

It takes a lot of concentration to ride this pace line properly. All the cyclists in the group must be able to ride steadily and smoothly. Just one cyclist out of synch can throw off the whole group.

To ride a circular pace line properly, the cyclist on the front should spend only a few seconds pulling before swinging off, no more than about 15 pedal revolutions.

The critical points in the circular pace line are when you swing off and decelerate and when you reaccelerate at the back. After riding this way and getting some experience at it, you will find it is best after taking your "pull" to start to ease off the front while you overlap the slower cyclist on your left by about a quarter of a wheel. By the time you are actually in position, enough space will have opened up so that he will be safely behind you.

And at the back of the line, start to reaccelerate as the leading edge of your front wheel is about parallel to the bottom bracket of the cyclist next to you. With these techniques, the transitions from faster to slower and slower to faster lanes will be made more smoothly and efficiently.

Echelon Pace Line

This is the hardest, most dangerous, but most enjoyable pace line to ride. The echelon is a circular pace line adapted for crosswinds. Instead of lining up one cyclist behind the other, each cyclist is staggered off the rear flank of the one ahead, in order to stay protected from the wind.

The cyclist on the front pulls off into the direction of the wind (for example, the right). He drops back until his front wheel has cleared the rear wheel of the next guy taking his pull. The cyclist in the decelerating lane then drops into the draft of the cyclist pulling just as he is beginning to drop back. When the cyclist reaches the last position of the slower lane, he then reaccelerates forward and into the slipstream of the cyclist ahead.

The rider moves diagonally forward and back, cyclists situated tightly off his handlebar and hip, with the cyclists directly in front moving in a different direction, at a different speed. As you can see, all this takes a good deal of timing, coordination, and bike handling.

Breakaways

Once a working group breaks away from the main bunch, it is very difficult for those behind to catch up, even though they may be equally strong and fit. Try to develop an instinct for predicting breakaways. Here are some tips:

- Note where all the top cyclists are positioned. If you see them moving up to the front of the working group, follow them.
- If there is a hill ahead, try to move to the front. As I've already mentioned, there is far less wind resistance at slower, uphill speeds than there is on the flat; being in front will cost you little or no extra effort, and you will be in a good position once you are over the summit.
- It is often a good idea to move toward the front before an intermediate road sprint, even if you are more interested in winning the later pan of the race than the prime itself. Commonly, breakaways follow immediately after a prime when cyclists who have not contested it attack.
- When there are crosswinds, keep as near to the front as you can; the better cyclists are likely to form an echelon that will be difficult to get into unless you are in a good position when they break away. Cyclists in an ordinary bunch will not be as well sheltered as those in the echelon.

Sprinting

There is no doubt that some cyclists are better endowed genetically than others and therefore are able to generate that brief burst of speed that brings victory. A preponderance of fast-twitch fibers in the muscular makeup provides that ability.

There is another factor in sprinting other than genetic ability, and that is learned skill, which is often the deciding factor. Any sufficiently determined cyclist can learn to sprint. Like any other facet of the sport, it is best learned by regular practice. No matter how far down the field you finish, try to win the bunch sprint from the group with which you finish. Only by learning to beat lesser cyclists will you build up the skills with which to beat better cyclists.

There are a few simple rules to follow in bunch sprinting. As the race enters the final few kilometers of the course, move up toward the front part of the bunch. Not into the front, but near enough to observe the cyclists who are still able to make the running at this late stage of the race. Among these will be some who can be discounted because they rarely contest the sprint, not believing they can do it. Others are noticeably struggling and will be glad simply to finish. Then there are those who regularly win or finish in the placings, and it is from this group that the winner will most likely emerge. The thinking cyclist will move in close to one of these and try to position himself so that he can watch some of the other likely winners.

By now the correct gear should have been selected. Often cyclists make the wrong decision and simply push the gear lever as far forward as possible to contest the sprint on a ratio as high as 54 or 53 $\times$ 12. Once rolling, this size of gear can be turned effectively for a short distance. The problem is to jump from a rolling speed of 55-plus kilometers per hour or faster. A cyclist on a lower gear will accelerate more quickly, and the gap he opens in the first jump may be wide enough so as to be impossible to bridge in the last 200 meters to the line.

With practice, it is possible to use a smaller gear to accelerate quickly with the initial jump, and then shift to a smaller cog in the final 100 meters. In the last kilometer, the tension begins to mount as the speed of the bunch creeps up. More cyclists will start to move forward, trying to get into a good position before the sprint begins, and this often will frighten a cyclist into leading out the sprint with too far to go to the line. Beyond 250 or 300 meters out, only a really strong sprinter will be able to lead and hold that lead all the way to the line.

Many cyclists try to "find a fast wheel" for the sprint. That is to say, they try to be behind one of the potential winners at the initial jump and let the slipstream pull them up to speed before doing their best to use the slipstream as a slingshot to get them past and into the lead just before the line. A better tactic for the cyclist trying to ensure such a tow is to try to be beside the person he selects as a "lead out," instead of being behind him, so that as the one jumps, there is a bike's length of slack to give the other time to match the jump and still get tucked into the slipstream.

In a big bunch that is panicked into starting the sprint too early (in excess of 300 meters), a cyclist will have to switch from one leader's wheel to another during the sprint, as a faster cyclist comes past. Once the bunch is committed to the sprint, every ounce of effort has to be poured into the simple task of propelling the bike at maximum speed over the last few meters.

The race ends only when the finish line has been crossed. This is an obvious fact, yet it is one easily forgotten. It is an all-too-frequent occurrence for the lead to change, literally, in the last half-meter to the line, as cyclists ease prematurely. That glorious gesture of hurling both hands into the air in victory can cost one dearly if it is done too soon.

Strategies

Bicycle racers have to combine basic cycling techniques with specific racing skills, techniques, and tactics in order to be successful in racing. To the beginner, a bike race looks like a confusion of activity with the best-conditioned athlete winning. Skills and tactics play a much greater role in bicycle racing than is generally thought by those outside the sport. As you gain racing experience, you learn that even a well-conditioned cyclist will not win if she can't employ a good racing strategy, execute timely tactics, and have highly developed bike-handling skills and techniques.

However, fancy tactical moves are of little use if you do not have the physical power to execute them to your advantage. Make no mistake, most tactical moves depend primarily on a high level of physical conditioning. But, developing your racing experience and "savvy" is critical to all cyclists. Experience is needed to develop the proper timing of an attack or to learn that patience is one of the most important tactics in racing. It's easy to panic and respond to every attack and breakaway forming in the pack. Such riding will leave you exhausted and unable to respond when the truly decisive attack of the race occurs.

I am a rider who wants to do his work well and remain at a high level, taking advantage of his physical ability. The rest is meaningless.

Mario Cipollini, self-proclaimed world's fastest cyclist,
holder of most stage wins in the Tour of Italy

Racers must have excellent bike-handling skills and techniques. As a racer, you must feel comfortable when riding in a pack. Most cyclists do not learn the proper techniques of drafting. Learning to ride close to another rider's rear wheel is a matter of technique and lots of practice.

Cycling is just as much a skill sport as baseball, basketball, or football, with the added penalty of a possible crash if maneuvers are not properly executed. With this in mind, let's look at some basic racing strategies, tactics, and skills that every serious cyclist should know.

This information comes from a lecture given by Chris Carmichael at one of his training camps held for cyclists looking to improve their racing skills. For additional information on training and tactics by Carmichael, visit www.trainright.com.

Developing a Race Strategy

It is important to note the difference between tactics and strategy. Tactics are specific maneuvers that help a racer attain an objective. You may use a tactic to win a sprint, break away from the group, or help a teammate bridge a gap to the breakaway. A strategy, on the other hand, is the overall plan for a race and employs a number of tactics.

The strategy you develop depends on factors such as the length of the race, the terrain, your competitors, and, of course, your own abilities. Tactics are based upon the opportunities presented to you during a given race situation. It has been said that "cycling is a sport of circumstance." This is true, for how you employ your tactics determines how you take advantage of race situations. It is the preconceived strategy that allows you to capitalize on your own strengths, or expose and capitalize on your opponents' weaknesses.

You should design your strategy in the weeks leading up to your competition. Include information such as

- the course profile,
- the race distance,
- the last 1-km sprint run,
- the distance from the last corner to the finish line,
- your competitors,
- the feed-zone locations,
- other teams,
- weather conditions, and
- your fitness level.

As you collect this information, apply some basic strategic principles to help you develop your race strategy. You can use these basic strategic principles to dissect the race into organized segments. You then can create many different tactical opportunities from which you can benefit.

Conservation of Strength and Energy

All athletes should be as economical with their energy as possible, for these resources are not endless. It is said that the doubling of speed requires a fourfold increase in energy expenditure. This is why during a high-speed race conservation of energy should be a priority. Remember, trying to break away during a high-speed race can be very "energy expensive." Conserve energy and wait until speeds are reduced before launching an attack.

Planning where you are going to attack and how much effort you are going to expend during the attack can be the decisive move that leaves your opponents defenseless.

"As long as I breathe, I attack."

Bernard Hinault, five-time Tour de France winner

The length of a sprint is important. Try to pick out a landmark somewhere in the last 500 meters, knowing that from that landmark, if you have a straight shot, you can continue to accelerate all the way to the finish line.

All energy expended should benefit you. Think about this while in a breakaway. Ask yourself, "Am I the driving force here?" If the answer is "yes," then chances are that someone in the breakaway is living to "level the playing field" and get you to take the brunt of the work. The break should not "live or die" by your energy. Try taking shorter pulls and maintaining the same pace as the rider who just finished pulling. It is possible to save considerable energy during a long breakaway if you reduce the length of pulls in the pace line.

 ## Rule of Thumb

All energy expended should benefit you. This rule of thumb can be applied in many ways. For example, if you are the strongest rider in a breakaway, try using your strength to wear down your opponents. If you are not as strong as your opponents, try maneuvering them in such a way that they are doing most of the work. For example, time your pulls at the front so that your opponent pulls during the headwind sections of the course. You will save valuable energy while wearing down your opponent.

Go for It!

Many athletes lose their chance of winning by not carrying out the plan or strategy that they designed. They recognize the correct move and initiate it, but they do not continue because they lack the courage to carry out the plan. They are often afraid to take the risk. Once a tactic is initiated, it should be carried out.

For example, Joop Zoetelmelk attacked hard during the last 2 km of the 1985 Professional World Championship Road Race and went on to win the race. During this attack, he stayed ahead of the group by only a few seconds. If he had hesitated for a split second in initiating his attack, he would not have won the World Championships.

Use the course or conditions to your advantage and stick with your plan. If you're a climber, attack on the most difficult part of the climb. A sprinter needs good positioning leading into the final kilometer of the finish, picking the right wheel of another good sprinter from which to receive a leadout.

Rule of Thumb

Don't calculate too much. Things happen very quickly in races. You must be able to react and employ the tactics quickly when necessary. Avoid thinking about the negative consequences of your actions. Focus on succeeding.

React to Changes

As previously mentioned, you should go into every race with a preplanned strategy and try to stick to that plan. However, if situations arise that make the strategy unworkable, you must be able to react quickly and initiate another plan. Race experience plays an important role here. Winning races is a matter of capitalizing quickly and intelligently, almost instinctively, on situations as they unfold. As you gain experience, you will develop race savvy that enables you to react wisely.

Take a Chance

The role you play during the race depends on how you feel at the time. If you are having a bad day, your available tactics will be limited. It is at times like this that you may choose to take a risk and attack. For example, during a stage race several years ago, I was coaching the U.S. National Team, and the stage was long and very hot. One of the athletes on the team was George Hincapie. On this particular day, he was suffering badly. As the field slowed for a feed zone, I instructed Hincapie to attack. He was successful in breaking away, although his break was caught within a mile from the finish line.

Hincapie was disappointed because he had come so close to winning the stage but hadn't. That evening, as I sat and counseled him, I reminded him of the poor day he had been having prior to the attack. The attack had rejuvenated his otherwise lackluster performance. By taking a risk when he had nothing to lose, Hincapie affected the outcome of the race for everyone and ended up with a successful race for himself.

Rule of Thumb

When there is no alternative, take a chance.

Calculate Your Moves

Taking an early lead in a race, particularly a stage race, may not be the wisest move. Consider the consequences of your move and your ability to defend your position. Can you afford to be the "marked rider" for whom everyone is gunning? Are you strong enough to defend your lead from the start of the race? Calculate carefully and look at the overall picture. What are the point standings of you and your closest opponents? Is it worth exhausting yourself to chase down a rider who is not even in contention?

If you are the first rider to reach the top of the first of many climbs in a single race, will you be able to employ an element of surprise later in the race when you might be able to break away and maintain the lead? Have you considered taking some other riders with you in a break so that you have some help?

Don't underestimate your opponents' strengths. If you are in a breakaway, sprinting for the finish, or grinding up a long climb, remember to remain fully aware of your opponents' mental and physical strengths. Winning a race involves not just what you do, but also what others do. Clearly, the strongest athlete does not always win. You have to be able to outwit and outride your opponents.

 ## Rule of Thumb

Don't be bluffed by your opponents. Always ask yourself, "Are my opponents showing me their true strengths, or are they bluffing me in order to hide their real strengths or weaknesses?" Competitive cycling is a thinking person's sport.

Capitalize on Your Opponents' Weaknesses

Gather race history on your opponents. Analyze the information and determine their physical, mental, and tactical strengths and weaknesses. Then use this knowledge to your advantage in the race:

- Force the race pace in order to exploit and weed out weaker opponents.

- Keep pressure on your opponents by constantly attacking. This will wear them out before the decisive moment of the race.

- Try opening gaps on opponents on hills, after corners, or when they slow to shift gears or reach down to drink from a water bottle. Your opponents will have expended so much energy closing gaps that they will have nothing left when you initiate the winning attack.

Rule of Thumb

Know your competition. Some athletes are very predictable. Study your opponents' faces and riding styles. You will learn to recognize when they begin to tire. This will be your signal to increase the speed and frequency of attacks. Keep up the pressure and soon your opponents will "crack." Winners are proactive, not reactive. Force your opponents to react to your moves!

Racing strategies and tactics involve constant and quick decisions. What is going on inside your opponent's head? Study your competition, and know their strengths and weaknesses as well as your own. Good athletes learn from their own mistakes, failures, and victories as well as those of their opponents.

Tactics

When planning tactics, first find out all you possibly can about the course to be used for the race. Are the roads hilly or flat? Exposed or sheltered? Narrow or broad? Winding or straight? It's amazing how many riders start a race without even knowing how many laps or miles they have to do. If the finish is to be off the circuit, find out as much as you can about it, or better still, have a look at it before the start.

Of course, it always helps if you can ride the course in advance, though this often gives a false impression; drags that seem hard when you are just plodding on your own often pass unnoticed when you are in a bunch hammering along at 30 mph. Similarly, corners that seem safe can assume a frightening aspect at full racing speeds.

Find out as much as you can about your opponents, too, then you'll know the people to mark on the hills, in the sprints, or when the breaks start going.

Enter every race with a plan. This can be fairly simple and should reflect your abilities and expectations for that event. If you excel on a flat road in windy conditions, for example, and the course provides those conditions, your race plan might call for maximum effort at that point where the terrain is open and flat.

A race plan might involve other cyclists in the event, whether they are team members or competitors with whom an agreement has been made before the start. If so, it should be clear in each rider's mind what is required of him in a joint effort to succeed.

The race plan might call for no more than an effort to win a prime or intermediate prize in the event. Whatever the plan is, you should know exactly what you are trying to achieve, and your goal should be measurable so that you can judge afterward whether you succeeded or not. It must therefore be something achievable in order to be meaningful.

You also should realistically reflect your capabilities in your race plan. Remember, while winning is the ultimate goal, it is not the only measure of success. The plan could simply be to finish within a certain time margin or within a given placing, or to better your previous best time.

During the event, you should concentrate continuously on what is happening in the race itself and on anything else that could affect it. You should keep close to the front even when you have planned to take no more than a passive role in the proceedings.

There are a number of ways in which a race may be ridden, and a race plan might well call for all or most of these tactics at different times. The plan should be flexible, for what others do is likely to affect your own race strategy. Success at the end generally will be the result of a well-considered plan, modified by the circumstances of the race itself and brought to fruition by a thinking rider seizing opportunities when they occur.

Most race skills can only be learned through regular competition, and they will only be learned by thinking cyclists who try to understand the changing patterns of races so that they can predict what is going to happen.

During a race, watch the cyclists who are regular winners, or who frequently finish high up in the placings. Try to identify the way they ride in the race at any given time, and try as well to discover their special talents. Having done that, see if it all points to a predictable race plan.

The Final Spin

Road racing is a sport that demands brains and techniques as well as fitness and strength. Experience is best gained through actual racing, but studying this chapter will help you avoid falling into some of the blunders of novices.

Read all you can, study the way other people race—both by watching them in action, either as a spectator or fellow competitor, and by analyzing race reports—and then you will get the full value out of the tactics this chapter presents. Use these hints as a catalyst for building your successful foundation of personal experience and practice.

PEDALING FOR OPTIMUM EFFICIENCY

Understanding the basic biomechanical factors involved in pedaling will help you pedal more efficiently and allow you to get more push for your effort. The problem with applying biomechanics to cycling is that the enormously complex web of physical and mechanical variables is completely interrelated. Physical factors such as the muscles used to pedal and your position on the bike are included. Mechanical factors of the bike can be adjusted. But the whole system taken together—position on the bike, frame geometry, crank length, cadence, power output, muscle-fiber type, and speed—is so interdependent that if one variable is changed, it affects several others, making the study of one variable in isolation impossible.

Most of the important determinations of crank length, frame size, pedal cadence, and so on have been empirically developed by cyclists, coaches, manufacturers, and scientists. These individuals have done a good job of filling our needs for improved performance and injury prevention. The challenge in the future will be to integrate our ever-increasing knowledge of cycling mechanics with rapidly improving computer and instrumentation technology to improve cycling performance.

Let's begin our exploration of the biomechanics of cycling with an examination of the physical factors in pedaling, in converting muscle power to pedal power. We then will examine the pedaling motion as it relates to ankle position and to your position on the bike. Finally, we'll draw some conclusions about optimal pedaling cadence per minute.

Pedal Motion: The Science Behind the Effort

The pattern of force applied throughout the complete pedal cycle begins at top dead center. Force output has been shown to change continually during one complete revolution. Figure 14.1 shows changes in the various forces as the crank rotates through the 360 degrees of a revolution. This figure represents one complete leg cycle at 20 points (about 18 degrees apart) in the crank revolution.

The crank (dotted line) and the pedal (short, bold line) are shown in correct relationship to each other. The angle of the pedal with respect to the vertical line is called the ankling angle. The size of the force being applied to the pedal, referred to as resultant force, is shown by the size of the bold arrow. This arrow's orientation to the pedal shows the angle at which force is applied. The scale of 600 newtons equals about 135 pounds of force on the pedal.

Not surprisingly, most cyclists attain peak force at about 90 degrees or with the pedal at about 3 o'clock. However, significant downward force is still being applied at the bottom of the pedal stroke (180 degrees); cyclists refer to this as trying to stretch the crank arm. Downward force decreases but is not totally eliminated during the upstroke, acting in opposition to the other leg.

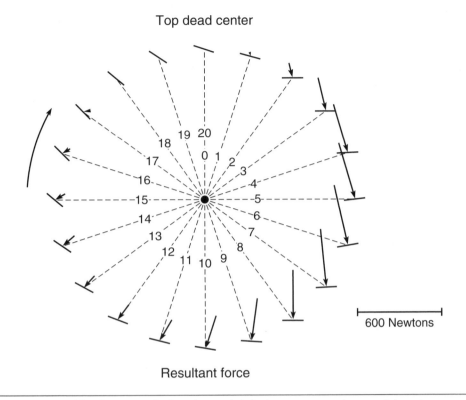

Figure 14.1   The force applied to the pedal during one complete pedal cycle.

From "The Biomechanics of Cycling: Studies of the Pedaling Mechanics of Elite Pursuit Riders" by P.R. Cavanagh and D.J. Sanderson. In *Science of Cycling* (p. 105) by E.R. Burke (ed.), 1986, Champaign, IL: Human Kinetics. Copyright 1986 by Edmund Burke. Adapted by permission.

Biomechanists use the different forces a cyclist applies to the bicycle pedals to characterize pedaling technique. These forces typically are measured with pedals that have built-in piezoelectric measuring devices and are described in component terms. Biomechanists refer to the force that is perpendicular to the pedal as the normal-force component and the force along the surface of the pedal as the tangential-force component. The effective component acts perpendicular to the bicycle crank arm and is responsible for powering the bike forward. The ineffective component acts parallel to the crank arm and thus only acts to lengthen or compress the crank arm.

Early research by Dr. Peter Cavanagh at Pennsylvania State University has shown that to be most effective, it is necessary to apply force perpendicular to the crank. The product of the effective force and the crank-arm length is called torque.

This research has shown several interesting observations, which can be seen in figure 14.1. The cyclist upon which this figure is based was seated and riding a simulated pursuit at about 100 rpm with close to maximum power output during a steady-state ride of four minutes. Notice that the force on the pedals is rarely vertical (a direct push downward to the ground). In the first 130 degrees of the pedal cycle (positions 0 to 7), the force is downward and forward. For much of the remainder of the pedal cycle it is downward and backward. At position 4, the force is close to a 90-degree angle with the crank arm and is very close to being 100 percent effective. This is the position that corresponds to where the most force is being applied to propel the bicycle forward.

From this point forward, the angle of the crank and pedal decreases and the effectiveness of the force put into the pedal decreases. By the time the pedal reaches the bottom of the stroke, a fairly large force exists, but you can see from its orientation that it is not very effective.

During the recovery phase of the pedal cycle (180 to 360 degrees), a force is still pushing down on the pedals. The weight of your foot and leg on the pedal is a negative force during recovery that tends to produce a countertorque, opposing the forward movement of the bicycle. Notice that, under the conditions of the study, during the recovery phase hardly any pulling-up force was applied to the pedals. Pulling-up forces would be shown on the diagram as an arrow underneath the pedal and would point upward.

Remember, though, that your legs are moving in a synchronous motion but 180 degrees opposite each other. When the right leg is pushing down in the propulsion phase, the left leg will be in the recovery phase. The small downward force from the leg in recovery is easily overcome by the other (propulsive) leg. During sprinting, climbing, and starting on the track, the recovery forces would probably indicate that the rider actually pulls up on the pedals.

From figure 14.1 we see that propulsion occurs whenever the effective component of the applied force to the crank arm is positive and in the direction of pedaling. It is obvious in the figure that the resultant force is still effective beyond bottom dead center. Your goal should be to make the propulsive phase of the pedal cycle as long as possible.

In this example, the fact that the cyclist was able to remain seated while pedaling indicates that his maximum steady-state resultant force was less than his body weight. If he had produced forces greater than his body weight, he would have lifted himself off the saddle unless he used his arm and back muscles to hold himself down.

Leg Movement Patterns

By using high-speed film, it is now possible to film pedal action while a cyclist is pedaling. The developed film then can be digitized (converted to numbers), and when these numbers are entered into a computer, the rate of leg movement and joint angles of the foot, ankle, knee, and hip can be calculated. Researchers have been able to give us clearer answers as to where maximum knee flexion occurs in the pedal stroke, how straight the knee is at the bottom of the pedal stroke, and how the cyclist "ankles" during the pedal cycle.

Figure 14.2 represents a composite of the mean data collected by Peter Cavanagh on six National Team pursuit cyclists as they rode their own bikes at 100 rpm in a 53 × 13 gear combination.

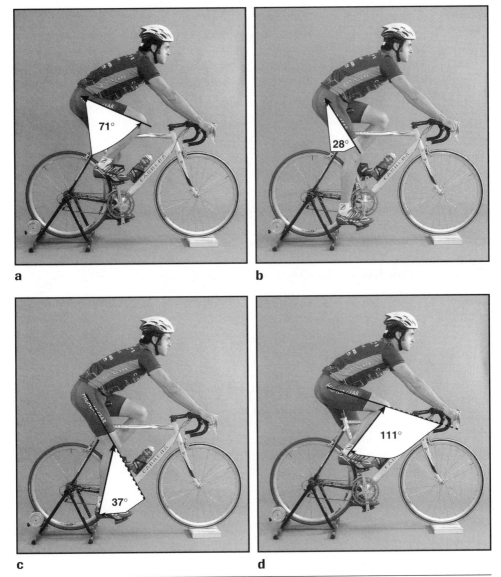

Figure 14.2 The body position and crank at the times of (a) maximum hip flexion, (b) minimum hip flexion, (c) maximum knee extension, and (d) maximum knee flexion. These values are the means from six different elite riders who had individually adjusted the cycle to their own requirements. The small light-shaded sectors represent the range of values for the particular position found among subjects.

Looking at one complete revolution of the crank cycle, we can see the range of motion of the major leg joints and segments. The thigh moves through about a 43-degree range of motion. It moves from about 71 degrees of vertical just after top dead center (TDC, figure 14.2a) to within 28 degrees at bottom dead center (BDC, figure 14.2b). Through this range of motion, the upper body stays relatively motionless at about 35 degrees of horizontal. This means that the hip joint never moves into full extension. (Full extension would be if the thigh moved behind a line drawn through the center of the trunk.) These observations have implications for designing your strength-training program.

The knee's range of motion is about 75 degrees. Near the bottom of the pedal stroke the knee is flexed at about 37 degrees (figure 14.2c), and at just before TDC, the maximum knee flexion is 111 degrees (figure 14.2d).

The shaded areas in all four diagrams show the variations in range of motion among all the cyclists in the study. It is quite small, about 10 degrees. This points out that the adjustments the cyclists made to their bicycles have fairly standardized their body positions once they begin riding.

Although the leg's range of motion is fairly constrained by the rider's position and the geometry of the bike's frame, there are significant changes in technique when the rider changes positions. When a cyclist climbs or sprints out of the saddle, for example, her joint patterns will be different. Even when she is seated and climbing or pedaling hard, as in time-trialing, the pattern can change due to body and bike movement.

"Bikes don't win races. Racers do."

Steve Hegg, professional cyclist, Olympic gold medalist, individual pursuit

Muscle Activity Patterns

Robert Gregor, PhD, and others from the University of California have identified the major cycling muscles of the leg using the technique of electromyography (EMG). EMG is based on the fact that contracting muscles generate electrical impulses. The unique advantages of EMG are that it reveals both the intensity and the duration of a muscle's action and it discloses the precise time sequences of muscular movement. The analysis of the EMG data shows that many major lower-extremity muscles produce hip extension (propulsion) (see figure 14.3).

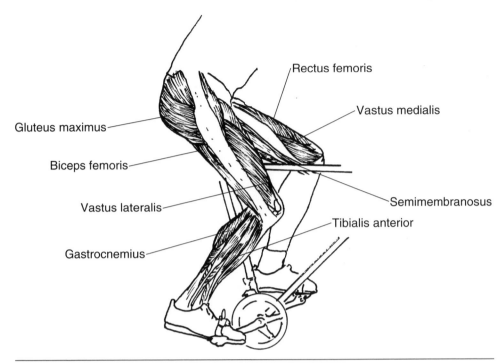

Figure 14.3   Major lower-extremity muscles used in cycling.

From "Effects of Saddle Height and Pedaling Cadence on Power Output and Efficiency" by R.J. Gregor and S.G. Rugg. In *Science of Cycling* (p. 74) by E.R. Burke (ed.), 1986, Champaign, IL: Human Kinetics. Copyright 1986 by Edmund Burke. Reprinted by permission.

Figure 14.4 shows that the gluteus maximus and biceps femoris play a major role in hip extension from 0 degrees (at TDC) to 180 degrees (at BDC). The rectus femoris, vastus medialis, and vastus lateralis—the principle extensors of the knee—are active at the same time as the hamstrings, from 0 degrees to 75 degrees, and during the last 90 degrees of the recovery, helping to flex the hip. Their primary use, however, is during the propulsion phase of the pedal stroke.

There is no doubt that knee extension and flexion are important in the production of force during cycling. The semimembranosus, biceps femoris, and gastrocnemius play a role in knee flexion. Many weight-training programs tend to ignore the knee flexors while working the knee extensors. The cyclist must plan a strength-training program (see chapter 4) that works both knee flexors and knee extensors.

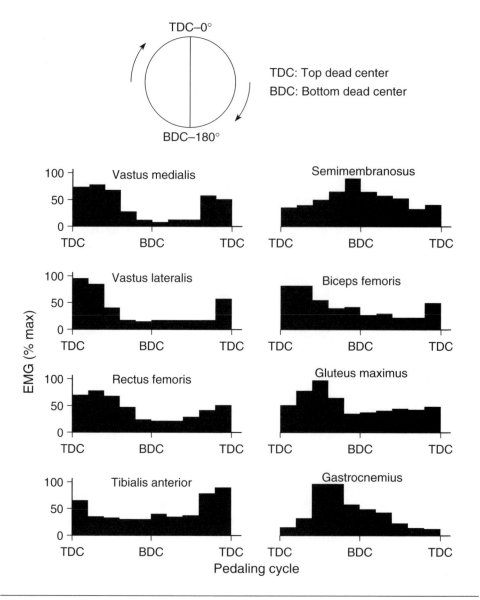

Figure 14.4 Mean normalized EMGs collected from 10 subjects.

From "Effects of Saddle Height and Pedaling Cadence on Power Output and Efficiency" by R.J. Gregor and S.G. Rugg. In *Science of Cycling* (p. 74) by E.R. Burke (ed.), 1986, Champaign, IL: Human Kinetics. Copyright 1986 by Edmund Burke. Reprinted by permission.

Ankling

Many traditional cyclists will tell you to drop your ankle as you pedal through top dead center (for example, from 30 degrees before TDC to 30 degrees after TDC) and to drop your toe across the bottom of the pedal stroke. From the information we've received from measures of pedal force (figure 14.1, page 271) and from high-speed filming, we know that the pedal varies from almost horizontal in position 3 to slightly heel-down in position 6, to a maximum toes-down position in position 16. The maximum toes-down position occurs at about 75 degrees before TDC.

The total ankling pattern that Peter Cavanagh and David Sanderson have measured is shown for one complete crank revolution in figure 14.5. The dark solid line is the mean, or average, pattern from seven elite pursuit riders; the two other lines represent values for a single rider. Notice that this rider is off of the mean pattern for most of the revolution. In general, he keeps his heel a little higher than average. This is particularly noticeable on his left foot during the recovery phase (180 to 360 degrees). There is also an approximate 10-degree difference in the range of motion of his left and right feet.

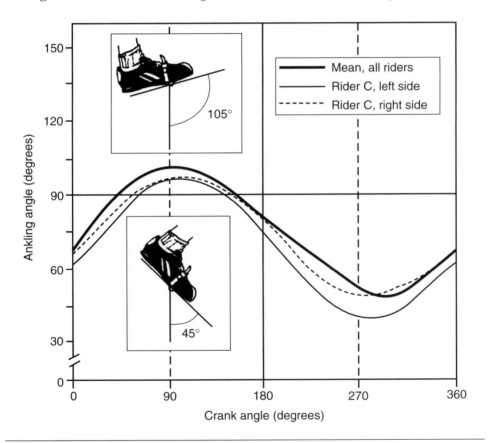

Figure 14.5   The mean ankling pattern as a function of crank angle for a group of pursuit riders during 100-rpm pedaling with a 400-watt power output. Zero degrees is the first top dead center, and 360 degrees is the end of one crank revolution. The inset diagrams show the conventions used for measuring the angle of ankling. Also shown on the diagram is the ankling pattern for a particular rider (rider C of the study).

From "The Biomechanics of Cycling: Studies of the Pedaling Mechanics of Elite Pursuit Riders" by P.R. Cavanagh and D.J. Sanderson. In *Science of Cycling* (p. 95) by E.R. Burke (ed.), 1986, Champaign, IL: Human Kinetics. Copyright 1986 by Edmund Burke. Reprinted by permission.

The ankling pattern used by the seven cyclists (figure 14.6b) and by other non-elite cyclists they have studied departs considerably from what has been accepted in the popular literature. The pattern suggested in some lay articles (figure 14.6a) is likely both anatomically and mechanically impossible if the rider remains in the saddle. Your ankling pattern should look like that in figure 14.6b, in which you can increase your effective force on the pedal by pushing through at the top of your stroke and pulling back at the bottom.

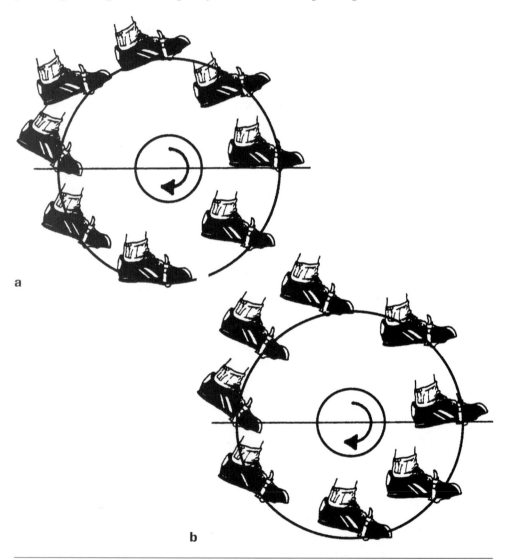

Figure 14.6 *(a)* The ankling pattern recommended in popular bicycling literature. *(b)* The ankling pattern that Peter Cavanagh and David Sanderson discovered highly successful elite pursuit riders use.

From "The Biomechanics of Cycling: Studies of the Pedaling Mechanics of Elite Pursuit Riders" by P.R. Cavanagh and D.J. Sanderson, 1986. In Science of Cycling (p. 95) by E.R. Burke (ed.), 1986, Champaign, IL: Human Kinetics. Copyright 1986 by Edmund Burke. Reprinted by permission.

Foot Position

Your foot should be positioned so that the ball of the foot is directly over the pedal axle. To avoid knee pain later on, adjust your cleats so that your foot rests on the pedal naturally. Experienced cyclists have their cleats set with a rotational adjustment device at their local bicycle shops. Most cyclists today use clipless pedals that allow the foot to "float" a few degrees inward or outward on the pedal as it moves through the pedal cycle. Research has shown that these new pedal systems put less strain on the knee and allow a more natural pedaling motion.

IS THERE A NEED FOR FLOATING PEDALS?

Bicycle pedal and shoe design has changed significantly since Bernard Hinault won the Tour of Italy and the Tour de France in 1985 using Look pedals, which he helped design and which helped him avoid falling on several occasions. Since then, clipless pedals have become the most popular among competitive, road, and mountain bike cyclists. In 1993, history was made again when Sean Kelly finally turned in his toe straps and clips for clipless pedals.

But with the introduction of clipless pedals in the mid-1980s, the medical community saw a rise in the incidence of overuse injuries to the knee, such as tendinitis, chondromalacia, and illiotibial band friction syndrome. The increase in injuries was attributed to clipless pedals that locked the foot more firmly in place and to the stiffer-soled shoes that were used with them.

Andy Pruitt, EdD, ATC, director of the Boulder Center for Sports Medicine, says, "In the old days, cycling shoes had soft leather uppers and the cleat wore in quickly, allowing one to have quite a bit of pivot around the ball of the foot. Most injuries occur in trying to make the knee adapt to a fixed pedal position, which puts chronic stress on the knee joint. The 'static' or 'fixed' clipless-pedal systems hold the foot and knee in a rigid position. The foot wants to move during the pedal stroke."

Because of the increased incidence of knee problems, in 1987 Jean Beyl, the inventor of Look pedals, created the Time pedal-and-shoe system and introduced the first "floating" pedal design. His floating system was the first attempt to make the pedal adapt to the cyclist. Now every major pedal manufacturer produces floating systems that allow as much as 37 degrees of lateral pivot in road pedals. Speedplay recently introduced a mountain-bike pedal with 54 degrees of lateral pivot.

The floating-pedal systems allow your tibia (the large bone of the lower leg) to move in and rotate as you push down on the pedal. In a fixed-pedal system, your knee and its ligaments must absorb much of this rotation, which can cause knee problems.

Pruitt says that any cyclist's knees are safer in a pivoting pedal. He adds, "The ultimate cycling position for maximum performance is secondary to cycling

(continued)

injury- and pain-free. The floating-pedal systems are ideal because there is no loss of power and they allow for some knee and foot movement. The natural rotation of the large bone of the lower leg [tibia] is to rotate in as you push down on the pedals. If your foot is fixed, your knee and supporting tendons and ligaments must absorb this rotation, which leads to chronic knee problems. Remember, chronic injuries in cycling occur over time. If your foot is improperly fixed to the pedal, and you pedal at about 95 revolutions per minute, you will complete 5,700 revolutions per hour, per leg. If you are riding about 10 hours per week, you will pedal approximately 57,000 pedal strokes per week. Do this for several weeks, and it is easy to see why knee injuries may occur."

During research at UCLA's biomechanics department, cyclists rode both "fixed" and "float" pedals on an instrumented-force pedal system, which shows the force placed on the pedals while cycling. Data from this investigation suggest that the torsional force applied at the shoe-pedal interface is attenuated with the use of the floating-pedal design. Cyclists who had existing knee pain exhibited more internal and external rotation of the foot while cycling. Although this is preliminary research, it confirms the need for floating systems.

If you are experiencing knee pain, first evaluate your cleat position with the use of the Fit Kit's rotational adjustment device and consider using a floating-pedal system if you do not already.

After you change shoes or pedals, be sure to recheck saddle height and fore/aft position. The only disadvantage is that some floating motions take getting used to. Some cyclists say they experience hamstring soreness in the first few days of use, but this eventually will go away.

If your knee pain is severe or continues after your adjustments, I suggest that you make an appointment to see a medical specialist who is familiar with cycling mechanics and injuries; you may have a leg-length discrepancy, excessive foot pronation, or another anatomical problem.

 **The Final Spin**

Cycling involves the repeated application of force to the pedals of the bicycle in order to go fast. This pedaling action requires you to put adequate force to the pedals to overcome air resistance, gravity, and friction. Your pedaling action is a repeated circular motion that is restricted by the design of the bicycle and your position on the bike.

INDEX

Note: The italicized *f* and *t* following page numbers refer to figures and tables, respectively.

ABOUT THE AUTHOR

Edmund R. Burke, PhD, has written or edited 11 books on health, fitness, and cycling, including *High Tech Cycling* and *Fitness Cycling.* Renowned for translating the latest scientific research into practical application, he serves as the executive editor of *Cycling Science* and is a columnist for *Adventure Cycling, Active.com,* and *Performance Conditioning for Cycling.* He has also written extensively on cycling physiology, training, nutrition, health, and fitness for *Velonews, Bicycling, Winning Magazine, MTB Magazine,* and *NORBA News.*

Dr. Burke was the physiologist for USA Cycling for seven years. During that time he worked with the 1980 and 1984 Olympic cycling teams that won nine medals. He consults with several companies in the areas of cycling, fitness equipment design, nutritional products, and fitness programs. A fellow of the American College of Sports Medicine, he served as the vice president of research for the National Strength and Conditioning Association from 1993 to 1995.

Dr. Burke holds a doctorate in exercise physiology from The Ohio State University. He is a professor and director of the exercise science program at the University of Colorado at Colorado Springs, where he lives with his wife, Kathleen. In his leisure time he enjoys mountain biking, road cycling, and hiking.

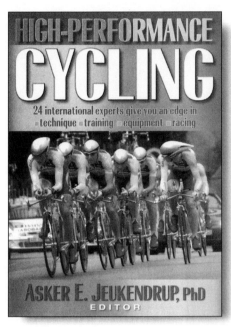